FIRST WORD

XXXXXXXXXXXXXXXXXXX

To Shelly Davis —
Stay strong and positive.

Brenda Person-Lynn, Ph.D.

(15 November 1996

FIRST WORD

Black Scholars • Thinkers • Warriors

Knowledge • Wisdom • Mental Liberation

JOHN HENRIK CLARKE

IVAN VAN SERTIMA

YOSEF A. A. BEN-JOCHANNAN

FRANCES CRESS WELSING

WILLIAM LaRUE DILLARD

ASA G. HILLIARD, III

ROBERT A. HILL

DEBORAH MAÁT MOORE

NA'IM AKBAR

LOUIS FARRAKHAN

BARBARA SIZEMORE

KWAME TURE (STOKELY CARMICHAEL)

LEONARD JEFFRIES, JR.

EDITED BY KWAKU PERSON–LYNN

HARLEM RIVER PRESS

NEW YORK
& LONDON

Published for **Harlem River Press** by:
Writers and Readers Publishing, Inc.
P.O. Box 461, Village Station
New York, NY 10014

c/o Airlift Book Company
26 Eden Grove, London, N7 8EF
England

Editor: Patricia A. Allen
Editing: D. Kamili Anderson
Jacket Design: Terrie Dunkelberger
Book Design: Tenth Avenue Editions, Inc.,
    Clive Giboire & Suzanne Cobban

Library of Congress Cataloging-in-Publication Data

First word : Black scholars, thinkers, warriors: knowledge, wisdom,
    mental liberation / edited by Kwaku Person-Lynn.
            p.   cm.
        Includes bibliographical references and index.
        ISBN 0-86316-335-1
        1. Blacks. 2. Afro-Americans. 3. Afro-American intellectuals-
-Interviews.   I. Person-Lynn, Kwaku.
CB235.F57 1996
973' . 0496--dc20   96-41295
                                                         CIP

ISBN 0-86316-335-1

Manufactured in the United States of America

For
Ravim, Ayo, So,
Jarim, Jaaye,
Roslind,
and
Latasha Harlins
and
Those to come

CONTENTS

ACKNOWLEDGMENTS

PAYING HOMAGE

In a work such as this, there are always people to thank. Gratitude always begins with the Creator, for giving us the tools needed to live and produce something that might be beneficial for the human race. Thank you, Isidra and our sons—what they gave no one else on earth could. I am grateful to Adele Mathias for being a beautiful mother. Very special thanks go to the Afrikan scholars, thinkers, and warriors who made time in their intense schedules and allowed me to sit down and talk with them on tape. Their words comprise the substance of this book. We all benefit from your work. I thank as well the ancestor who turned on the light: Minister Malcolm X (El-Hajj Malik El-Shabazz).

Love and thanks to: Shelley Palmer of the Herb Alpert Foundation, for engineering the generous gift that enabled me to complete this work; James Fugate of Eso Won Books, for guidance; Larry Obadele Williams, for his great bibliographical work; Wazir Aziz, of Renaissance Multimedia, for his expert computer assistance; Sylvester Rivers of Uhuru Communications, for his tape copying services; and Jendayi Malachi Kwakye, David Martanelli, and Dr. Joy Williams, those hard-working transcribers. To those Afrikan musical ancestors who laid the foundation for all the music we hear today—Bob, Féla, Jimi, Bird, SWV, and Luther—thanks for accompanying me during the trying times. Of course, there were good friends who helped and inspired me along the way: Kofi Opantiri, Dr. Billie Jo Moore, Louretta Walker, Ashra Kwesi, Nzinga Heru, Diana Hill, and Moses Adewole. Thank you "Spirit Flight" and "Afrikan Mental Liberation Weekend" family for your continual encouragement. Extreme thanks and props to Patricia A. Allen, Editorial Director of Harlem River Press, for making things so easy; and to Kamili Anderson, copy editor, for being one of those rare, spectacular word people.

To the hip-hop generation, all those players and gangstas out there: I hope you read this book, scope the phat history and culture thing, gain something, and realize that there is a reason to care about yourself and be positive. Your reality causes me to try harder.

INTRODUCTION

Knowledge without permission, compromise, or apologies

In the dawn of the twenty-first century, a child is born in the Western Hemisphere. She grows and experiences television, movies, video games, virtual reality, and the World Wide Web. She is trained at the best schools available. One day, she goes to a friend's home and hears a tape. On it, a man passionately discusses global Afrikan history, culture, science, and a host of other things.

The content of the information shakes her beyond belief. Her first reaction is doubt and suspicion. She has never heard such things before. They were not even hinted at during her entire educational experience.

She asks her friend where he got the tape. He tells her that he attended a lecture and bought the tape afterwards. Her curiosity bulges. She becomes obsessed with finding out more. She goes to a former teacher and asks her about this material. The teacher tells her that it has always been available, but school systems and other institutions do not embrace it. She tells her that some people called it "Afrikan-centered" or "Afrocentric" information, but that she should not pay attention to how the material is labelled but concentrate on its content. She also tells her that if she wants to find out more about her history and culture from the perspective of people of Afrikan descent, the path of her investigation will be an arduous one. She leaves her former student with these words: "Understanding who you are is the clear light. Without it, you are walking in the dark, the unknown."

When I did my first public interview, I did not recognize the significance of the person I was talking with. I knew he was a young man at the pinnacle of his art form, and he shared his revolutionary, spiritual, positive vision with me for the world to hear and see. That first interview was with Robert "Bob" Nestor Marley, the reggae music genius who would become an icon in both the Afrikan world and the world at-large. Over time, I came to see that such interviews could reveal much that is important and necessary for universal Afrikan survival and success. I continued my quest to record the images, knowledge, wisdom, and experiences of other significant Afrikan individuals. In Los Angeles, I produced such radio specials as "Afrikan Mental Liberation Weekend," a thirty-hour

broadcast featuring lectures and interviews with the best universal Afrikan minds available.

Year after year, requests were made to transfer the recorded word into the written word. This effort was inspired by those years and those requests. Indeed, the purpose of this work is to present, in book form, the knowledge, wisdom, and life experiences of some of the most significant Afrikan scholars and thinkers. Those included in this volume are Afrikan men and women whose work has had an incredible impact and influence on changing, correcting, and expanding the higher consciousness of Afrikans and other people throughout the world. Their pioneering works and experiences have contributed to the creation of a mind-set that balances the scholarship and thought of those who think Eurocentrically and who claim that the knowledge of people from other cultural groups is inferior and not to be taken seriously.

Certain individuals flow in the path of many views with a single purpose. They ignite our consciousness and help us to transcend beyond mediocrity. All the scholar/activists included in this work operate out of a universal Afrikan experience, both spiritually and intellectually. They adhere to the Afrikan collective responsibility statement that says: "I am, because we are; and since we are, therefore I am." Their work is changing the way people look at history, the Afrikan world, and its descendants. They are heading movements to change curricula to be more culturally equitable. They are the vanguard of the scholarship to come. They are bringing forth the truth, the hard-fought recognition of the achievements and ideas of Afrikans in America and throughout the Diaspora. They are the nucleus, the heart, the very center of the modern Afrikan perspective. For the first time ever, their ideas, in their own words, are included in a single work.

The enduring battle these individuals have faced in dealing with a history and culture that has been maligned, distorted, hidden, omitted, and changed more than any other begins with the birth of humanity. Each maintains that the creators of civilization and the greatest achievements in antiquity, along with momentous modern accomplishments, were black—Afrikans to the first degree. Thus, as soldiers—indeed, as generals and chief strategists—in the war of interpretation, their work reflects information about a people who have been virtually written out of world history. For doing so, most of them have been savagely attacked by the leaders of those elements most resistant to change, justice, and truth who want the story of the beginning and building of humanity to remain the same. But these men and women are scholars of knowledge as well as scholars of struggle. They have fought white supremacy and emerged with rock-solid fortitude.

All the interviews were conducted—the large majority in hotel rooms—in Los Angeles, California, or in the surrounding areas of Compton, Culver City, North Hollywood, Hollywood, Monrovia, and Santa Monica, between the years 1985 to 1994. They averaged a little over an hour. All the participants were open and receptive. At no time were any negative feelings or ill-will expressed. Of course, there were some emotional and heated moments when the situation commanded. This was dictated by the seriousness and passionate commitment of each to their work. Unfortunately, that enthusiasm and emotional character does not always translate into the written word, but it was definitely there.

When uncovering old concepts and creating new ways of looking at the self, the world, history, and other areas, new terminology is bound to develop. New definitions for old words and new words for old definitions will necessarily evolve. Spelling Afrika with a "k" instead of a "c" grew from my study of Afrikan languages. For instance, the Yoruba alphabet does not have a "c" in it.

The definition of who is an "Afrikan" has also been expanded. As Peter Tosh, the Jamaican Afrikan reggae artist, states in his song "Afrika," as "long as you're are a black man, you're an Afrikan." That lyric also applies to black women. No matter where one is born, if that person is black, their ancestral origin is in Afrika, making them Afrikan, although the citizen of a particular country. When relating to a particular geographical area, the terms American Afrikan, Jamaican Afrikan, Brazilian Afrikan, or European Afrikan may be used, putting the emphasis on *Afrikan*, like one's last name.

"Scholar" is another term that is broadened in this book. The Western definition refers to a scholar as a "learned person in an advanced field," one who has received training from an academic environment. Here, it will also include a person trained or learned through experience and a lifetime of struggle against oppressive and racist elements. Some of the individuals in this book have devoted their lives to fighting racial oppression and nothing else. Their knowledge and experience are beyond the instruction of a classroom teacher.

The first teachers, who were in Afrika, always taught that "knowledge is sacred." That is the spirit from which this information exchange springs forth. That same spirit also dictates that this knowledge serve as a catalyst for human beings interested in regaining their humanity and morality, which were serious-

ly diminished when their ancestors were taken from their mother/fatherland, and which have not been reinforced in Western civilization.

Lastly, when I first started thinking about a title for this work, I wanted to call it "First Person," but that just didn't sound or feel right. Then it hit me. I said, "Wait a minute. If Afrikans were the first people, then they must have uttered the 'First Word.'"

KWAKU PERSON–LYNN

FIRST WORD

JOHN HENRIK CLARKE
HISTORIAN, EDUCATOR, AUTHOR, EDITOR, LECTURER

Dr. John Henrik Clarke is one of the original architects of modern Afrikan-centered scholarship. His work has influenced more young scholars and activists than that of any other in the field. He is well known for his volumes of writings, his massive library, and his close relationship with Minister Malcolm X. As a warrior/philosopher, he has stood up to every attack on his work and character to reap the highest levels of respect in both the academic world and the everyday working communities of his people. He is one of those rare educators who has the ability to incorporate wisdom and grace into all of his scholarly endeavors. Yet, as Dr. Clarke humbly notes, "I am just adding the missing pages of world history."

My work began with my desire to become a Baptist Sunday school teacher, and with my search for the image of my own people in the pages of the Sunday school lessons and in the Bible itself. Being told that God is love and God is merciful, and also being told the Bible is God's book, I could not believe that a loving and merciful God had left an entire people out of his book. I began to search for my own people inside of the Bible, only to discover that someone had tampered with the book, and that the illustrations in it weren't drawn by us or for us—that religion very often can be misused as an instrument of oppression.

I began to investigate the role of my own people in history and the role of religions in history as a power factor. I think this is what ultimately led me to a consideration of the works of the historian John G. Jackson and the old Harlem History Club that later became the Blyden Society. I was a long way away from John Jackson at the time, and I did not know that the weekly Sunday school lesson was printed by a white Baptist publishing company in Nashville and distributed to black churches. I did not know that control of an image was part of the weaponry in the control of the mind. Once you control what people see, you often control what they do.

I began my investigation while working for a white lawyer in Columbus, Georgia. I wanted to do something exceptional for my fifth-grade teacher, who is a deity in my life to this day, Ms. Evelina Taylor. She taught me to believe in myself. I wanted to do something exceptional in the current events period on Friday. I had been accustomed to bringing in magazines and newspapers so others could be aware of current events. I worked for white people before and after school, so when they threw away the *Atlanta Constitution*, I would bring that to

school, along with *Literary Digest, Reader's Digest,* and newspapers about the Japanese invasion of Manchuria. My gang, my grouping, got ahead because of my information. I became kind of the leader of a little group we called the "Black Brigade," as against the "Light Brigade," that generally got all the privileges, including the privilege to speak in the assembly.

I first began with the suspicion of the belief that my people had no role to play in history. When I asked this lawyer for a book about Afrikan people in world history, he shook his head sadly, and spoke to me kindly and said, "I'm sorry, John, your race has no history." I could not believe that I came from a people with no history! So, a few years later [circa 1932], while doing chores in the new Roosevelt High School—the Black Brigade always did the chores— that is something which is beyond this discussion, because it's something black people generally do not talk about, intracolor prejudice—but I was doing chores. This high school was new, and they had no coatroom. I held the books and coat for a recitalist. That was my little job. He had a book called *The New Negro.*[1] I opened that book to an essay by Arthur Schomburg, a Puerto Rican of Afrikan descent. His essay was called "The Negro Digs Up His Past." That essay made me believe, for the first time, that I came from a people who had an ancient history. That I was older than my oppressor. I became kind of smug, because I realized we came from the senior people of the world. And if people had left us out of God's book, then they had misused God's book.

I remember the one single thing Schomburg said to me.[2] He was on his lunch hour, and I asked, "I want the history of my people, all of it, henceforth, within the hour." He looked at me pitifully and said, "Sit down, son. What you're calling Negro history and what you're calling Afrikan history are the missing pages of world history." He said, "Son, go study the history of your masters. Study the history of those who have enslaved you, and you will learn that no one can successfully oppress a consciously historical people. In order to set our people up for oppression, they had to make them apolitical. They had to read them out of respectful commentary of history. Read their history and you will find out why."

I began to read European history and how they systematically programmed the world to give the illusion that the world waited in darkness for them to bring the light and created the myth of their people spreading civilization. I would later learn that civilization is never innocently spread by one people onto another people, that people spread their way of life in order to control. To be civilized, you have to first be civil. The presence of the European, outside of Europe, infusing himself, interfering with the civilizations of other people, has been and still is a protracted act of oppression.

The fact that they could not admit there were heroes in history other than Europeans revealed to me that there was something wrong with their history. They had a good relationship with Afrikan people before the fifteenth and the sixteenth centuries, when they invented the "savage." The savage was an invention, because if you read their history, they tell you of the periods when they had good relationships with Afrikan people.

They contradict themselves in their history, because there were three Afrikan emperors of Rome. There were three Afrikan popes. The father of church literature, and maybe church social thought, was St. Augustine, an Afrikan. When you look at the facts, the Roman Empire was born in Afrika and fell in Afrika. Look at the European mismanagement of Christianity. Roman taxation, the brutality and oppression with taxation, forced the European concept of Christianity into being. St. Augustine reminded them, after the conference at Nicea in 325 A.D., that the European was giving the world a religion the Afrikans had three thousand years ago. Christianity had emerged in the world under different names. John Jackson would later confirm this in a little pamphlet called "Christianity Before Christ," now a major book called, *Christianity Before Christ*.[3]

When I read the history of the Middle Ages and saw how the Europeans were dying of famine and plague, and read about the slave trade and their move to the East and to the spices of the East, I saw that the goods and services of the slave trade not only saved Europe from starvation, but with those resources they laid the basis for the modern industrial, scientific, and capitalist world. They advanced to a Commercial Age, tantamount to an Industrial Age of that day.

We have to remember that an Industrial Age, by European definition, means a different thing by other peoples' definition. Afrikans built the pyramids without a great network of factories. We have to understand that people have handled different industries different ways. Afrikans laid the basis for a great agriculture. They laid the basis for a great age of art and science, without any great art colonies.

When people, any people, fail to adjust to the nature of change, they decline. The Romans failed to adjust to the nature of change. They declined. The Greeks, they declined. Europeans, especially Americans, cannot go all over the world taking what they want, knocking over people who object. If you understand this, you'd understand the tragedy of this little drama in the sand in Arabia,[4] where nobody could win. The winner will be paying for his winnings for three hundred years. So will the loser.

One of the things Afrikans did not adjust to was the rise of gun technology and weaponry. Afrikans were very brave, but they were no match for the new gun technology Europeans had developed to protect themselves from each other. The Europeans turned on the Afrikans. Afrikans were going through a period—we're talking about West Afrika, mainly—of a difference of opinion on statehood, a difference of opinion over territory. Had Europe stayed out of Afrika fifty more years, the Afrikan would have adjusted because there were periods when Europe was in much more turmoil within itself. The European took advantage of this dissension between Afrikan and Afrikan. They pitted one against the other and ended up conquering both. They corrupted the Afrikans with things they had never seen before: habit-forming alcohol, shiny bric-a-brac. Some Afrikans began to sell each other to get these goods.

It's almost like looking into a mirror of time. It's almost like something that is happening right now. Crack is an element of re-enslavement of the mind, and is hitting the most important factor in our continuation as a people the hardest: the women, the childbearers, those who must produce the next generation.

Europe began to pour its degeneracy over the world. Its leftover population, its discarded, its unwashed, its unwanted, the scum of Europe went into the slave trade. They got it established and well under way. They broke the structure of Afrikan governments because many Afrikans did something that they should have learned not to do and something they haven't learned to fight against successfully to this day: never, absolutely never let an outsider settle a family dispute. If we didn't learn anything else from "The Godfather" movies, you should have learned that lesson. The cohesion the Mafia has is in its own internal security. All disputes must be settled within the context of the family. The outsider is *never* to be brought into such disputes.

Before the Nicene Conference in 325 A.D., Christianity was basically North Afrikan and Afrikan. The Romans, who had been killing Christians, killed more Afrikans in their amphitheaters of North Afrika than in the arena in Rome. After a while, Europeans stopped killing Christians and became Christians themselves. They adopted the religion for political reasons, and they still hold onto it for political reasons. Just like the communists in Russia. Communism was adopted for political reasons. When it no longer served its political purpose, it was discarded the same way you discard an orange after you've squeezed out all the juice.

The European is politically practical. Unfortunately, we Afrikans are politically naive. What the world needed then, and what it still needs, is not another religion, because in form, formation, and use, all religions are fakes. What the world needed was spirituality.

JOHN HENRIK CLARKE

These foreigners to Afrika fashioned religions out of spirituality and sometimes a misinterpretation of spirituality. They turned all organized religions into what they are right now: male chauvinist murder cults. Name me the religion, and I will name you the murder. These Western-organized religions, including Islam, were brought into being by men who feared the power of women. In all these religions, the woman takes a seat less than the man and has a place less than the man.

I have no romance with either Islam or Christianity. I think all religions can be good and should be good. Every religion in the world that has not been used as a rationale for the enslavement of Afrikan people will be, when it is to the conqueror's convenience to do so. The same thing is true of every form of Western politics.

The Arab had a fear and a disrespect of women before Islam. He merely took what was in his culture and transferred it to Islam. So the separation of women occurs within Islam. The role of women in Islam had nothing to do with Islam. It had to do with Arab culture. Most of what we think is Islam is Arab culture. A lot of what we think is Christian custom is European custom.

The European woman had a different role in history, coming out of that thawed-out icebox that is Europe. The Afrikan woman lived in a society where she had more freedom. She did not have freedom to dominate, but freedom to come to power when it was her turn to come to power. You can understand why the matrilineal society developed in Afrika, and why the first woman to head a state came out of Afrika. The first woman to ride at the head of her armies came out of Afrika; the first woman to get respect. Nearly all of these women rode at the head of all-male armies. When women tried to reach for power in Europe, white men began to burn them as witches.

We who were imprisoned by the woman-fearers began to adopt some of their obnoxious traits. A few years ago I was asked to lecture on the historical origins of black teenage pregnancy. I did the lecture correctly. I did not mention the black man at all. The women were shocked, because I told them that in the culture that produced them there was no teenage pregnancy. There was no wife-beater, and there was no wife-deserter, because the family was structured such that all these things took care of themselves within the context of that structure. I told them that when one is taken out of one's own cultural incubator to live in the cultural incubator of another people, one lives by the rules of another people. You adopt some of the worst traits of the other people, including the traits alien to the culture that produced you.

In the post-Nicene Conference period, the Romans were in North Afrika. Remember now, they had been there since the fall of Carthage, in some form, nearly two hundred years before the emergence of the formal Christ-oriented Christianity that we now know. Christianity then was a practice that stemmed from the normal customs of the people. All of these rules and everything in Christianity already existed in these societies before Christ. The concept of Christianity as a white creation came out of the Nicene Conference. They were preparing Christianity to be a weapon of Europe. Europeans adopted it as a political weapon. They still hold onto it as a political weapon. When it fails to serve them politically, they will discard it as readily and as quickly as they discarded communism.

In the 1500s, Michelangelo painted his picture of Christ. Prior to that, there were no extensive pictures of Christ painted white. Michelangelo painted the Holy Family white using his own relatives as models. The Jesus that hangs in your churches and some churches in different parts of the world, especially black churches, is the creation of Michelangelo, who lived 1500 years after Jesus was dead and had no way of knowing how Jesus looked. He obviously did not even do any research on the descriptions of Jesus during his lifetime. The Biblical description of him tells us of him having hair like "lamb's wool" and feet of "burnished brass."

We Afrikans are the keepers of America's truth. We are the victims of America's lies. If the truth about us were known and taught, Western scholars would have to take back the lies they have been projecting as history and truth. You might have to tell the real story about George Washington, who purchased a slave for a barrel of molasses. He had a number of slaves. You might have to tell Thomas Jefferson's real story, about his black mistresses. You might have to investigate J. A. Rogers's little pamphlet called *The Five Negro Presidents*.[5] The ones Rogers pointed out as having our blood were not especially outstanding, as far as I'm concerned. I wished he'd kept quiet about four of them. We live in a country where the silly, stupid racial laws say that one drop of black blood makes you black. Well, if that is true, that would give us five presidents.

Internationally, if you apply that same reasoning to hundreds of years of Afrikan and European intermingling, what with Hannibal's move into Europe and all that Mediterranean and Mongolian mixing, they too would be Afrikans. If you apply that reasoning—that one drop of us makes you a whole of us—to Europe, at least one-third of Europe would be black. We would have all the Spaniards, hands down, no questions asked. Afrikans hung out with them nearly a thousand years and didn't go home for that biological necessity. We would get all of the Italians. Maybe we should read the *Journal of Afrikan Civilization*, edited by Professor Ivan Van Sertima, and his work, "The African Presence in Early Europe," which explains that Afrikans had a European connection.[6]

Earlier, I reluctantly mentioned the subject of intracolor prejudice and the problem of light-skin preference. Fact is, many of the early black schools were created to accommodate light-skinned blacks who didn't want to go to Indian schools and couldn't get into white schools. That would include Shaw University in North Carolina and other historically black colleges in the South that maintained that prejudice up until the eve of the civil rights movement, and some a little beyond that. But even in schools that were not established solely to accommodate this preference, light-skinned Afrikans got preference in these schools. The same thing happened in the Caribbean Islands. It's still happening today, but to a lesser degree.

Years ago, I started writing a book in my mind, but I've never put a single note on paper. It's called *The Role of the Bastard as a Factor in History*. I was going to deal with bastard offspring throughout the ages in Europe and Asia, where you have three million Eurasians—that is, Asian children with white fathers. I would also deal with the Coloreds in Afrika. I was going to deal with how the mulattos almost destroyed the Haitian Revolution, and how even today they keep Jamaica from being a great island nation.

The skin-color factor among Caribbean people today is downright sickening. Their worship of whiteness is also downright sickening to this very day. Many Caribbeans look arrogantly at black Americans and say, "Where I come from, we have no race prejudice. A person is a person." Well, blacks may be in the majority in the Caribbean, but they are still discriminated against. The British colonialist, the British governor, the British civil servant had his choice of almost any black woman or any other woman he wanted.

If you study Brazil, especially the works of Gilberto Freyer, who wrote *The Shanties and the Mansions*, or Arthur Ramos's work on *The Negro in Brazil*, you find that a mulatto class emerged in which most of the mulatto women were prized as mistresses and prostitutes.[7] The same thing developed in New Orleans, where they had octoroon balls and mulatto balls. We have not dealt with this sad factor in our history as a people.

As we Afrikans approach a revolutionary period again, we will have to ask for the loyalty of everyone. We have to tell those who have any doubt as to whether they belong to us to come into the house and stay or to go out and stay out. If you can get entry within the house of your white father, go knock on his door and see how well he accepts you. He will not accept you in his house. Our house is the only house you have. You will stay in this house, on our terms, or you will take your chances in your father's house, where the door has already been closed.

We don't have to really talk so much about the color question, there's a literature on it. Read Mavis Campbell's work on the Jamaican free coloreds—she's a brilliant Jamaican person, but a lot of people don't like what she says.[8] It's really a good covering of the situation and of how the mulattos in Jamaica tried to make a deal with the British to protect them. The deal was this: If the British gave them special privileges, the mulattos promised to protect the British against the blacks. When the British failed to give them that protection, some of the mulattos went over to the blacks.

The loss of Chancellor Williams is significant. The importance of Chancellor Williams and his work, in addition to his being a senior scholar, is that he was one of those scholars who looked in the neglected corners of history and brought out things other scholars objected to, things other scholars did not know or care to research. His last book, *The Destruction of Black Civilization,*[9] is uneven in its presentation because it was supposed to be a two-volume work. He was losing his eyesight and crammed it into one volume. That explains the unevenness of it. He decided that he would stop extensively quoting white writers—he'd quote himself. He was just as much an authority, or more so, as the people he was quoting. We differed on this, because I think you can take white references and beat them over the head with it. You can take their own references and prove them wrong. I thought he should have mixed it up, but that's not the main point.

It's a fact that Williams's book was the first to deal with the impact of invaders on early Afrika. His most devastating chapter deals with the impact of western Asia on Afrika. Afrika had enemies from western Asia well over two thousand years before Europe was an entity in the political life of the world. That enemy from western Asia devastated Afrika to a great extent. They are still in Afrika, in the presence of the Arabs, those white "wannabees," who are still not too clear about which side they're on in this world struggle.

All people, to be sovereign and free, must own their own soil. We have to make up our minds to ask the vital questions and be in a military position to force the right answer. We must ask everyone, "What is your mission in my house? What is your loyalty to my house?" This is the responsibility of all the people who walk this earth. We Afrikans are the only people who permit others to live among us for hundreds of years without declaring any loyalty to us. Arabs have never had any Afrikan loyalty. None of these western Asian people have ever had any Afrikan loyalty. In the fifteenth and sixteenth centuries, the Europeans had no Afrikan loyalty.

The house of Afrika is our mother home in the world, all of it. We should never concede North Afrika to an invader. We should look at Afrika holistically. All of it, not only our home, but all of it is our Holy Land. Long before the birth of Jerusalem, at Abydos, in the country the Greeks called Egypt, we produced the world's first spiritual Holy Land. We need to go back and restore to our historical memory: what we did before outsiders interfered with us, disrupted the structure of our society to the detriment of our societies forever. This is precisely what happened in Somalia.[10] Afrikans can feed Afrikans. Afrikans can put Afrika's house in order. But Afrikans have a structure imposed on them, and they are under the illusion that that structure is the salvation. There are no Afrikan-structured states in Afrika, there are only imitation-European states.

The structure of the present-day Afrikan nation-state is European. The Afrikan, at his best, before this interference from western Asia and subsequently Europe, lived in territorial states, not nation-states. There were several states within territories, with different religions, different belief systems, and different customs, yet they co-existed side by side. The Afrikans in those states never used the word "democracy," yet they practiced it. They never used the word "Christianity," yet they practiced it.

We have to look back in order to look forward, but we're not looking back far enough. No one, with all the talk about Somalia, no one mentions the fact that Somalia was once a part of the Greater Ethiopian Empire. So was Eritrea. These countries were fragmented by foreigners. They were cut in half, in some places arbitrarily, with one cultural group on one side of the border, another cultural group on the other side of the border. Afrika has to put itself back together again. Afrika has to learn how to relate to itself.

I'd say Chancellor Williams, more than any other black historian in this century in the United States, left us a blueprint for liberation, salvation, and the restoration of the best aspect of these Afrikan states. *The Destruction of Black Civilization*, his best-known book, is not his best book. He would admit this. His best book is *The Rebirth of Afrikan Civilization*,[11] which he wrote while his health and eyesight were intact. That book is almost an academic architectural blueprint for what Afrikans will have to do to recover what slavery and colonialism took away. And it is Pan-Afrikan in its perspective, both of his books are. But the basis of his Pan-Afrikan nationalism is something many of us talk about without thoroughly understanding.

Afrikan people embrace European ideas because many of them are politically naive. They think that concepts like socialism and communism are new.

These concepts are not new. They were old in Afrika before Karl Marx was born, before Europe itself was born. Afrika had brought into being sharing societies, where each person got according to his needs and not according to his ability to earn. Afrikans have failed to study their traditional societies and how those societies made sure that every person living in them had enough to eat, enough land for food, enough cloth, and access to basic distribution. In many of these societies, most of them, there was no rich or poor. Either the whole society was rich or poor, but no individual was rich or poor. These were collective societies. When Europeans use the word "collective," or when they say "each according to his own," we fail to understand that Akhenaton preached this from his throne 1300 years before the birth of Christ. It's nothing especially new for Afrikans. They knew that a collective society is the most practical society.

Now that Europeans are throwing the idea of collective societies away, we are picking it up. We always pick up what Europeans throw away. I think our solution is going back and looking within ourselves. There is no European solution for Afrika's problems.

Most Afrikans on the continent were trained by missionaries, mostly Europeans. They were trained to think they had nothing to contribute to their own salvation. We have to look at this matter because powerful people never train powerless people in the arts and techniques of taking their power away from them. We need a generation of Afrikans trained in Afrika, by other Afrikans, for the express purpose of serving Afrika, who will not care whether the Europeans like their methods or not. We care too much about being accepted by people who enslaved us, who demeaned us, and whose propaganda slanders us in the eyes of the world. And yet, in our political naivete, in our lack of knowledge about our own culture, we care about their attitude towards us.

Europeans have presented an image of themselves to the world that is the image of the achiever, of the problem-solver, the hero—the image of success. This menticide, this conquest of the Afrikan mind and the mind of most of the world's people, is Europe's greatest achievement. I call this "the manifestation of the evil genius of Europe." An inadequate people, a bunch of grown-up juvenile delinquents, took over the world and convinced a whole lot of their victims that they had a *right* to do it, that it was good for the world to let them do it. They decided that Europe was their home. Enclaves like Canada and the United States were their homes outside of Europe. The rest of the world was their servants' quarters.

What is disturbing in the world right now is that the gloss of this shiny propaganda is wearing away. There is a revolt in the servants' quarters. Other people are asking, "Am I not also entitled to the goods and services of the world the same as the European?" The European's day in the sun and his triumph over the

minds of most of the world is coming to a close, but we are ill-prepared to assume our proper place.

This is why, sooner or later, we Afrikans might question the wisdom of having Afrikans educated in Europe or the United States. Afrikans should use their resources to build big universities in Afrika. If they want to hear what a foreign teacher has to say, then they should import the teacher. Afrikans must stay at home and be educated in the traditional Afrikan ways of life and of administering justice. All of this must be integrated into the totality of our being. Afrikans are not Europeans. What is in Europe may well be good for the Europeans, but is not necessarily good for Afrika or Afrikans.

The tragedy of modern Afrika is that every single Afrikan state is a poor imitation of a European state. Nearly every Afrikan head of state has been either educated in Europe or influenced by Europe. Afrikans have to turn within themselves and find solutions for themselves. They have to look for Afrikans outside who have gained some technical knowledge. Afrika might hold the lock to its own future, but the key that will open that lock, that will industrialize Afrika and free Afrika systematically of dependence on others, might rest in the hands of the Afrikans who live outside of Afrika.

The mass media, especially the movies, television, and videos, spread missionary propaganda. No one in Europe has a vested interest in Afrikan people coming together. If Afrikan people came together, then Afrikans would be the beneficiaries of the great mineral wealth of Afrika, the great iron in Afrika's body, the oil in the body of Afrika. This would lessen the European hold on Afrika and free Afrika from its consistent dependency on Europe.

To maintain control, Europe must spread the kind of propaganda that makes one Afrikan on one side of the world question an Afrikan on another side of the world. A survey was taken in Ivy League colleges. The most anti-black American of those students were Caribbean students and continental Afrikan students. Both have fallen for that propaganda.

Afrikan people throughout the world are ignorant of each other. We're ignorant of the vast amount of Afrikan people in Asia. We cannot take advantage of the fact that once we come together as a single people we constitute over a billion people on this earth. If you want to create an economic system, make shoes for a billion people, or make bread for a billion people. Fully two-thirds of all Afrikans on the face of the earth can be employed furnishing goods and services and building and maintaining living quarters and offices for other Afrikan people. Once we are not economically dependent on Europe or whites in general, Afrikans will achieve a new political voice among ourselves, a political voice in the world. Then people would not dare plan the future of the world and leave us out.

If we woke up tomorrow and there were no white people, there would be sudden confusion. Our dependency is so deep, the move would be too sudden to deal with. I think rejoicing and some sober thinking among some people would take place. Some Afrikans would start looking within themselves to find solutions they once searched for other people to find for them. I don't think it would be too disastrous. We could survive it.

History is not only for Afrikan people but for all people. History is a clock that people need in order to tell their political and cultural time of day. It is also a compass that tells a people how they should be located on the map of human geography. The role of history is to tell a people where they have been, what they have been, where they are, and what they are. The most important role of history is to tell a people where they still must go and what they still must be. History is essential not only to our people but to all people. How do you fit within the historical scheme of things? This you have to know first before you begin to move forward and chart your course.

The Europeans made an evil decision in the fifteenth and sixteenth centuries: they decided that whoever controlled the world was going to be a person of European descent. It could be one who calls himself a communist. It could be one who calls himself a fascist. It could be one who calls himself a Christian. Or one who calls himself a democrat. But it's going to be a European. The period when Afrikans and non-European people nullify that decision is at hand, yet a lot of people who are supposed to be among those who will nullify it are so in love with European cultures, European ways of life, European thinking, and European women, they will not be participants.

Still, there's an awakening throughout the world, a desire among non-Europeans to be the masters of themselves. The most fortunate thing about this awakening is that while these people insist on being the masters of themselves, they do not think that this gives them the right to be the masters of others. There may be some individuals who think the opposite, but in general, no one has any plans. It is wild and unreasonable to gain our freedom and then take away the freedom of white people. I think this is a fortunate circumstance of history. Yet, I know there are Europeans who would rather see the world blown apart than see black people free. If they can't rule it, some Europeans would rather ruin it.

There are forces in the universe, including forces among Europeans, who are willing to recognize that the period of European dominance of the world is over. But there are a whole lot of blacks, many of whom are called conservatives—and I never knew what Black conservatives were conserving—who are defenders of the European's point of view. There are a whole lot of captive blacks who would sell their entire people for thirty pieces of silver, or even less, if you bargain with them.

In spite of all of these negative factors we can point to, I think, in the main, including those blacks who are confused, that we Afrikans are ready to begin to think out our own destiny on our own terms. There are a whole lot of blacks who are Muslim who think we've got to think it out in Islamic terms. They're dead wrong. There are those who think they're going to think it out in Christian terms. They're also dead wrong. It's a political solution, not a religious solution, we are looking for.

Christianity was used as a rationale to start the slave trade. Read the papal edict of 1455, when the pope said to Spain and Portugal, "You are authorized to reduce to servitude all infidel people." Why were we Afrikans declared "infidels" and enslaved? The Arab took the same attitude. Their leaders said everything within Islam is the abode of peace, everything else was the abode of war and thus fair game. The Arab slave trade started one thousand years before the European slave trade. The brothers today who are Muslim won't deal with that. They will not read an elementary book like Eric Williams's *Capitalism and Slavery* or C. L. R. James's *Black Jacobins*.[12] They will not reclaim our revolutionary tradition. We have a world revolutionary tradition we can use to free ourselves.

My association with Malcolm X really began when I was director of an Afrikan heritage exhibit at the World Trade building in New York City after I returned from Afrika in 1958. Malcolm X's group, the Nation of Islam, was one of the exhibitors. He would come in to watch the exhibits and see how his people were getting along.

It actually began when a Caucasian lady came into my booth to wait for someone. She was waiting there, anxious to meet the person who showed up. Malcolm walked over to me and asked, half-confidentially and half-openly, "Is that your woman?" I said, "No." He said, "Good. I've gone down that street. It's a dead-end street." I said, "Well, it's not my street, and I pretty much know both the joys and the dangers of going down wrong streets." He laughed. That was the beginning of our friendship.

Malcolm said, "They tell me you know a lot about history. Do you know anything about Islam?" I started telling him things about Islam he didn't know. He appreciated it. He wasn't offended. From then on, when he wanted to know something about not just Islam but history in general he would turn to me and my files. I would go through the files and find it for him. When he had to debate college professors, I told him, "Never let people find you wrong on your facts. What you *do* with your facts is another thing."

Malcolm X had a lot of non-Muslim assistants. They never told him what to do or how to interpret information, they simply made sure his information was available and correct. Being a part of Malcolm's history cabinet, I know this to be true. One day—this is the most outstanding case—Malcolm had to attend a debate on the Congo situation. He sent to me for some information. His man picked up the information around seven, but Malcolm said he didn't see it until nine. Of what I sent, he only read some newspaper clippings and one small book called *King Leopold's Soliloquy* by Mark Twain.[13] Yet he went on the air, and for two hours he made college professors sound like crying children. He pinned them against the wall each time they took the conversation into an area where he had no knowledge. He brought it right back to the area where he had knowledge, such as about the casualties in the Congo wrought by Leopold—the number of women who had their breasts cut off, the men who had their hands cut off because they weren't collecting enough rubber. He dealt with those statistics ruthlessly. He made the most effective use of statistics I've ever seen.

From then on, I was part of Malcolm's "shadow cabinet" of non-Muslims who fed him information behind the scenes. That would continue until his death. We had a warm and human friendship. He had a case against me that he never stopped stating though. To the last day of his life he always hit me on the back, and with that playful laugh of his, he would say, "Well, John, you're a good man, and I appreciate you. I'm going to give you a ninety-nine. If you ever stop visiting that swine you can get a hundred. One thing I got against you, you're a pig-eater. Straighten up your diet. If your diet was as sturdy as your historical information, you'd be alright."

The historical portion of the charter for Malcolm's organization, the Organization of Afro-American Unity, was drawn up in my living room. I got the charter of the Organization of African Unity, and we patterned it, almost word-for-word, after that. When we hit upon this idea, and could phrase it in pure context with Afrika, Malcolm was like a child discovering a new toy. That was a side of his personality the public never got to know. He was a beautifully shy human being. There was a childlike quality in him that reinforced his manhood, his humanity, and his relationship to other people. It's hard to explain that to some people because they interpret it as a weakness. I'm talking about a strength!

I know of occasions when Malcolm turned down upwards of three million dollars because a certain monied group wanted him to pull away from Elijah Muhammad and form a separate Muslim group, financed by the Arabs, that they could control. The Arab is interested in controlling all Islam, just like the European is interested in controlling all Christianity. Christianity is the hand-

maiden of European world dominance, and Islam is the handmaiden of the attempted world dominance of the Arabs.

Today, Malcolm X is coming back to us. It is fortunate he will not go away as a symbol of a pure, uncompromised freedom fighter. But already, the books demeaning him are being written and pushed on the market. There are people who don't want black America or the Afrikan world to have an untarnished hero. He is such a hero in the eyesight of millions of Afrikan people, including those in Afrika and the Caribbean. He's partly of Caribbean extraction, his mother coming from Grenada. Millions of Afrikan people look at Malcolm X as the one pure hero we produced in the twentieth century.

This film about Malcolm, I've offered my suggestions and my advice as best I could. I admire Spike Lee and his film technique, although I have some questions about the subjects he uses and his use of those subjects. I don't think Spike Lee is mature enough as a filmmaker, as a human being, to really give the world the Malcolm X I knew, though I wish him well in his attempt. He's going to attempt it whether I like it or not or whether others like it or not.

There's a "star system" people seem intent on following. For years, we could only have one star in the movies. Once, it was Sidney Poitier. Right now, the star in filmmaking is Spike Lee. He has become the end-all of everything. We're a diverse people, and I think to make this film you need a diversity of the best talent we have in cinematography. It has to go beyond Spike Lee, his ego, and his perception. He would have to be humble enough and strong enough and gracious enough to be one of the persons, but he could absolutely not be all of it.

There's been some talk of a romantic scene with Malcolm X and a Caucasian woman in the movie. It would personally offend me. I don't see what useful purpose it could serve. I can understand Betty Shabazz opposing it. I would personally oppose the making of the film if that happened.

[After seeing the film] Well, my view hasn't changed drastically. I'm willing to admit that Spike Lee has done a mature film. He's done a remarkably good film. However, the essence, the meaning, and the definition of the Malcolm X I knew and the period in which Malcolm X lived wasn't in the film. There were some things relevant to understanding Malcolm's life that were left out. A lot of emphasis was placed on his North Afrikan or Islamic *hajj*, the pilgrimage. Then, the end of the film tries to make Malcolm seem like an integrationist, which he was not. It cleans him up for a white audience, so he could be digestible. It diffuses and de-revolutionizes him. That's not the Malcolm X I knew and not the

Malcolm I believe needs to be transferred to our children as a spiritual image. I think we need to go back and dig up the real one, read the actual speeches, and study the period we're talking about.

Malcolm X outgrew the Nation of Islam. His calling was too broad for that narrow stage. That was part of the internal conflict. The external conflict was that Malcolm X had done something that once you do it in this country, you're either assassinated, driven into exile, or driven to suicide: he showed black people the real face of power and told them what they would have to do about it. His "Message to the Grassroots" speech was part of that revelation. His "Ballot or the Bullet" speech comes straight to the point, letting us know that we're not going to wish up on freedom—that freedom is something we have to take with our own hands.

Those of each generation must secure freedom with their own hands. It's not left to us in a will. No people can hand it down to another people. Even if you inherit it, you have to secure it with your own hands. It becomes yours to the extent that you put enough safeguards around it. You safeguard the people who bring you to the brink of freedom. Had we had this knowledge, we would have guarded Malcolm twenty-four hours a day, and he might still be here.

I think the planners of Malcolm's murder got clean away. I don't think the Nation of Islam had the kind of intelligence, the kind of contacts, to set Malcolm up to be murdered the way he was. The fact that some of them pulled the trigger is one thing; the planning was obviously not our planning. Fortunately or unfortunately, we Afrikans are passion killers. A black man typically doesn't kill you at the moment he says he's going to kill you. If you avoid him for twenty-four hours, he may change his mind. His passion may cool down.

The murder of Malcolm X hasn't been thoroughly investigated. There's a new book called *The Judas Factor* that appears to be the best examination I have read.[14] I haven't had time to go over it or many of the new books on Malcolm with any degree of thoroughness. The anthology I did on Malcolm, published soon after his death, has been republished. A lot of people think it is a new book. It was really done over twenty years ago. It's called *Malcolm X: The Man and His Times.*

Sometimes I write an article inside of my mind. I take notes and then I say, "Well, I've got something else to do," and discard it. One such article was titled, "Will the Real Malcolm X Stand Up in Order to Lay Back Down in Peace?" These new books are giving this generation a Malcolm X I didn't know. I knew him about as well as quite a few other people who say they knew him intimately.

I still think Spike Lee could have made a better and a more honest film about Malcolm. It would have been a commercial success. It might have been

shorter too. Good filmmaking sometimes is like good editing. It's also learning how to say a lot in a limited space of time. The film was interesting. I'm going to see it again.

When I think of some of the most significant historical events during the ancient period, I probably would start with the Third Dynasty in Egypt that saw Pharaoh Zoser and his advisor Imhotep introduce a great Afrikan intellectual age. Imhotep was more than just an advisor to the Pharaoh, he was an architect. He designed the step pyramids of Saqqara. He was a medical doctor and the first one to perform an operation on the stomach. Today, we would call him an abdominal specialist. He may have been the first doctor to use wine as a stimulant on a patient. He started the school of thought that later developed into what Europeans mistakenly call the "mystery system." Anything Europeans can't understand becomes a mystery.

I think the emergence of the Third Dynasty and the great multi-genius Imhotep was a great step forward for human beings. Imhotep lived two thousand years before the Greek Hippocrates, who is now called the father of medicine. But even Hippocrates said, "I'm a child of Imhotep."

The Afrikan intellectual development in the Nile Valley, stretching from the Third Dynasty up until about the Sixteenth Dynasty, that would be another great period. Western Asia's invasion of Afrika in 1675 B.C. was the beginning of the mulattonization of Egypt. The recovery from this invasion two hundred years later was also a great event in history. The Assyrian invasion in 666 B.C. and the Iranian invasion in 650 B.C. ushered in the Greek encroachment into Egypt under Alexander, who subsequently opened the door for the Roman invasion and the so-called Punic Wars.

The Roman Empire rose up in Afrika and fell in Afrika. They stopped killing Christians and became Christians in Afrika. Their mismanagement of that religion, because they didn't have the temperament for Christianity, helped to introduce Islam. But Afrikans, thinking they would get the Romans off their back by adopting Islam, merely replaced the Roman conquerors with Arabs and Islam.

In the A.D. period, I think a great moment in history was when Abrahol of Ethiopia broke with the Coptic Church of Egypt, thus setting up the Independent Ethiopian Church apart from that of the Europeans. During that charade called the Crusades, with its marching across Europe, Abrahol did not see Ethiopian Christianity as having any part in this European side show and decided to stay at home, to stay out of it. It was the Independent Ethiopian Church that kept Ethiopia free from foreign domination.

The A.D. period also saw the last great king of the great independent state of Ghana: Tankamanin. His reign ended in 1076 with the invasion of Muslims from Mauritania, thus marking the first Muslim destruction of a non-Muslim nation in Afrika. The same thing happened in southern Sudan—Muslims killing Afrikans solely because they were not Muslims. We need to pay a great deal of attention to this invasion of a western Afrikan independent state by an army of North Afrikan Muslims against Black Muslims of inner Afrika.

The destruction of the last of the great independent states, Songhay, facilitated the spread of the slave trade inland. Afrika's doom was a fact. Afrika was in a trap it wouldn't get out of after that. Those who romanticize Islam need to understand that the Muslims from the North brought about this event by attacking the Muslims in the South. Those who say there is no discrimination and color prejudice within Islam need to have the lie flung back into their teeth. There is color prejudice in all religions.

There are a thousand and one events we need to talk about. The ascendancy in Rome of Septimus Severus, the most noted of the Afrikan emperors. The ascendancy of the three black popes of the Roman Catholic church. The beginning of the slave trade—that was a catastrophe. The entry of the British into the slave trade during the period of Queen Elizabeth I gave the slave trade organizational solidity and put the Afrikan in a bind he wouldn't partly come out of for the next three hundred years.

Looking at the United States, slavery itself was an historical event. For the first one hundred years, it really wasn't chattel slavery, it was a form of indenture. However, some of the misconceptions about it obscure what we did in spite of it. We not only had 250 revolts, we effected numerous partnerships between the indigenous Americans, mistakenly called Indians. We produced craftsmen. We built some of the great houses of the South, under brutal supervision, but we did build them. Some blacks were independent craftsmen.

If there is any people who have proven their patriotic love for this country, we are that people. Afrikan Americans participated in every American war—in the American revolution, in the Civil War. After the Emancipation Proclamation, which was bogus, we participated in the rebuilding of this country during Reconstruction. The Emancipation Proclamation is an interesting piece of paper, but it didn't emancipate. Sometimes emancipation is like shifting the deck chairs on the Titanic—it's going to sink anyway, no matter what deck chair you sit in. Regardless, blacks tried to put themselves back together again. We just moved

from one form of slavery to a form of servitude called sharecropper peonage, out of which my own parents came.

The emergence of Booker T. Washington was a great event in American history, as was the building of Tuskegee Institute. The opposition to Booker T. Washington is still not understood. The emergence of the greatest intellect produced in this country, that of W. E. B. DuBois, and his critical analysis of Booker T. Washington, were also important. Likewise important was the emergence of two great Black journalists: T. Thomas Fortune and William Monroe Trotter. Black participation in the two world wars and the fact that America did not even want her Afrikan citizens, or alleged citizens, to participate in combat is also significant. They had to participate in combat under a French general, yet DuBois called for Afrikans to show patriotism in spite of this.

Then there is the emergence of Marcus Garvey in 1916. And the "Red Summer" of 1919, when black children were burned in bonfires by white bigots. Between World War I and II, Afrikans were still fighting for their basic rights in this country. The nature of our fights between these wars is still terribly, terribly misunderstood by Afrikans and by Caribbean people, in spite of the fact that a great Caribbean personality, Marcus Garvey, was to accentuate our struggle by developing the largest black organization ever developed, before or since. Garvey called our attention to the fact that we are *all* Afrikan people, wherever we are on the face of this earth.

The emergence of Marcus Garvey and his teachings, the concept of going "back to Afrika," of owning our own ships, our own factories, even having black dolls as opposed to whites ones, were revolutionary events aimed at turning our minds back to ourselves. We can learn again what we lost, namely, how to structure and manage the state, which is the cultural and political container for the people, the infrastructure that holds a people together. The people's allegiance is always to the state. When you have no state, you become, as we are in the United States, a large nation within a nation, searching for a nationality.

The 1954 *Brown vs. Board of Education* Supreme Court decision is another event in our history that we need to look at and examine some more. I question whether the Supreme Court meant what they said. The bus boycott in Montgomery and the emergence of Martin Luther King, Jr., in 1955 is another. We also need to take a look at the 1963 March on Washington, which some people called "a picnic on the grass" because it was glamorous and all that. King had a dream, but he never had a plan.

Then, we cannot ignore the emergence of Islam, Malcolm X, and his adopted father, Elijah Muhammad. Second only to the Garvey Movement, the Nation of Islam called attention to our needs in this country and our needs in the world. It pointed to us as a lost nation away from home. There's a lot about it I disagree with, but there's a lot about it I agree with. A whole lot of Afrikan people, using that framework, cleaned themselves up and became whole again. They refocused themselves to a point where they could get back their peoplehood, their humanhood, their manhood, and their womanhood. Irrespective of the religious aspect, which doesn't interest me very much, I really think that, at the heart of it, most of the followers of Elijah Muhammad were disgruntled Baptists calling themselves Muslims.

I recently set out to do a cycle of three books on the liberation movement outside of Afrika. The first book in that cycle is called *Africans at the Crossroads: Notes for an African World Revolution.* The second book in that cycle I'm still working on; it's called *Conditioned Reflex: The Dilemma of the Afrikans Away From Home.* The third will be called *Immigrants Against Their Will: Afrikans in the Americas and in the Caribbean Islands.*

I have recently finished a book in between these other books called *Christopher Columbus and the African Holocaust.* I also revised a book of short stories that is almost a definitive study of the contributions of blacks to the literature of the short story. I have a small book that will be published by Kent State University Press; it's a book of my speeches called *Who Betrayed the African World Revolution?* I'm also working on a larger book of speeches called *In Search of Liberation,* which will include ten of my most relevant speeches on the concept of Afrikan liberation over the last twenty years.

I'm always writing something. I've written a number of introductions recently. Some are reprints and some originals. I wrote the introduction to Michael Bradley's latest book, *Chosen People from the Caucasus,* and to Leo Weiner's work, *Africa and the Discovery of America,* and to another work originally published in 1902 called *The Arab Conquest of Egypt.* I just finished an introduction to Jacob Carruthers' work, *MDW NTR: Divine Speech.*[15] I keep active.

I didn't do it this summer, but maybe next summer I'll finally do the editing of my novel and update it. I also have two books of short stories, *The Boy Who Painted Christ Black and Other Stories,* and a book I started at the Clinic for Professional Writers at NYU called *A Gallery of Lonely People,* dealing with loneliness and estrangement in the twentieth-century U.S.A. With that, the speeches, the travels here and in Japan—plus I'm now preparing for a Caribbean tour—I'm gainfully employed a little bit.

Being legally blind has brought about some limitations. At first, I thought it would drive me insane because I was losing my finest tools: the power to read; the power to observe so that my analysis could be correct; the power to analyze audiences, to study faces, and determine what people meant, no matter what they said, by the serious study of their expressions. Now people can hide their expressions from me. I can't exactly know what they mean. You cannot always tell what people mean by what they say.

I'm self-educated. I've been an avid reader most of my life. I've schooled myself in the literature of the world, new and old literature. I miss having the ability to pull ten books down from the shelf and go through all of them in one evening, extracting from them what I wanted or needed for a given lecture or for a lesson. I trained myself how to dissect and extract information from great bodies of knowledge, how to condense it and go into a classroom, teach the essence of it, and stimulate students to read more. Reading is the finest tool you need in teaching.

Teaching is the finest thing I have done. When I think of the different things I have done in my journey on this earth, I think my finest performance and my most useful service was as a classroom teacher. When I realized the facility to do that at its best was going, it was all I could do to hold on to my sanity.

Then one night I was upstairs in my house. Someone had left the TV on. It was an offbeat station, and Thurgood Marshall was being interviewed. Near the end of the interview, the interviewer turned to Thurgood Marshall and said, "In the final analysis, Mr. Marshall, what do you think needs to be said about you and your career?" All Thurgood Marshall said, very casually, was, "Just say I did the best I could with what I had."

That was a fortunate circumstance. I just sat there for an hour after the program ended. I turned the TV off and was thankful for just having that moment. I made my decision: my career would not end. My life would not end. I still had a good mind. My health was deteriorating, but I was doing the best I could to hold onto it. I was still a servant of my people, and still a lover of my people. I decided that I would continue to do the best I could with what I had. I will complete the mission or go as far as I can with the time and energy I have. My life will be a political statement, a cultural statement, for young people coming after me.

I've gone this far, yet I remain one semester short of finishing grammar school. I have three libraries named after me, including a major library at Atlanta University's Woodruff Center: The John Henrik Clarke Afrikana Collection. Seven thousand books have been contributed already; six thousand have already been catalogued, and more are on the way. If I've left that kind of a stamp, coming from a family where the largest sum of money my father made in

one week was eighteen dollars, what excuse do other people have who had more than I started with? Why not do the best you can with what you have left?

Poor health, poor diet—the bad use of salt, sugar, and fats— rushing so much to save other people and forgetting to save myself has taken away the best of my eyesight. My brain is as good as it ever was, and that will be my defense. I will use it well.

Looking back over my life, would I have changed anything? No. I would not have changed, but the things I have done I would have done better, if I had it to do again. I'm over seventy now and most of my vision is gone, yet I have enough intellectual industry to produce four books since I've been legally blind. I'm still active as a lecturer, as a writer of articles, and as a participant in activities relating to Afrikan world liberation.

If I had it to do over again, I'd pay more attention to my health in general. As a researcher, I'd pay more attention to languages. I think language gives you an entry into the cultures of other people in a way that nothing else gives you. I would study cultures as well as history. I would study in depth something that I've only had time to study occasionally: the role of migrations, cultural infusion and diffusion, and how cultures fertilize other cultures to become a single culture.

I think the cultural history of mankind has not been written. I don't even think the political history of mankind has been written. I think we need to point out directions for clarification. I think people need to be in training at a much earlier age for the things they need to be. We need to stop asking people to be certain things, and find people with certain aptitudes and say, "You *will* be an engineer. You *will* be a chemist. You *will* be a doctor. You *will* be an astronaut." Tell them, don't wait for them to develop the traits of being! If you get only half of them, you've still got more than you can use.

We have to look at this issue of relationships. You can explain what is obvious and true, even to the layman. If we did any thinking about it, we would see that this crisis between black men and black women is an engineered crisis. It is one of the instruments of oppression. If the male of any people emerges, that means the warrior class has emerged. The attempt, then, becomes not only to destroy our warrior class, but to destroy the woman who must produce that class. It is part of an international genocidal war against Afrikan people, and we find it very difficult to accept this as truth. AIDS is part of that war. Crack is part of that war.

To end the war, to win the war to turn our people in the right direction for their own salvation on this earth, some of us are going to have to give up something. Some of us won't be here when the solution is found. Some of us are going

to have to put some life on the line to end this war against us, this war of anni-hilation. Then, if we are powerful in the world, there are other people who think that they cannot coexist with us as a powerful people.

How would I want people to think of me? Understand that I was a dedicat-ed scholar. A scholar is nothing but a worker, an academic worker. I could have been many things other than a scholar, but I had the choice, and I made the choice. I don't regret having made it. I've never met a rich man who had a better mind than me, so I could have made it as a rich man, if that's what I had want-ed. I never met a crook who wasn't also a fool, so I could have made it as a crook, if that's what I had wanted to do. I chose to be an explainer, a teacher, a researcher. I chose to try to chart the way and to leave some kind of maps that people can use to move forward and beyond me.

I want people to remember that I did the best I could with what I had. That was my mission. I leave that to you as my legacy. And the role of your generation is to improve on what my generation left behind. Prepare the way for your chil-dren and their children still unborn.

I say to the children like Jaaye [Person-Lynn's son]: You are tomorrow, and you are part of a generation still to come. You are our future, and without you, we have no future. I hope you take this responsibility seriously, and I hope you wear it well. I hope you achieve it. I hope you are able to accomplish what I have worked all my life for—to make this a better world.

✕✕✕✕✕✕

[1] Locke, Alain, *The New Negro* (New York: Atheneum, 1968).

[2] In 1933, Clarke moved to Harlem and visited Schomburg at the 125th Street branch of the New York Public Library.

[3] Jackson, John G., *Christianity Before Christ* (Austin, TX: American Atheist Press, 1985).

[4] Dr. Clarke is referring here to the 1990s Gulf War.

[5] Rogers, Joel A., *The Five Negro Presidents* (New York: Author, 1965).

6 Van Sertima, Ivan (Ed.), "The African Presence in Early Europe," *Journal of African Civilizations* (1986).

7 Freyer, Gilberto, *The Shanties and The Mansions (Sobrados e Macumbos: The Making of Modern Brazil* (New York: Knopf, 1963); Ramos, Arthur, *The Negro in Brazil* (Washington, DC: The Associated Publishers, 1951).

8 Campbell, Mavis C., *The Dynamics of Change in a Slave Society: A Sociopolitical History of the Free Coloreds of Jamaica, 1800–1865* (Rutherford, NJ: Fairleigh Dickinson University Press, 1976).

9 Williams, Chancellor, *The Destruction of Black Civilization: Great Issues of a Race, 4500 B.C. to 2000 A.D.* (Chicago, IL: Third World Press, 1987).

10 Dr. Clarke is referring here to the recent famine and war in Somalia.

11 Williams, Chancellor, *The Rebirth of Afrikan Civilization* (Chicago: Third World Press, 1993).

12 James, C. L. R., *Black Jacobins: Toussaint L'Ouverture and the San Domingo Revolution* (New York: Vintage, 1989); Williams, Eric E., *Capitalism and Slavery* (Chapel Hill, NC: University of North Carolina Press, 1994).

13 Twain, Mark, *King Leopold's Soliloquy* (New York: International Publishers, 1991).

14 Evanzz, Karl, *The Judas Factor: The Plot to Kill Malcolm X* (New York: Thunder's Mouth Press, 1992).

15 Bradley, Michael, *Chosen People from the Caucasus: Jewish Origins, Delusions, Deceptions and Historical Role in the Slave Trade, Genocide and Cultural Colonization* (Chicago: Third World Press, 1992); Butler, Alfred J., *The Arab Conquest of Egypt and the Last Thirty Years of the Roman Dominion* (Oxford: Clarendon Press, 1978); Carruthers, Jacob, *MDW NTR: Divine Speech* (Chicago: Karnak House, 1995); Weiner, Leo, *Africa and the Discovery of America* (Brooklyn, NY: A & B Books, 1992).

IVAN VAN SERTIMA

ANTHROPOLOGIST, LINGUIST, EDUCATOR, AUTHOR,
EDITOR, LECTURER

Professor Ivan Van Sertima's phenomenal book, They Came Before
Columbus: The African Presence in Ancient America, *changed American
history. Using various categories of evidence, this work accurately demonstrates an extensive Afrikan involvement and influence in the civilizations
of the Western Hemisphere and virtually destroys the myth that Columbus
"discovered" America. Of equal importance is Van Sertima's distinction as
founding editor of the* Journal of African Civilizations, *a comprehensive
and definitive scholarly publication that addresses issues related to the
Afrikan contribution to cultures around the globe.*

*T*hey Came Before Columbus: The African Presence in Ancient America taught
me a lot about the prevailing climate of prejudice that inspired the many
attacks that were leveled against it. The attacks are becoming fierce again, now
that they see the book is beginning to make its mark. For example, it's now in its
twenty-first printing. I am thinking of bringing out, once again, the collective
work, edited in 1986, *The African Presence in Early America,* which presents
important new data. My contribution would be much larger than it was before.

A great deal has happened over the last almost two decades. What the reaction to *They Came Before Columbus* revealed to me is that it does not matter
how well-documented, how well-supported the new facts one presents to the
world may be, the old habits of thinking about the Afrikan do not easily change.
It is important that the vision of the Afrikan be changed, our old-fashioned
vision of the Afrikan ancestor.

I began to realize the reason why it was so hard for people to see the Afrikan
on any other plane, before the European arrived, except that of the primitive, the
static primitive: most primitives do not easily make transcontinental,
transoceanic movements. It took thousands of years for the very early primitives
to move across the spaces of Afrika, across the spaces of Europe, across the
spaces of Asia. By conceiving of the Afrikan as a relatively static primitive, it is
hard to accept that they could be on a continent other than their own unless
someone brought them there. Especially when a vast and virginal ocean stands
between. Therefore, it is claimed that they not only made contact with distant
civilizations, but influenced them. That would start a momentous controversy. I

realized that I would first have to revise, in the minds of millions, the popular vision of the Afrikan.

That is why I got involved in the *Journal of African Civilizations*, which has produced more than a dozen volumes, nine of which are titled. I am now working on the tenth. I have stretched tentacles into Europe, into Afrika, into the Caribbean, all across America, to draw from the very best of our scholars. There's the issue, *Blacks in Science: Ancient and Modern*, which is now accepted by nearly a hundred schools and universities. There is *The African Presence in Early Europe, The African Presence in Early Asia* (co-edited with Runoko Rashidi), *The African Presence in Early America, Great Black Leaders: Ancient and Modern, Black Women in Antiquity, Great African Thinkers* (co-edited with Larry Williams), *Nile Valley Civilizations, Egypt Revisited*, and *The Golden Age of the Moor*. We, and I really mean we, have developed a kind of school. It has made a tremendous difference.

Now what these volumes have done is to make people aware that the Afrikan we have been dealing with, the Afrikan we've been focusing upon, or rather the Afrikan that our Eurocentric vision has created, is one-sided and false. The Afrikan we were taught to envision as the true Afrikan is the peripheral creature of the forest zone or the colonized survivor of the slave trade.

The more sophisticated centers of Afrika were shattered. The great achievements of mainstream Afrikans were ignored. So we have a comparison between the mainstream European and the primitive Afrikan. Even people of Afrikan descent have come to the conclusion that what is special about the Afrikan is his simple, raw humanity, his exotic little rituals and costumes, etc. They are not aware, for example, of his scientific tradition. Most people have been made to think that it was the European, because of his so-called theoretical and abstract thinking, who alone learned to master and transcend nature.

When we go back in history we begin to realize that this is not true. We have found, within the last twenty years, Afrikan astronomical observatories, one going back in Kenya three hundred years before Jesus. Of course, in Egypt, it's much earlier than that. In the area we usually call "south of the Sahara," we have found an observatory dating three hundred years before Christ. On the basis of the alignment of this observatory, these early Afrikans built one of the most accurate of prehistoric calendars.

We found steel-making machines that were in advance of Europe. We have found tetracycline, used 1,400 years ago in Nubia, when we in the West only started to use it in the 1950s. We found the use of aspirin among the Bantu centuries before us. We found Afrikans developing vaccines before us. A smallpox vaccine was brought here by the Afrikan slave Onesimus, as reported by his master, Cotton Mather.

We find Afrikans were performing eye cataract surgery long before other people. The Arabs report this performed in Mali in the fourteenth century. We find Afrikans giving us physostigmine, a drug that is still used in the treatment of glaucoma. We find what is probably the first drug to treat hypertension and psychotic disorder—reserpine—developed by Afrikans.

We find their navigation was far more sophisticated than we had come to assume. Carthaginian-type vessels were found on the Niger. Phoenician- and Egyptian-type vessels were found on the Afrikan edge of the Indian Ocean. We find the Chinese reporting Afrikans bringing elephants to them in ships, two hundred years before Columbus.

Our whole vision of the Afrikan, his capacity, his potential, his ability to move and to affect and influence other peoples—all that had to be changed. All that had to be revised before people could look again at the hypothesis of an Afrikan presence in early America. And it is not just a mere hypothesis. A vast body of evidence has accumulated, and in this discussion, I would like to deal more systematically with some of that evidence.

Before I do that, let me tell you of some significant things that are happening in the world related to this research. I want to point to two major developments. There is a very serious growing movement to rethink the curriculum in many of the major educational systems in this country. I have been advising teachers in the major school systems of various cities: St. Louis, Cleveland, Detroit, Indianapolis, Portland, Atlanta, Boston, Newark, etc. I spent a whole week last summer teaching the basics of this new revision of history to 350 teachers in the St. Louis school system, both white and black. This goes across the boundaries of race, across the board.

All of us have to be affected by this. It is not just a black thing. It affects blacks more than anybody else, of course, because we have been practically excluded from history. Everybody has to become aware of this revision of history. The disrespect for us, the kind of prejudices that have been built up upon that disrespect and contempt, is what is at the root of racism. It makes no sense talking about man being equal when we have history books that show us repeatedly that it is not true.

The concept, the idea, the vision of equality cannot be based simply upon liberal clichés or Biblical fantasy. We have to realize that it is rooted in hard historical realities. The movement in Atlanta, in Portland, in Detroit, in Grand Rapids, in Columbus, in St. Louis, in New York, in New Jersey, in Maryland, in Washington, D.C.—these are just a few I know of and have been involved in. It makes us aware of a new movement, a real attempt to change the traditional curriculum.

There is resistance in certain places, and here is where I want to sound a note of caution. There is so much that has been developed, and responsibly developed, in these years by this school. There is no need for people to make up things or to ride upon half-known or half-sure things. There is a body of hard evidence about the great achievements of Afrikans and Afrikan Americans upon which we can build this new curriculum.

The curriculum is not simply Afrocentric. That term is being misused. Our Afrocentricity, or rather our new vision of the Afrikan, which is what this Afrocentricity is about, should be used to counter and correct Eurocentricity. Eurocentricity has brought so much falsehood into our present curriculum. But you cannot exchange a biased Eurocentricity for a biased Afrocentricity. This shift of vision must be corrective. The Afrocentric vision comes as a corrective, so that you get nothing that is exclusively Eurocentric or exclusively Afrocentric. You get a balancing, which brings you closer to the truth. You come closer. You cannot totally capture the truth, but you can come closer to a more balanced truth as a result of this corrective vision.

I want to make that quite clear because some people are saying, "Why are you exchanging a Eurocentric for an Afrocentric curriculum?" It is not an Afrocentric curriculum. It is an Afrocentric perspective, which helps us to correct the present Eurocentric curriculum, so we get something broader, fairer, more all-inclusive. We get a more inclusive curriculum. The word "inclusive" is used because, instead of excluding us and merely including the achievements of others or excluding their achievements and saying we did it all, the curriculum becomes all-inclusive: it pulls the various elements or fragments of the human condition together. We have been pushed out of it altogether. We are the invisible chapter of history. That is one of the foundations of racist thinking.

The second significant event is something that is beginning to happen in Europe. I know there have been some great upheavals recently in Russia, then there was the fall of the Berlin Wall, the end of the Cold War, which many of us seem to think is just a passing phase. It's no passing phase. A new Europe is being born, and that new Europe, especially Eastern Europe, even though it may seek economic models from the West, is very much aware of the kind of stifling, racist prejudices that bedevil the West.

The Europeans soon held a conference in 1993, for example, in the Netherlands. I was invited to attend this. I was invited to this so that the participants could have a new vision of the Third World, a new vision of history, particularly of Afrika. I want you to be aware of the change that is occurring, not only here in America but in the world. The Russians—let us pray their movement does

IVAN VAN SERTIMA

not come to a sudden halt—have spent the last year revising their history curriculum. They actually banned history exams for a year so that they could bring into being a more all-inclusive curriculum that could include more objective truths and not repeat the Stalinist falsehoods of the past.

We have to carry on our own thing as well. Carry on a subterranean movement under the conventional structures of the system. We have to make our people aware of these things and be inspired by them, not to be inspired by mere hollow chauvinistic boasts, but inspired by a genuine awareness of achievement so that we can emulate that achievement. So our children do not have to feel they only half-belong to the world. They do not have to feel as though they're on the backside of the world, as it were. It is very important that we all be aware, particularly our people.

People of Afrikan descent should become very much aware of what is going on, very much aware of these developments, of this record of achievement. It is affecting us profoundly. It's not only the ignorance of this that is making people despise us, push us aside, and treat us as second-class citizens--but our ignorance of it also makes us treat ourselves in a certain way. It has affected the way we approach everything.

For example, I have seen many instances where there's a new enterprise or a new type of publication. Our people may think it is good enough simply because it's a black thing, regardless of whether it is operating on the lowest level. In other words, mediocrity has become the ideal. They do not realize that we are not a second-class people. We are not a mediocre people.

When you go back in history to the great West Afrikans, the West Afrikans at their best, the Egyptians at their best during the ancient dynasties, the black-dominated period--and I'm not talking about modern Egypt, which is an entirely different thing--if you see these people at their best, you will see their passionate quest for excellence. Their legacy of excellence, their ideal of excellence, is so remarkable. When I first went to Egypt, for example, I particularly wanted to find one of the things they had been building centuries ago, an obelisk, which they had abandoned because it had a slight flaw. It would have taken centuries for the flaw to make a difference, but it had to be perfect. It had to be as perfect as they could make it. That is the kind of mind, that is the kind of imagination so critical to us in this time.

Now, in the face of all the evidence presented, there may still be a backlash. That is always possible in history. It is for us to become vigilant. It is for us to push on with such great force that such a backlash either does not occur, or if it does occur, it does not have any lasting effect. You see, one has to be always careful in any movement, in any revolution. One has to be always careful about the

old flesh creeping back. Look what happened in Russia. All these great liberals, everybody got so excited. Look what's happening today in eastern Europe.

In the liberal wing, which had a chance to harden itself, consolidate itself, and push forward, serious divisions occurred. It could be it was just the nature of the society and the time. I am not blaming anybody, but there is always the possibility for backlash. Backlash seems to have come.

The group that is fighting for a new life, for a new deal, the vigilance of that group is critical. One doesn't just fall back and say "Okay, everything is going fine now. At last they are changing the curriculum." That is why I say, hand in hand with the mainstream shifts, there must come a subterranean group arming itself with these facts. If anything happens in the mainstream, they could push forward again. They could keep this thing alive. One cannot predict the future because there is always a danger. One has to be vigilant.

Let me now deal with the evidence I mentioned earlier, on the subject that I have become most associated with: *They Came Before Columbus.* One of the things I may not have mentioned with as great a force in the past as I do now is the fact that even though we have to build up the evidence by going into many disciplines, most people seem to think there was no documented evidence. They think nobody wrote about this, that nobody mentioned these early Afrikan explorers. In fact, at least a dozen people who came during the time of Columbus saw or heard first-hand reports of blacks among the Native Americans.

Christopher Columbus himself was the first person to suggest that there were blacks in America before him. He said that when he was in Haiti, Native Americans told them there were black-skinned people who came from the east and southeast in large boats, trading in gold-tipped metal spears called *guanin.* Samples of these spears were sent back by Columbus on a mailboat to Spain. They were inspected by Spanish metallurgists who found that they were identical—not similar—identical in terms of the ratio of gold, silver, and copper alloys found in spears then being forged in Guinea. Ferdinand Columbus, the son of Christopher Columbus, wrote a book about his father, in which he said that his father told him he saw "Negro" people north of the area we now call Honduras.

Vasco Nunez de Balboa, in September 1513 the day after he claimed to have discovered the Sea of the South, was coming down the slopes of Quarecua, when he saw two black men among the Native Americans. They were very different from the natives, and so he asked them, "Where did these black men come from?" They said they did not know. All that they knew was "that these blacks were living in a large settlement nearby." That's in the Isthmus of Darien, which we now call Panama. They were in this large settlement there, and they were wag-

ing war with them. Lopez de Gomara reports that the blacks Balboa saw were identical to the blacks of Guinea.

Peter Martyr, the first major historian of America, tells us that they found Afrikans living in the mountains. He called them "Ethiopians," the word generally used for people with burnt skin--that is, black people. He was not talking about modern Ethiopians. He said that they were probably shipwrecked long ago and had taken refuge in the mountains.

Rodrigo de Colmanares reports that one of the pilots of Balboa said he saw blacks east of the Gulf of San Miguel. Riva Palacio reports on blacks near Tegucigalpa, on the Nicaraguan–Honduran border. All these are people coming before the slave trade, you know. L'Abbé Brasseur de Bourburg says that two distinct people were indigenous to Darien--one of them, Mandingo; the other, Tule. The Tule were the red-skinned type, Native American, with straight black hair; the other, the Afrikan type.

Apart from all this, the Smithsonian Institute discovered two Afrikan skeletons in the United States Virgin Islands in St. Thomas, at a place called Hull Bay. When they dug up these skeletons, they said that they were in a layer or stratum dated 1250 A.D., which is more than two hundred years before Columbus. They said that these were the skeletons of Afrikan males in their thirties. They said their incisor teeth were filed, which was a peculiar dental ritual used by some pre-Columbian Afrikans. They said, in addition, there was a pre-Columbian Indian ornament, a Native American ornament around the forearm of one of these skeletons. Yet, when they took them into the lab to date them, they couldn't date them. They found an interference that didn't make any sense. I'm not allowed to talk about what caused that interference. It's a secret and has nothing to do with the subject.

Going into the Virgin Islands, I found at the bottom of the Reef Bay Valley in St. John's, a pool. Carved on the side of this pool, along the water line, I found a dot and crescent script. It was deciphered by Dr. Barry Fell. A shadow has fallen over Dr. Fell. A great deal of criticism has been leveled against his work. I therefore had the decipherment checked out with the Libyan Department of Antiquities. They gave it a reading that was almost identical to the one Barry Fell had given me. It was written in the Tifinagh branch of the Libyan script that was used by the Tamahau Berbers. It was also used by a people in medieval Mali and by a people in southern Libya. These were all mostly dark-skinned peoples. It read: "Plunge in to cleanse yourself. This is water for purification before prayer." They have found, so far, seven examples of this type of inscription with the dot and crescent formation across the United States. The one I discovered was deciphered. Mine was the longest found.

Apart from that, there is botanical evidence. The Portuguese, who entered Afrika half a century before Columbus, found a cotton growing plentifully on the Guinea Coast. They naturally assumed it to be an Afrikan cotton. They took it and planted it in the Cape Verde in 1462. Note the date, thirty years before Columbus. A study made in the twentieth century established it as an American cotton. How could an American cotton get into Afrika before Columbus, one must ask, unless there was a crossing? Now this cotton is *gossypium hirsutum var. punctatum*. It was only found growing in the Caribbean and South America, not in Afrika. It is not indigenous to Afrika. It cannot get to Afrika without a human crossing.

There are certain things that can cross from Afrika to America without humans. The bottle gourd, for example. It has a thick shell, and it can fall from a tree or boat into one of the currents. There are three currents that take things from Afrika to America. The gourd could fall into one of the currents and come to the Americas. Salt water doesn't affect it. But that is not the case with cotton. Cotton cannot cross in the current without losing its potency.

An Afrikan jack bean also got into South America. This jack bean, *canavalia virosa*, intermarried with an American jack bean, *canavalia plagiosperma*, to produce a new world jack bean, *canavalia piperi*. This was long before Columbus. Then there is the banana. It's not an Afrikan plant, it is Asiatic. It is found on the Atlantic side of South America, not on the Asian side. It came into Afrikan trade in the twelfth century, when the Arabs introduced it to Afrika. They found it pre-Columbian in graves in South America. They also found widespread cultivation of the plantain—the banana's sister—along the Amazon coast when they came in. It had nothing to do with the later post-Columbian introduction of the banana and plantain. Bananas in South America all have Afrikan names.

Remember, this was not a once-and-for-all affair. The currents that traverse the Atlantic, that move from Afrika to America, they are massive and they've been continuous in the Atlantic Ocean for thousands of years. Voyages of intent, as well as voyages of accident, occurred over a long period. The period I've been talking about so far is the period of the late pre-Columbian voyages, dating from the early fourteenth century right down to the time of Columbus himself, when people began to sight these blacks among the Native Americans.

The early voyages, the early contacts, some of them are very important. They are not just simple shipwrecks. They involved a substantial body of people. The more significant of these is found among the Olmec, the very earliest of American civilizations. This had nothing whatever to do with the Mandingo voyages. It is absolutely removed in time by centuries. These very early voyages

involved Egypto-Nubian types or other Afrikan types affected by Egypto-Nubian civilizations. They occur between 948 and 680 B.C. We know that because the first sequence of stone heads begin to appear in ceremonial centers in the Olmec world, and the first pyramids also begin to appear there.

When we deal with the pyramids of Mexico, we are dealing with a much earlier period and a different type of Afrikan voyage. I want to make something quite clear. The American pyramids were not built by Afrikans, they were *influenced* by them. The first pyramids that appear in America appear in a strange coupling on the same platform. They appear linked to the first sequence of stone heads, with both Afrikan and Mongoloid-type features. Not all of the stone heads can be classified as Afrikan, although they have broad noses and very full lips. But some of them are definitely Afrikan, especially the Tres Zapotes head, with its braids; and another one, in black stone, in a sort of Osirian pose, practically lying on his chin, showing no helmet, only a crown or tuft of Africoid hair.

The hair evidence is very important. Sometimes you could have an Asiatic type with broad features like the Afrikan, because the Afrikan type entered Asia very early. Fortunately, you have lots of terra cotta—that is, clay sculptures of Afrikans—in which the texture of the hair, even the coloration of the skin, is skillfully reflected in the texture and dyes. You also have skeletal evidence where the bones of the face, the texture of the hair, the brow ridge, the nasal aperture, the nasal fossae, and the structure of the jaw—all sorts of things in combination—indicate the Africoid-type, as distinct from that of the Native American.

The first pyramid to appear in America has no predecessor in America. It appears right on the platform where the first sequence of stone heads appear, at La Venta. It is on a north–south axis. That in itself is very unusual because all the major ceremonial centers and pyramids in Egypt and Nubia are also on a north–south axis. Never before in America was any ceremonial center built on a north–south axis. Never before in America had a pyramid appeared. Now all of a sudden, and just where the first sequence of stone heads appear, we have a miniature step pyramid as well as a conical pyramid. Some experts say, "Oh, that's not a conical pyramid, its a fluted cone." If you go and look at it now, you're going to find deep depressions, of course. You'll see that it has a cone, but the sides have sort of caved in. So they say it's a fluted cone, not a pyramid. That's nonsense. The reason it has deep depressions is because it was built of clay, not brick or stone, as the pyramids of Egypt were. The Americas didn't have that much stone, not in that area anyway, where they built the first one. It's built in the swamps. The sides would naturally fall in with time, as do most earthen hills.

There are no more fluted cones in America after that. So if they planned it as a fluted cone, in order, as the experts say, to represent a volcano, where are the other fluted cones? If the pyramid at one end of the platform is meant to represent a volcano, then what is the step pyramid doing at the other end of the same platform? Is that then a baby volcano? Again, experts have argued, "In America, the pyramid is a temple. In Egypt, it's a tomb." That is not true. The tomb and temple combination is reflected in both complexes of pyramids, in the Old World and the New World.

The greatest pyramid in America, the one at Teotihuacan, although not built by the Olmecs, but was influenced by them and has roughly the same base, is off by one meter. Some experts are now allowing that meter for mistakes in the reconstruction. It has roughly the same base as the Great Pyramid of Egypt. It also has moveable capstones, like the one in Egypt. It was also used as a geodetic marker. It has all the relationships and functions you find in the greater pyramids of Egypt.

Apart from the stone heads, there are thousands of terra cotta clay sculptures of Afrikans in the Americas. The Americans left more than a million terra cotta bodies and heads. That is what survives, their remarkable lifelike clay sculptures, so we have pictures of them. We can't say, "Oh, because they didn't have the camera, we don't know what they looked like." We know what they looked like. Most of them did not look like Afrikans, so the Afrikan type, when it appears, stands out. When Dr. Andrzej Wiercinski went down into the graves in the dry areas where the skeletons survived—places like Tlatilco, Cerro de las Mesas, and Monte Albán—he was able to make significant cranial measurements that show you have a type here that is very distinct from the native type, that had come in and crossbred with the native type.

In spite of all this evidence, Afrika obviously is not as influential as it was before the slave trade. Remember, Afrika is no longer what it used to be. Afrika is an exploded world, an exploded star, a shattered continent. It is only in this century, within our own lifetime, that it has started to stumble back into any kind of coherent, independent form. Even independence has not yet truly come to Afrika. The richest part of Afrika is not yet economically independent. So bear in mind, you can't compare modern, shattered Afrika with the Afrika that was. There is no place on the globe, at the moment, where the Afrikan figure has the kind of power and prominence the old Egyptians had when Egypt was dominated by Afrikans. There is no empire in Afrika, at the moment, that has the cohesion and the power such as we find in the medieval period in places like Mali or Ghana. Bear in mind, we are dealing with the Afrikan before the crash of their world, okay?

What is remarkable about the Jews is that they preserved the past, even though they were shattered and almost destroyed. Millions of them were wiped out. The only thing that kept them together was the bond of their history. Whatever reservations one may have about the policies of the present Jewish state—I'm not interested in the politics of the moment, I am dealing now strictly with the human spirit and how it preserves itself, how people remake themselves—the only thing that preserved them, that enabled them to hold their center, was their memory of the past. The preservation of the past, the glorification of the past, the consolidation of the past—they can go back to something that was thousands of years before their shattering, before their explosion into fragments, before they were scattered over the earth, before the attempt to destroy them. They could go back to that and hold it, like a light before and within them, until they became, in spite of their small numbers, a central force in the world.

That is something you have to understand. Just because something happened thousands of years ago does not mean it is insignificant. In fact, the past is more significant than the present. The present, after all, is a passing, fluid thing. Only the major events of the present are going to really leave any marks. The past has already left the blight or the bloom of major events. That is the nature of the universe. Every major sound and light event in the universe is preserved. We photographed a doomed star about five years ago. This star had exploded 160,000 years ago, yet we photographed it because the light of that event, the mark of it, is still with us, still traveling through the universe. Even the sound of what people call the "Big Bang"—the birth-boom of the universe, the sound behind all sound—Bell Labs picked it up some years ago. It is still with us. We can actually hear that primal explosion that occurred in the beginning of time.

Let me mention and clarify my presentation before Congress, and how it relates to this work. I appeared on July 7, 1987, before a Congressional committee that was overseeing the work of the Christopher Columbus Quincentenary Commission. I was called upon to show due cause why they should not refer to Columbus's accidental stumble into the Caribbean as a discovery. I pointed to the fact that Columbus was the first to suggest there were Afrikans in the Americas before him. I stated that the Afrikan voyage was significant. I also pointed to the fact that the International Congress of Americanists, meeting in Barcelona as early as 1964, had ruled that there "cannot now be any doubt that there were Old World visitors to the New World before 1492." I pointed to the

testimony of nearly a dozen Europeans who had come to the New World in the first phase of the European contact period.

I pointed out some other things. I pointed to a map that shows the correct latitudinal and longitudinal coordinates between the Afrikan Atlantic coast and the South American Atlantic coast, with certain prominent Caribbean islands drawn in, long before Columbus. They could not have been drawn at the time of Columbus, or even two hundred years after 1492. Nobody in Europe could plot latitude and longitude in that way. In fact, 150 years after the death of Columbus, encyclopedias in Europe reported that longitude had not been discovered and was probably undiscoverable. With the short time allowed me—twenty-five minutes—I presented a range of things to this Congressional committee that indicated to them that it was insulting to use the word "discovery." It was not only insulting, it was inaccurate.

One of the things my testimony led to was the chairman advising the commission *not* to use the word "discovery." I'm not sure they are going to follow that to the letter, but they were strongly advised not to. One of the commissioners got very angry and left the chamber! He did an interview with *The New York Times* and reported the next day, "Even if Columbus was not the first to discover America, he was the first person to go back and give a press conference." He got his jollies out of that.

I also managed to get the Bahamas into the commemoration; at first, they just wanted to include the mainland United States. I also pointed out that they did not have any Native Americans on the commission. There was only one black, I think. The result was a larger, more multiculturally diverse kind of commemoration of the fusion of Old World peoples in the New World, rather than a celebration of the mythical discovery of America by Columbus. Those inclusions emerged as a result of my testimony.

Of course, everybody knows that the movement, the massive, continuous movement of Old World peoples to this continent led to the destruction of the Native American civilization. One of the things I would like to touch on now is what happened to the Native American. Today, we only find them in the reservations, or we find them in certain other areas of America.

One of the things a lot of people don't understand is why Montezuma, who ruled a great empire, was so easily defeated by Cortes. The ragged army of Spaniards under Cortes, who landed here in 1519, could not defeat the Aztecs, who were the Native American power at the time. It was impossible.

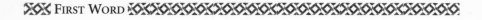

What Cortes saw in the center of America startled him. Here again, we have the same general ignorance about what Americans were doing as we have about what Afrikans were doing. When Cortes saw their pyramids and places, their aqueducts and their zoos, their running baths, their chinampas—the most advanced agricultural technique then in the world—he said, "I have not seen its like anywhere."

The reason why Cortes defeated Montezuma is that several tribes—or rather, small nations—were being oppressed by the Aztec, the ruling power. They therefore joined with the European to defeat Montezuma in the same way Europeans joined with the Afrikans, under Hannibal, to defeat the Romans. Some unseasoned European troops joined with the Afrikans to defeat their own European Rome. The Romans, after all, were an imperial power oppressing other European people. It had nothing to do with race. The reason why Cortes won had to do with the fact that he could draw upon the support of the dissident tribes pitted against Montezuma.

You know, doing this kind of work brings about some highs and some lows. One of the things I've been excited about is the emergence of some of the most remarkable scholars out of Afrika. I was very pleased by the tremendous respect accorded me by Cheikh Anta Diop and later by Théophile Obenga. Cheikh Anta Diop very much wanted me to bring out his latest book, *Civilization or Barbarism*, but he had already given the rights to the French.[1] The most he could do was to give me permission to have two major chapters of his work translated and published in my journal. I am very happy about that.

The book I wrote, or rather edited, on Diop had quite a profound effect. I was assisted by Larry Obadele Williams. Larry Williams did a remarkable job. While a lot of people were just going around enjoying themselves during Diop's visit here, Larry Williams collected everything he could. He made photographs, collected tapes, all sorts of things about Diop, which were very helpful. There were interviews that were extremely important in giving us a vision of Diop. Diop was profoundly affected by the reception and honor he received from Morehouse College in Atlanta. That was the last great moment of his life. When he went home, his wife wrote and told me he talked about that all the time until he died. It was a marvelous thing. That was one of the great high points, because Diop really was the most important Afrikan in this field.

I am very impressed by Théophile Obenga also. I was surprised that God had sent us another contemporary soul to light the way. Théophile Obenga is the true successor to Diop. He gave me his whole manuscript in French. I had two major chapters translated. It was rather expensive, so I couldn't do the whole book. I brought it out in *Egypt Revisited*. That has been one of the great high points.

The other high point is the participation of European scholars in our venture, people like Basil Davidson and John Pappademos. They are not Eurocentric, even though they are European. There are black scholars who are Eurocentric, like Frank Snowden. Many of the major figures in this field are white: Claudia Zaslavsky, the mathematician; John Pappademos, the physicist; Martin Bernal, the linguist and classicist; and Basil Davidson, a very remarkable historian who is among the best Europe has produced on Afrika. All of these people found a platform in my journal. They represent a new wave of European, not the European interested in putting the Afrikan down and excluding him, but Europeans dedicated to rebuilding Afrika and Afrikans by struggling against the prejudice of their disciplines and even, in the case of Davidson, their own early prejudices.

Now, I don't want to dwell on the low points because every struggle has its anguish. But I sometimes have been pained by statements made by American Afrikans or Afrikans who are still Eurocentric and who, instead of revising their thinking, go out of their way to destroy what we are doing and keep us where we have been. I don't want to call names, but I have sometimes been very pained by that. It has taken years to fight one's way back.

Yet, the negatives have been my greatest help. That is the one lesson I learned over the years: the negative is very important, sometimes more important than the positive. Sometimes, if something is highly successful instantly, it makes you facile. If something meets great negatives, it can be even better in the end. Unless it is destroyed, it is far better if it meets with negatives. The negative makes you go back and check out everything. You find a whole lot of new things. If before you came with a revolver, the next time you come with a cannon. The time after that you come with a nuclear bomb. So the negatives are very important. To know the enemy is larger than you think, more formidable, makes you go back and build a bigger arsenal.

The negatives made me realize, for example, how very alone I was and how necessary it was to have a community of scholars. When I wrote *They Came Before Columbus*, there was not a single writer who later wrote for the Journal that I knew personally. Not one. I did not even know who John Henrik Clarke was until he came to speak at the book party. I was not aware of anyone here who was doing anything. I did not know Asa Hilliard. I did not know Charles Finch. I did not know any of these people. So it built, for me, a community. Being attacked in that way built a whole community that was really very critical. It welded a great many of us together, people whom I never knew.

You see, if as a child and all through your adult years you have been accepted for doing a certain kind of thing, and the people who have tried to do some-

thing else have been crucified, it would take something very extraordinary, something tremendously traumatic for you to change. I have known one or two scholars, and here I can't call names, who attacked me at first, then found through their own research that I was on the right track. They were so upset they never said anything. They quietly died. It is not until you look at their posthumous papers that you find they made discoveries that brought them around. They preferred to be silent, until death, than to say that they found what I found.

People deal with these things in different ways. I myself have pointed this out over and over. I wasn't born with any revolutionary vision of the Afrikan. All the prejudices, all the Eurocentricities that had become part of the flesh and blood of man's thinking in the Western world were part of mine. I only began to wake up in my thirties. All through my twenties, all through my teens, all of the falsehoods about Afrikan people like myself and other people of Afrikan descent, all of these fictions I believed. I believed in them as one believes in the Bible, meaning they were like biblical truths to me. It was only the trauma, the real tremendous internal upheavals, and personal catastrophes that accompanied my going to Afrika when I was thirty-two that led me to swing around. Even the actual revolution in the Caribbean and in Afrika, which had a temporary effect on me, I suppressed. It came up in me again later and dismembered all of the myths I held, which had become the foundation of my life. It had been a foundation for centuries for billions of other people.

Take my brother, for instance. Things that happened in his life made him see the truth, the larger truth of what I was saying. He had been traumatized by his experience, so he jumped out of his shell and was able to transform himself. I think it is very important to note that people are not to be attacked because they are locked into this sort of thing. One still has to attempt to change them, you know. This change has to occur at various levels in various minds.

Even among scholars, ego, jealousy, and envy can play a role in some of their attacks. I know that is something that happens everywhere. You find, for example, people who feel you are getting too much attention, that your ideas and so forth are becoming too popular or are affecting other things. Sometimes it's just a plain bread-and-butter issue. They feel that if they were to say your kind of thing, they would lose their jobs. All of that plays a part and contributes to the loneliness one sometimes feels. To follow up on some of the things one discovers calls for a lot of thinking. You can't think easily if your life is a social thing. A lot of people are very surprised they can get in touch with me. They may speak with

me for a moment on the telephone, but I don't have a social life. I don't go to parties. If there is a reception for a talk, I'll go. I meet very few people face to face.

Some of the people who have written for me, some of the people with whom I have had the most profound relationships, I have never met. Like Diop, for example. I didn't meet Diop until about a year before his death. I had a long correspondence with him, I spoke with him on the telephone, but for ten years I never saw him. Not until it was absolutely necessary to meet him face to face. I met him in London, then I met him in Atlanta, when he came over here for the big celebration for him.

It is very important to realize that in order to pursue certain things in life, one must often be alone. When I was doing *They Came Before Columbus*, I saw no one. I forbade meetings. I would see my chairman and colleagues once a month at faculty meetings. For about six to seven years, I met no one properly.

I am very fortunate in some respects. I have a remarkable wife. She takes care of half of my business. She is busier than I am. She often goes to bed at one or two in the morning. She is not my secretary, because she has as much work to do in her own business as I do in mine. The one thing I do regret is that so much of my time is spent on little things. I do not get as much time for research without having to separate myself.

For example, I spend about five hours a day on mail, in addition to my full-time lecturing, my research, etc. It is all very well for people to say, "But why don't you have a secretary?" I do have a secretarial assistant, but you have to directionalize things, otherwise the whole thing falls down. You have to make all the big decisions—about what book is being published this year, who will participate, who has expertise in this or that area. How can a secretary do that? My work calls for a lot of exploratory work, work I just have to do myself. Who decides what is going to be the issue? What is the most feasible issue? Who decides what your interest is going to be? Who decides where the experts in the new area you are exploring are? You can't get that from a secretarial assistant.

I am doing a book on the Moors. These are areas that are not charted. They are virginal areas, you know. Europe was in a kind of European Dark Age when the Moors—that is, the Afrikans and Arabians—invaded. The Moors had a profound influence on Europe. During that period some of the most significant developments occurred. The European Renaissance should really be called the world scientific revolution. For example, we saw the beginning of the gun. The gun is not European. The father of the gun was the firestick, which the Moors

brought into Europe. There were also many developments in map making. There were developments in trigonometry. There was the beginning of early Egyptian geometry and algebra. There was the beginning of optics. Windmills, crankshafts, and hydraulic worm-and-pinion gears were developed. The game of chess were introduced. The lighting of city streets was introduced, hot-and-cold water systems, all these things happened. But I don't want to give away everything in my book. There were so many surprising things. I don't want people to just pick up a few bits and pieces of it now. You have to really look at the impact of the Moors on Europe, on the edge of the new thing that was to happen in Europe.

After months of work on this book, I had to start all over again because I began to realize that many of those who wrote about the Moors had excluded Afrikans, not just the European historians but some Arabs actually assumed the Afrikan had nothing to do with this. I had to create a section called "The Egyptian Precursors." What the Arab invader of Egypt was starting with was the Greek heritage, not realizing that the Greeks took it from the Egyptians. While there were certain refinements and extensions, due to Greek genius, it was not merely a transmission of Greek heritage but a critical part of the Afrikan heritage. One had to really probe deeply to begin to realize this was a truly multicultural tradition. Elements were coming in from all over the world to build the world scientific revolution, which we have come to believe was largely a European thing.

I say today to young scholars just starting out, first of all, realize you have a far greater advantage than I had. You have before you a body of work which was not available to us in our time until rather late in our lives. Also, a word of caution: please do not accept everything. Do not assume that merely because someone is of your own race, everything they have to say about what Afrikans or people of Afrikan descent did is true. Our revolution has to be built up responsibly on a body of hard facts. You have to look very closely at evidence. You have to become self-critical. It's important that you do.

Life is not simple. The simpler you are, the more you are involved in the simplification or facile falsification of things, the harder life will become and the more it will surprise you. The capacity to look at things with great care is critical to the scientific mind. It's critical to human development. Since you have this body of material before you, you do not have to go through the terrifying searches some of us had to go through. Examine everything closely so you can build upon a hard base.

Do not become chauvinistic. It is very important that those people who are against us or those people who are not of us learn to respect us and learn to respect these discoveries. It is equally important that you also become aware they had their achievements too. We have got to lay emphasis on our own achievements, of course, because we have been excluded from history for centuries. Therefore, nobody can accuse us of being racist simply because we emphasize what we have done. They would have good cause to accuse us of being racist if we tried to denigrate everything they have done. Let us be able to see clearly what claims were false and what claims were valid.

Also, we must realize that scholarship is not a separate entity from our relationships. You see, one of the things that leads to extremely difficult relationships, and this is not something that is going to vanish overnight, is self-contempt. This is very deep among American Afrikans and Caribbean Afrikan people. Our "historylessness"—and by that I mean our assumption that we have no significant history—our lack of belief in ourselves, our lack of belief in having something of value, something substantial of value, to support us leads to all sorts of anxieties, angers, and insecurities that are bound to affect relationships. No relationship in a highly troubled psyche or shattered psyche, no relationship with people who nurse or nurture troubled or shattered psyches, can be easy. That is why it is so critical to use history to rebuild, to bring a healthier wholeness to that psyche. So even though no one will come and tell you directly, "Well, look, if you study this history, you are going to have a better relationship," the study of history can give you a sense of wholeness and a different quality of mental health. It will almost inevitably lead to healthier relationships.

One of the problems we have is our misunderstanding of Afrikan polygamy. This misunderstanding can flatter and foster gross male chauvinism. Afrikan polygamy is a complex thing. It is not a ticket to sexual license and treachery. It was a social institution that was less of a sexual than a protective or social welfare type of institution. First of all, not everybody could be polygamous. You had to be fairly prosperous. You had to be able to support the unhusbanded females in your harem. You are not necessarily sleeping with all of them. As a protective institution it may have included, for example, your unmarried sister and your widowed mother. You would not even dare to dream of touching them.

Incest is a far more serious offense in Afrika than in any culture in the world. You could be executed for incest. Incest is so serious, the restrictions extend beyond the immediate family. You cannot even marry you\r cousin. Sometimes, in some places, you cannot even marry someone in your own clan. Incest was only allowed in ancient times as a royal prerogative, in those extreme situations

when it became connected with certain religious assumptions about divine royal blood. The blood of the pharaoh was the blood of God because he was the representative of God on earth. Those were religious exceptions and oddities.

When black people were brought here to the Americas, our women were kept fairly close to the children most of the time. Some of them became concubines of their masters by force. The man was sent wandering all over the place. Liaisons developed at times between him and women in other places. Those liaisons, or his so-called polygamous behavior, grew out of something totally different from the situation in Afrika. Not out of prosperity and stability, but out of insecurity. American Afrikan men should not use this example and say, "Well, the Afrikans are polygamous, and that is why I am polygamous." Those things are not genetic, they are not even fixed cultural imperatives. They are responses to situations.

On the other hand, you have the Afrikan woman, who may pride herself on the fact that she had a certain measure of independence in relation to her man, a measure of independence that was often comparably greater than that of the woman in the traditional European family. Particularly in the American context, because of the wandering or unemployed black man whose economic opportunities were sometimes less, the American Afrikan woman has sometimes been in the unusual position, unusual in terms of our convention of becoming the chief breadwinner. All sorts of tensions develop in those relationships. You have to see, therefore, the unhealthy or unhappy types of relationships between men and women, particularly black men and black women, as part of all sorts of social situations and crises.

It's not confined to us, by the way. Marriage, at the moment, is undergoing a revolution. Many people have never investigated the fact that there is a dramatic increase in the break-up of marriages among whites. There has been a tremendous shift to single-family households headed by women not only among blacks, but whites as well. If you see the latest statistics, you would be utterly surprised how much of that is happening. You have a relationship that has been stretched to its limits. The battle for woman's equality, on every level, has led to all sorts of redefinitions of marriage. This has profoundly affected all of us. The family is in crisis. It is not only the black family. One has to see in what way the new historical information can heal or help to heal the black psyche or can be used to help the family.

I just want to end by saying that to think this historical information stands as a separate area of knowledge, and that it can only peripherally impinge on relationships is not true. It's just that nobody could come and map out your relationship for you. They can give you certain information that can help

change your consciousness, and a changed consciousness automatically remaps its relationships.

✕✕✕✕✕✕

[1] Diop, Cheikh Anta, *Civilization or Barbarism: An Authentic Anthropology* (Brooklyn, NY: Lawrence Hill, 1990).

YOSEF A. A. BEN-JOCHANNAN

KEMETOLOGIST (EGYPTOLOGIST), HISTORIAN, EDUCATOR,

AUTHOR, LECTURER

"Dr. Ben," as he is affectionately known, is an elder scholar who has raised the consciousness and body of knowledge in one of the most fiercely argued areas in Afrikan history, namely, the origins and contributions of Afrikans to Nile Valley civilizations. Through his volumes of writings, physical evidence, lectures, and tours, Dr. Ben has convincingly demonstrated that Nile Valley civilization, prior to any invasions and during their golden eras, were indigenously Afrikan. He has also proven himself one of the great influences on developing young scholars.

I was born in what is nefariously called the Falasha community of Ethiopia, East Africa. In fact, it is the Beta Israel community of the Hebrew people in Ethiopia. We call ourselves Beta Israel: people of the House of Israel. There are two groups of us: the Kaila and the Falasha. My people are Kailas, predominantly.

What is the distinction? The Kaila, my group, do not associate with non-Jews in the community. The term "Falasha" is a dirty word—it shouldn't be used—that means "don't touch me," "strange," or "funny people" in Amharic. That's my background, Ethiopian Hebrews. That's what I was born into. I don't express that at all anymore. I have withdrawn from Judaism. The reason being evidence in Ethiopia, Sudan, and Egypt told me there was no justification for me to be Hebrew. Why eat the dregs that have washed off the plant and not the main food? Judaism, Christianity, and Islam are outgrowths of principles laid down by the Afrikans along the Nile. When I didn't know any better, yes, I followed Judaism. I can't follow it after seeing the facts about where the basic foundation comes from, and the distortion of it. So I withdrew. If I am to be religious, it's going to have to be of the pure Nile Valley religious thinking or spiritual thought, the zenith that was reached in Egypt. This is the same sentiment I have for the kind of work I do.

Observing the removal of the Afrikan from the Judeo-Christian Bible was the first thing that grasped my mind in terms of scholarship. According to this Bible, one of the rivers, the river Gihon, is supposed to pass through the land of Ethiopia. That's supposed to be the word of God, yet Afrika is not mentioned. When parts of Afrika are mentioned, not as Afrika but as Ethiopia or Egypt, it is

presented as if they are not in Afrika. The people who are presented in any picture Bible are always blond, brunette, or something else, but never black.

In the same Bible, there are so many racist stories. Such is the one in which the Queen of Sheba, Makeda, is supposed to be sorry that she's black. She makes the complaint that the reason she is so black is because her mother kept her in the vineyards, whereas her sisters were not kept in the vineyard. We could go through many other things in the Bible, where black is treated as if it's bad or dirty or the worst thing. White is always the best and clean.

I'm told constantly what the Greeks did, the Greeks just having come here in the world yesterday. The Adam and Eve story and the Jehovah story have always been told to me as something coming from Jews—come to find out, it's plagiarism. The person they created called Moses was supposed to have gotten the Ten Commandments on Mount Sinai. In fact, he stole them from the Egyptian "Negative Confessions" that long preceded his birth. You could find them everywhere in Egypt. Those ten were already made, because you find them in the *Egyptian Book of the Dead*, in a rare section called "The Osirian Drama."[1]

I was told in school that Hippocrates was the father of medicine—come to find out, that, too, is a big lie. Hippocrates was only around during the 300 B.C. era. Imhotep, to whom Hippocrates gives homage in his "Hippocratic Oath," swears that he will practice medicine accordingly. Imhotep preceded Hippocrates by more than two thousand years. I could keep going on and on, revealing this mirage of lies that were told to us as Afrikan people. This kind of knowledge had a lot to do with my change in belief system.

One can pay a price telling the truth though. This line of work exposed me to a tragic reality: hunger. I've been fired forty-seven times—we counted them. I would get a job and be fired before the end of the semester. My wife, children, and I used to eat potato soup three or four days a week. My children are professional people and went to college. Sometimes they make potato soup because they like it. They've had it so much, it became a part of the family.

I know what it is to wash a suit by hand because the one on my back was the only other one I had. I know what it is to have three jobs at the same time, for seven years, without a day off. One at the United Nations, one doing private engineering on the side, and one teaching at Teachers College, Columbia University and other places. I washed cars in a pit at 105th Street and Grand Central Parkway, in the Bronx. I had four girls in college at the same time, one studying medicine, and I had to support my family. I know that I did all that, and I don't think I'm supposed to be given any applause. That's a man's duty. No other man supported my children. We never had to hire a baby sitter, because

socially, if you invited me, you invited my wife and children. If they couldn't come, I couldn't come.

One of the big reasons I could do this was because I had the right wife. I got a woman who didn't need fur coats, Rolls Royces, and condominiums. I got a woman who was satisfied with a cotton coat like the one I am wearing. That's why I'm so adamant about the greatness of the black woman.

I could have gone and decided to get the money, but I had seen what people with the money got: alcohol, drugs, excesses with women. I love women too, but when I walk down the street, I want them to say, "Here is a brother that acts like a brother." I'm not going to try to make a date with her to go to bed. If I don't like a woman enough that I could marry her, I don't want to go to bed with her. Any woman I go to bed with, I got to feel I could marry. I wouldn't just go for a lay. So when you got those kind of values, you're going to be fired sometimes.

In 1939, I wrote *We, the Black Jews*. I was a youngster, just finishing at the university in Puerto Rico. I recently expanded that book to a two-volume work to make it more commensurate with current events. Volume One deals with Afrikan Jews and other black Jews of the world in Asia and Afrika. Volume Two deals with the black Jews in the Caribbean and the United States.

Although the Torah doesn't mention the exact color of the people in it, it does mention the places they came from. For instance, Abraham, the first of the Jews, was supposed to have come from a place called Ur, in Chaldea. At the time, Chaldea had changed to Elam. The people were called Elamites. They were the conquerors who had come from the Nile Valley peninsula area and captured territory all the way into India. That would mean there were Afrikan people ruling at the time. There are inscriptions dealing with that.

In the case of Moses, he challenged Jehovah's decision. Jehovah was showing Moses how powerful he was when he said, "Put your hand in your bosom, and I'll show you how strong I am and how powerful." Moses did that and, lo and behold, the Bible says, "he pulled his hand out of his bosom and it had turned white." Now, if it turned white, then it couldn't have been white from the beginning. It meant it was some other color. It didn't say it was black, green, purple, or technicolor, but one thing we know, it wasn't white.

Then we look at the area Moses was from. Let us take one of the early historians, Herodotus, Europe's first historian. Herodotus speaks of that area in terms of the Colchians, Egyptians, Ethiopians, Nubians, and so forth. He said they had "broad noses," "woolly hair," and they were "burnt of skin." So, based upon these facts, they were Asians and Afrikans, and obviously they were black and brown, not Caucasian or white.

When Rome took over Christianity, that religion lost its full, correct, and true meaning and became Christendom. Several Christian concepts were changed at the Nicene Conference, which was called in 325 A.D. by the Roman emperor, Constantine—a man who was never a Christian! Some writers try to tell us that on his deathbed Constantine professed Christianity, but during his life, he was a persecutor of Christians. Constantine called the Nicene Conference to end the fight between the North Afrikan church, the western Asian church, and the European church, and to settle a dispute among the 219 bishops.

Before the conference, Jesus was believed to have been born in a cave in Ethiopia; that was changed to a manger or stable in Bethlehem. Before the conference, Mary, the mother of Jesus, was worshipped over her son. The Book of Mary, which spoke of Mary's mother having Mary by an Immaculate Conception, was expunged. The Immaculate Conception story was changed to say it was Jesus who was born via Immaculate Conception. Mary was demoted from her status as a deity. Eighteen books, most of them dealing with Afrikans and genealogy, including one called the Book of Genealogy, were removed from the Bible. They allegedly returned in the Roman Catholic *Apocrypha* after being thoroughly edited. There were quite a few other minor things, but to me, those are the major changes that took place at this conference.

The oldest practicing Christians are called Coptics. The largest group of Copts in the world today are in Ethiopia, but Egyptian Coptics maintain they are the head of the church because that's where it originally started. The whole Christian church movement started with Pantheus and Boethius in Egypt. There was a thriving church in Egypt. Rome got into the Christianity business late. The Black Madonna and Child are examples of Christianity before Jesus. The Jesus story is a copy of the Isis, Osiris, and Horus story. That takes place as early as 4100 B.C. The advent of Christianity, as it was being practiced along the Nile, was preceded by thousands of years of Christianity in the ancient form and hundreds of years in the modern form.

The ancient people didn't have such a thing as religion. They would say, "Well, I worship Isis, I worship so and so." The worship of Isis and Osiris, the Immaculate Conception, and the virgin-born child was just said to be that. It wasn't the name of a religion. Religion, in its organized form, is like a business. Religion today is nothing but a business, and the product being sold is organized spirituality. I wonder how much spirituality is in it. It's organized theosophy, being sold in a package, under control, as if it were any other kind of business.

The origins of the Nile Valley civilization points to as far south as northeast Zaire, among the Twa and the Hutu people, whom people call "pygmies." Many of their symbols, for instance, the ankh, the crook, and the flail—these signs are

54

YOSEF A. A. BEN-JOCHANNAN

all related to these small people whose history goes back thousands of years before the establishment of Egypt, at least before the dynastic period. We don't even talk about Rome and Greece in that conversation. They were baby nations. You can't talk about Rome before at least 833 B.C.—well, let's be favorable and give them a few hundred years—you can't talk of Rome or Greece before 1000 B.C. They didn't even exist in human history until then.

When you're talking about the Nile Valley, you're talking about history, authenticated and documented history, where there are artifacts and so forth going back at least 4100 B.C., to perhaps 10,000 B.C. For a major revision of history we could go back to the language itself, to the writing and mathematical figures, and to the number system. We're talking about six to ten thousand years of documented history. Europe doesn't come near that.

There was no Adam, and there was no Eve then, no god named Jehovah at that time. Yet, the ancient Afrikans along the Nile had gods. They had, for example, the hermaphroditic god/goddess Bes, who later, in about the Third Dynasty, was called Hapi, and who is shown with both penis and vagina, breasts, and so forth. There is nothing like that in Judaism, but the first Jew, Abraham, wasn't even born during this time. You're talking about thousands of years of civilization and history before there was even Judaism, Christianity, or Islam. Before there was Greece or Rome.

"Egypt" is the English version of the Greek word "Egypticus." One of the many names that Greece called the land now known as Egypt was "Kemet." Kemet would be, in literal translation, "Black Land." That's just what it means. I use the word preferred by the intellectual or priest: "Ta-Meri." Ta-Meri could be written in two ways: Ta-Merry or Ta-Meri. I use it because it is the one the writers, the priests, and the priests' scribes used. These were the people society depended upon for their knowledge. There were various other names for what is today called Egypt. The current population of invaders' children call it "Mizreer." The Hebrews, in their mythology, call it "Mizrain." The Muslims changed that to "Mizreer," all meaning the same thing.

The ancient people called Afrika by various names, depending on if one was Asian, or European, or whatever the case may be. The one that stuck is "Afrika." It came from the Greeks. As early as 400 B.C., we find the Greeks using that term. I don't know the origin of the Greek word, why the Greeks used it, or where it came from. I know there's literature dating back that far where the Greeks used the term. Ivan Van Sertima says he has some information that it came from the use of the word "Afrilka." I don't have the evidence for it, he does. The Romans, they used "Afer," which means the same thing. "Alkebu-lan" is the oldest name I've seen. It was used by the Moors as well as the Ethiopians at various times. Ortega, Hesperia, Lebos, Ethiopia, all these are names Afrikans and other people called the continent. We're talking about a continent now. At that early time, most of the writers had no concept of how large Afrika was. They thought the Sahara was the most southern limits of the continent.

Look at some of the early maps, especially the maps by Eratosthenes in about 200 B.C. Herodotus's map of Afrika (circa 450 B.C.) ended at the southern part of the Sahara. They felt that below Ethiopia, there was nothing. They saw the world as being rectangular, with the Nile taking a sudden western turn as it wound toward Ethiopia. Going across, they show boats where the Sahara was.

Several cultures migrated out of the Nile. The Yoruba, for example. Yoruba history and folklore speaks of their coming from the Nile at various times for various reasons. In terms of their religious structure, they have the exact same structure Egypt had. The whole structure of the relationship of the god Olodumare and his son Shango, was copied by Judaism. The Yoruba have other gods and demi-gods, and so forth, with various powers attributed to them. They even have an *ankh* similar to that of the Egyptians, but in their ankh, they put the face of a woman. They call it the "symbol of fertility," whereas the Egyptian ankh is the "key of life."

There are many interpretations of the ankh. Among the Sudanese and others, as well as some Egyptians, the tear drop is at the top. It represents the woman's vagina, or the woman's value. The stem that continues down is the male phallus or penis. The two arms, the two stems that reach out, are the male and female child. You have the exact same interpretation in Sudan, only the female part, the loop, is always held at the bottom. It's held from the shaft, which is the male penis. This is considered the natural position. That means the male shank or penis is on the top. The female ovum, or the female vagina, is at the bottom. The two children are on each side. They don't specify the right side or left side belonging to whatever sex. When you go into Central East Afrika, among the Twa and Hutu, the small people, they use the same symbol. They use the Sudanese interpretation; thus, they carry it by the stem, with the male part on top and the female part at bottom.

We know the Fons of Dahomey came to West Afrika from East Afrika, running from the Arabs. It isn't impossible that people would have come all the way across. They did that in the western Sudan. There were voyages all the way to Mecca as late as the time of the West Afrikan empires: Ghana, Mali, Songhay, and so forth. You had various voyages from Mali to Mecca. There's nothing impossible about the journeys of Afrikans during ancient times. They are well-recorded in several places.

There are a lot of debates as to who the ancient Egyptians were. In the first place, I wouldn't care about what anyone thinks. They can think whatever they want. Who are they? If I said the ancient Greeks were anything other than white, the same fellows would laugh right out of the school. Why didn't the Greeks come forward, and why didn't they say these things at that early stage?

The Greeks themselves explained that the ancient Egyptians were black. One piece of evidence of this was written by an ancient Egyptian in the Papyrus of Hu-nefer, in which Hu-nefer, the high priest and scribe, wrote, "We, the Egyptians, came from the beginning of the Nile, where the god Hapi dwells at the foothills of the "Mountain of the Moon." Let's break that down, and see where he's talking about. The beginning of the Nile we find in two different places, the farthest being the White Nile in Uganda; the second being the Blue Nile in Ethiopia. Both of these waters join together at Khartoum in Sudan. They continue north where they join another body of water coming out of the Ethopian highlands called the Atbara River in Sudan. From there the Nile empties into the great sea now called the Mediterranean. The ancient Egyptians themselves stated where they came from. Are we to assume the Euopeans, the Caucasians, were also the first people in Egypt?

Some of the greatest people in the Nile Valley have been given a negative image. The British used the term "pigmies" to refer to some of the people from this area. They said they looked like little pigs, always wallowing in the dirt. Many of us resented it and protested it. They changed the "i" to a "y." Normally, you change a "y" to an "i." This time, they changed the "i" to a "y" and called them "pygmies." That was supposed to mean something to us. The people they are referring to are actually the Twa and Hutu. They also were known, as they went down to Egypt, as Sybunetos. Farther down south, they are known as Kalahari people, like the desert people. Within that group, there are two sub-groups: the Khoi-Khoi and the Grimaldi, the latter known as the first Europeans. We see some of their etchings and stone carvings in the Museum of Natural History in New York. The Dutch and what-not have funny names for them also. The Dutch called them Hottentots and Bushmen.

These people brought down to Egypt and Sudan many of the most basic religious symbols we have—the crook, the flail, the ankh. These things have a Central East Afrikan origin, not an Egyptian origin. They came to Egypt as these people came down the Nile. The Nile flows from the south to the north. Egypt is down, lowland; central East Afrika is up, highland. They started what is called the Nile Valley high culture. We don't use the word "civilization" because there's a presumption that if they brought civilization, the people who were there were not civilized. That is pure nonsense; everybody's civilized. The word "civilization" had its origins in the word "civitat," which means a person of the city. That's all it means, no big deal. Some of the most uncivilized people are in the city.

Human need was the motivation for many of the great creations. Nobody sat down at the table and said, Well, let us develop these things because we feel we're going to start a high culture. Papyrus, for instance, the first paper, was developed in order to transport information by messenger. It became impossible to walk around with those big stones. They had to find a better way to send messages, to deal with things from place to place. It also became important to the Egyptians to keep dates and records of what's going on; thus, the calendar. They needed to record the moon and different aspects of its format, when the rain was going to come, when they had to plant, to tell time, and such. To do the calendar, they studied the movement of the stars, the moon, and other planets in relationship to the earth. They developed the science of chemistry to deal with the soil.

The Egyptians were also the first to deal with stone houses. That started with Imhotep. He wanted his Pharaoh not to be buried like any other Pharaoh. He thought the Pharaoh had to be buried differently from the people and to remain long after they were gone. Therefore he decided to build the Pharaoh's tomb out of stone. He did the first things leveled in stone. He found it stronger, better, but it wasn't good enough. It had to be bigger! So he put on a second tier. He wasn't satisfied until he reached seven tiers and it looked like a wedding cake. That started the first pyramid. Then, of course, as pyramids continued, they went to become what we call "true pyramids." The sides were equally slanted, but smooth. That set back the "step pyramid" and started a whole new thing in building temples and other things for the worship of gods and goddesses.

God and goddess were always the same, male and female. The Egyptians didn't have just a god. Their gods and goddesses were always married and had children. It's not like Judaism's and Christianity's God—always homosexual or nonsexual, always surrounded by a bunch of men or alone.

All of these things happened not from a master plan or the idea of any one man, but according to human needs. As they say, the mother of invention is need. It causes you to invent what you don't have. But like many high cultures, quite a few things can bring it down. One, you could say, was invasion. In Egypt, the first invasion was by the Hyksos, an ancient group of people. There's a lot of argument about this because in America everything is related to race, color, and so forth, so you have to come up with a race. I have no evidence at all showing that color, or whether lips were thick or thin, meant anything in ancient times. That kind of reasoning is very recent.

The Hyksos had been given an opportunity to live in Egypt and learn, but they wanted to take the whole thing around the thirteenth dynasty, about 1675

B.C. This was about the same time Abraham was supposed to have been born. Remember, there's no Judaism, no Jehovah, no Jesus Christ, no Allah, at this time. Nobody had mentioned or written a book about any of these people or religions. The Afrikans had the only book on religion known at that time. It was called *The Book of Coming Forth by Day and by Night*, which Wallis Budge, in his translation, called *The Egyptian Book of the Dead*. Well, the Hyksos came and they were repulsed. The Hyksos are from Asia, around the Oxus river, where there's a little tributary off the Tigris and Euphrates, around there. There are some statues and sphinxes at the Egyptian Museum of Antiquity in Cairo showing some Hyksos. All of them look like any Afrikan you would find. Their features are called Africoid. You don't hear much about them because they were repulsed.

Then came the Assyrians. They're another Asian people. At the time they came in, the Ethiopians were ruling Egypt, the whole Nile Valley. The Nile Valley was ruled by different Afrikans at various times. The Assyrians came in, and they were repulsed.

Then for quite some time, the Afrikan ruled again, until the Persians came in around 525 B.C. They took over Egypt. The Egyptians and Greeks came to an agreement to fight Persia, but Persia attacked both of them and more or less ruled both of them until they were expelled.

The Greeks wouldn't go home according to the treaty. They stayed instead in Egypt and remained until the Romans, under Augustus Caesar, expelled them in about 47 B.C. That ended the common era, the dynastic period. The last of the Egyptian monarchs was Cleopatra VII, the daughter of Ptolemy XII. From then on, we see the destruction of ancient Egyptian culture.

What many do not know is that the Ethiopian Empire went all the way to India. All the way up to Egypt, into Kenya, and possibly part of northern Tanganyika. What made this empire expand was its better military equipment. When others weren't thinking about war, they saw it coming.

Throughout history, you always have one country thinking about war, and thus its war machinery is better than the rest. It could be like, let's say in modern time, an Uzi up against a .38. It has nothing to do with the intelligence of the people, it has to do with the condition of the people. For instance, the United States defeated the Japanese. It wasn't a matter of intelligence, it was that the United States had more materials to pursue the war than did the Japanese. Like this recent thing with Saddam Hussein. Saddam Hussein didn't lose because of lack of intelligence, he lost because the whole Western world, and some other people not in the Western world, joined together to fight poor little him. It wasn't a one-to-one. No one nation, one-to-one, could have beaten him.

Yes, my work does cause me to go over the limit. I would like to say that I have cut down, but the reality is that I don't think I've done too much of that. I want to say, No, I'm not doing what I used to do, I'm now taking care of my health. But then I find myself going as much or more than I did even before.

One thing I learned is that I don't sleep necessarily by the clock. I eat when I'm hungry, sleep when I'm sleepy. That may be the thing. I do travel as much, probably more, than before. I find other things to do that cause me to cross the Atlantic Ocean quite frequently. I must plead guilty to not taking the proper care, probably. I said probably, because how can I do it differently and accomplish the things I want to do? At seventy-something, how much more time do I have? I wish there was a way to do less and accomplish as much. I would have gladly done it.

If you notice, you seldom see me at conferences. Most people don't invite me to conferences. I'm not conference material, particularly when you have interracial groups meeting. My political philosophy—you could classify me as more of a Garveyite than any of the other names out there. I am not acceptable to many academicians, especially those who consider themselves classical academicians. I don't want to be a part of it.

You'll never see me on a picket line, either. I don't go to picket lines. I'll give you an example. I will never go to picket a Korean store for anything. I'll just pass the store. I don't go into Korean stores. I will pass one next to me and go down the street to an American Afrikan store. I tell people, I don't see this nonsense about picketing any store, just don't go. If you don't go in, the store isn't going to stay there.

All this thing about the police killing a brother unjustly—I say we just kill the policeman, or his family, or somebody in his family in revenge, and it will stop. If I know the only thing you're going to do is pray, I'll kill you when I feel like it. If I know you may off me or my brother or my sister for killing you, then I'm going to think twice before I do it! I can't see it any other way.

For instance, this whole thing about picketing the South Afrikan delegation to the United Nations, laying down and praying. I don't do that. The day when they are ready to go down to blow up the South Afrikan mission, you can depend I will be in that group. I will contribute to buying guns for that purpose, like I'll contribute to buying guns in South Afrika to fight the South Afrikan government. I back the Pan-African Congress. I don't back the African National Congress.

People forget a leading member of the Pan-African Congress was in jail about seven months before Nelson Mandela got there. He came out the same

time with Mandela. His sentence was seven months longer than Mandela's. How come everybody forgot him? Everybody forgot that the PAC was the group that said, "One bullet, one invader, one settler." It's the PAC that calls for the land, not for a vote. I don't want no damn vote in South Afrika! The government of South Afrika is no legal government for Afrikans. Nelson Mandela's an integrationist and amalgamationist. I am not an integrationist nor an amalgamationist! I'm satisfied with black women. I don't want white women. The basis is Afrikan land. The PAC program calls for the return of Afrikan land, one way or the other. I say, if we can't get it by negotiation, then one bullet for each settler!

Martin Luther King has been praying, everybody's been praying to the Lord. The Lord ain't worried about such nonsense! If there's a God watching over this and is conscious of it, that God is too busy keeping the sun and the moon from bumping into each other! He don't want no damn nonsense about some black people on the earth supposed to be taking care of business and calling out, "Lord, please help me with these white folks." That's nonsense! The Lord didn't help you all these four hundred years with white folks; what makes you believe he's going to help you now?

This discussion about multicultural education sounds more reasonable than inclusive education. When you say inclusion, that means there's something that exists and you must be included in that thing that exists. Suppose that thing is crooked, say it's racist and dehumanizing, do you want to be included in that? Multiculturalism says, "Okay, I bring my culture, you bring your culture." I accept multiculturalism much easier than inclusion because I don't want to be included in a cesspool. American history, American education, they're cesspools!

How are they going to include me? They're going to include me by talking about the one God. They're going to include me by showing that I must respect the symbol of the American one-dollar bill, which shows the ever-seeing eye of Horus in the pyramid. Will American education ever say, "Yes, that belongs to Afrikans?" Are they going to include the United States Supreme Court, which has stolen the symbol of justice, turned it upside down, making one scale up, one scale down?

You get what I'm saying? First, you've got to scuttle the whole American system of education and start from scratch with all cultures, all people. You're going to have a history of the indigenous people as written by an indigenous person. You understand? Just as the Americans would not accept an English patriot writing the history of the War of Independence, I wouldn't want a European to write the history of the war of Afrikan people or the Moors.

The Moors are two or more different people at various times, depending on what time you are speaking about. They were once part of an ancient empire, the Khart–Haddas Empire, which later became what the Europeans called Carthage. You can see that they're a very old nationality. The time when people most speak about them is during the time when the Arabs came carrying the theory of Islam. The Moors were the ones that stopped the Asian Muslims, primarily the Arabs, from further conquest in Afrika by going northwest.

They had a queen at the time. Dahia was their leader, a woman. Her grandson was the young man who was responsible for establishing the first fort in the conquest of the Iberian Peninsula, which is today called Spain, Portugal, and southern France. His name was Tarikh. Dahia, seeing that her country was going to be overrun eventually, continued to fight to stop the Arabs and Islam, yet she prepared her grandson to become a Muslim. She realized that, according to Muslim teaching, Muslims would not invade a Muslim territory. She herself was a member of the Manichean religion, to which St. Augustine belonged.

So that group of Muslims or Moors were the ones who invaded the Iberian Peninsula for the first time, under Tarikh's leadership. They also had one among them by the name of Aadmir, who made the barges or rafts to carry the people across. From him, the words "admiralty" and "admiral" come. Between he and Tarikh, they invaded Mons Calp, "the Mountain of Monks," and changed the name to Gibral Tarikh, "Mountain of Tarikh." Of course, the Spanish couldn't write that, so it became "Gibraltar."

The Arabs also carried the name Moors because they came to the Iberian Peninsula from Mauritania. They were originally called Mauers, which later was changed to Mohrs by the Germans. The Spaniards and the Portuguese called them Morros. The blacker ones, the darkest ones, were called Blackamoors in the English language.

A lot of change took place in the literature of Europe after the Moors came. You'll find a whole different bunch of literature if you study in Spain as opposed to studying in the United States. There's very little about the Moors in the United States. The book most people who speak English deal with is Stanley Lane Poole's *The Moors in Spain*,[2] but there are so many beautiful books about the Moors written in Spain, by Spanish writers, that they make Poole and others look sick.

Of the three so-called Western religions, Islam is the youngest. If you're talking about Islam, you're talking about Muhammad Ibn Abdullah. Anything else is theoretical nonsense. If you're going to say somebody started Islam before

Muhammad, then you're just being a theorist. Anybody who wants authority goes to Al-Azhar, the university in Egypt, that is considered the Muslim university of the world.

Islam causes debates. Yes, Muhammad started Islam by building on other things that existed before. Take the Adam and Eve thing, the beginning of all the Jews, some four or five thousand years ago. Jews were nowhere to be found. You talk about Moses and the Ten Commandments, in which Judaism and Christianity established the Moses theory. Akhenaton died before Moses was born, and he was talking about the one and only God who goes by the name of Aton. There was no Moses yet. He wasn't born. The so-called Ten Commandments can be found in the admonitions to Goddess Maát, otherwise called the "Negative Confessions."

Most of what I see, particularly in the West, has a base in these things. The evidence is still there. People can go and see it for themselves. For instance, you can go and see the Temple of Herodotus at Philae Island, which is called Ajilaka Island. You see, that's another thing. What I try to do is to show what the Greeks said, and then show what we're using, as opposed to what the original is. Philae Island, there's no such thing as Philae Island in reality. That's what the Greeks called it. The Nubians called it Ajilaka Island before the Greeks got there. There's a temple in Aswan, it's called Kolaboyo Temple, or the "temple of God Mendulosee." Everybody called it Kalabsha. The Germans called it Kalabsha. But I won't call it Kalabsha. I will call a name by error if I don't know the original name. The pyramids at Gizeh—again, I don't use the Greek name, I use the indigenous names: Khufu, Khufra, Menkara. I never talk about what the Greeks call them: Cheops, Chephren, and Mycerinus. I won't call them that.

I am not interested in proving to any white people that I'm a scholar. That's nonsense! I am writing, not to white people, but to *black* people. I am writing for all Afrikan people to know. I don't care if people think I write at a first-grade level or second-grade level. The point is, I write! As a result, more Afrikans every day will know their background because the more of us who know our background, the struggle becomes that much stronger and better.

There are some brothers who want to debate me, but I won't have any debate with any brother! I do my research, and my research stands for itself. I don't do my research out of a textbook in a library—I go to the source. If I want some documents on the Moors, I go to Spain and look for the original document, then I check it out for myself! If someone wants a name, he should build it by his writing. He's not going to build it arguing with me. I don't argue with brothers or sisters in public just so somebody to get their orgasm out of it!

It would be a waste of time for me to condemn a brother or try to make him look small—that's something to be done in the family. If he wants to discuss with me and talk with me, okay. But I won't have a debate with him. He needs "Oprah Winfrey" or one of those programs, he doesn't need me!

Many black people who consider themselves scholars want to have a debate with me. Why? I'm not the person to have the debate with. I don't give a damn if no white people recognize me while I'm alive. I care that my people, on a large scale, know their history—Egyptian history—the most ancient history that's documented. That's why I don't pay any attention to this nonsense when they talk about Babylonia and Sumer being the oldest societies. You know what I tell them?: "Bring me the artifacts. I got artifacts older than anything you could show me. Don't give me your theory." I go *beyond* theory!

My work has caused me physical setbacks. I did it to myself. I ignored the fact that I was sixty-seven going on sixty-eight. I had a stroke one June. That May, I went to San Francisco. I flew in, got off the plane, and jumped into a car going to Santa Cruz to lecture. I came back the next morning and lectured in San Francisco. I jumped on a plane, went back to New York, then to Ithaca to teach a class. The next day I got on a plane at La Guardia to go to Dallas, Texas. I left Dallas to come back to New York to give a lecture, then went back to Houston. From Houston, I went back to New York. I dropped my bags for one day, then picked them up again to go to London with John Henrik Clarke to do a series of lectures.

When I arrived in London, I went from the airport directly into the lecture hall. With the five hours difference in time, it was literally two o'clock in the morning, and I'm in a lecture hall lecturing. I left the lecture hall and jumped on a plane going to Williamsboro to give another lecture. I came back to New York for a day or two then went back to London to finish up a series of lectures. Back in New York, I went to pick up my son's wife and new child and bring them back to the house. Then I went to visit a friend of mine in the hospital.

When I got there, I was totally disoriented. I couldn't remember when I went to the hospital or what I was there for. I left the hospital and couldn't remember where the house was. Finally, I got home. I felt bad. My wife came, and I tried to speak to her. I knew what I was saying, but she couldn't understand a thing I was saying. I went to lie down, and a friend from Philadelphia came by. I spoke to her, and she couldn't understand me either.

My wife called my doctor, Dr. Lewis, a friend of my family. He came over and checked my pressure. It was 265 over 150. He said "Let's go." I said, "Where?" "To the hospital." We walked right into the Emergency Ward. They grabbed me, knocked me down, and stuck things all over me. I went to Intensive Care, and the rest is history.

Gil Noble from television came to see me and said, "You know there were over four hundred people downstairs in the lobby trying to get up here in the hospital. Your daughter said only ten could be up here at a time. The doctor said they've got to give you some time to sleep." I was glad. I was happy to know four hundred people came.

My daughter said, "You are a helluva man. But if you die, Mom just told us you've got just enough to bury you in the bank." She said, "You ain't leaving us a damn thing! You spent all your life writing for people, spending time where we couldn't go. You were always someplace else for somebody else's business. But you know something?" she said, "When we saw the people downstairs, we would have been mad if you had left us money and no integrity." That really got to me.

One of my grandchildren came by to see me, and she said, "You hate us. How could you hate us so much?" I said "Girl, what are you talking about?" She said, "Who the hell gave you permission to die? You can't! We haven't had any time with you! Who the hell gave you permission to die?" She was just upset with me, and she said, "Granddaddy, what the hell are you doing with yourself? You got no business dying on us." Just like that. She had never used such harsh words with me before. She started to cry uncontrollably. I had to reevaluate my life. I had to realize that I was nearly sixty-eight, that I had to continue on, but at a slower pace.

When I got up, I called my wife and my colleague, Professor George Simmons, together. I told George, "George, you are going to run Alkebu-lan Books, my publishing company, from now on. I will come and do things some days, but some days I won't come in at all. Right now, I am going to walk out of this hospital and go home. I'm gonna go to the zoo with my little camera or something. Go someplace. You're the boss. I will work with you, but I just can't go on like I was going."

I told Ms. McDonald, my secretary, "Cut my program in half. I am not traveling two places in one week. I'm not doing five lectures in one week." I didn't stop, but I cut down drastically.

I am conscious of the fact that I slipped in my maintenance of my health, before the stroke. I could run the streets, but no. I do drink a lot of water. I do take some time for rest. I'm beyond seventy, and I'm now having some problems

with my arthritis, especially my right knee. But I can't settle down but so much. I must do something!

I've got nine unpublished works, some of them going back fifteen, twenty, thirty years ago. I'm trying to bring them up to date. I'm doing new work. I went back to archaeological work. I went digging in Egypt. I've got some writings on that.

I don't have the luxury of a research assistant. I have to do everything myself. I write my own books. I take my own photography. I do my books from the handwritten to the typewritten to the marking up. I do the whole picture work and everything. When I finish a book, it's camera-ready. I do it myself. I do my art work, my covers. There was a time when I couldn't get anybody to print my books, so I printed them myself. Now we're lucky. I got brother Paul Coates from Black Classic Press in Baltimore to print them. I got a brother in New York who's now helping me. And, of course, I've got tapes upon tapes of me out there, oral and video. But I don't get a dime from any of this.

I subsidize a village in Nubia, and much of what's going on there could not go on without the money I gain from my lectures or from donations. Whatever I get goes straight to the village. I don't use a penny of the lecture money. The profit from my book sales goes to the village.

When people think of me, first of all, I want them to know that my greatest triumph is my family. I am an Afrikan man who has married three different Afrikan women. One died, so I married another. You may hear people talking about me. There's a rumor that I married a white woman in Egypt. Heaven forbid! The woman they're talking about in Egypt is much darker than my mother. I have a light-skinned mother who would have killed anybody who told her she was anything but an Afrikan. Of these women I've mated with, I've had twelve biological children; eight girls and four boys. I went further and adopted eight more Afrikan children, giving me a total of twenty children, from which I have forty-seven grands and eleven great-grands. One was born three nights ago. I'm going to see the baby tomorrow.

I want to be remembered as an Afrikan man who raised his family, stood by his family, and did the best he could with the limited funds he had to make them self-sufficient. I want to be recognized as an Afrikan man who saw heaven through his Afrikan woman and respected her such that he never laid a hand on her in anger. That would be the first thing I would want to be remembered as—

as a father, a husband, and so forth—and then as an Afrikan nationalist, one who adored Afrikan women to the highest.

As far as my involvement in Afrikan people is concerned, I would like to be remembered as an Afrikan who fifty-two years ago decided to take up the mantle of freedom for my people. At that time I was in Puerto Rico writing my first book. I have never swayed one iota from that. I have never swayed one inch to the other side. I never wanted a white woman's body, never had one, and don't care about having one. I would like it to be said that I've never destroyed or beat an Afrikan woman, never disrespected one or called her "bitch." I would like it to be said that my work, everything I did, was toward the glorification of the Afrikan woman and the Afrikan family.

1   Budge, E. A. Wallis, *The Book of the Dead: The Papyrus of Ani in the British Museum* (New York: Dover Publications, 1967).

2   Poole, Stanley Lane, with Arthur Gilman, *The Moors in Spain* (Beirut: Khayats, 1967).

FRANCES CRESS WELSING

PSYCHIATRIST, AUTHOR, LECTURER

Frances Cress Welsing is one of the most prominent and brilliant behavioral scientists in the world. Her pioneering work, articulated most cogently in her "Cress Theory of Color Confrontation and Racism," stands alone as one of the most penetrating discussions of white supremacy ideology available today. Her book, The Isis Papers: The Keys to the Colors, *spells out in detail the various strategies by which racism is played out in the real world.*

I was born in Chicago, Illinois. Both my parents were born in Chicago. I grew up there attending Chicago public schools. My father was a physician. My mother was a public school teacher. My father's father had also been a physician. I guess I'm a third-generation Chicago physician. My grandfather and my father are now deceased.

I knew very early that I wanted to be a physician. When I was in the first or second grade, I remember coming home from school and telling my father that I wanted to be a nurse. He said, "Well, if you're going to be a nurse, you might as well be a doctor." I just said, "Fine." Since I look like my father, there are three girls in my family, everybody was saying, "Who's going to be the doctor? I guess Frances is, she looks just like her father." I just accepted that. I had a tremendous amount of respect for both of my parents, but certainly my father. I used to work in his office when I was in high school. I knew I was going to be a physician, and that really is what I consider myself. I consider myself a physician who is dedicated to the well-being of black people.

My father's father was such a physician. He was a physician/politician in Chicago. He died in 1909, very, very interested in medicine and in the racial oppression of black people. My father was very well read in and outside of medicine. I think I'm just continuing in that tradition. Both my parents and both sides of the family have always been involved in political ideas—ideas to help develop the community, develop respect for ourselves as black persons, respect for our communities, that kind of thing. So I was shaped and molded in that form. My mother tells a story about a time when the FBI or somebody went to her to question her about my activities. My mother told them that she raised us to protest injustice. So that's my tradition.

I went to Antioch College in Yellow Springs, Ohio, and got a B.S. degree in pre-medicine. Then I went to the Howard University College of Medicine. I did

an internship at Cook County Hospital in Chicago and planned to stay there and do pediatrics. At the last minute, because of circumstances, I went back to Washington, D.C., and did a residency in general psychiatry at St. Elizabeth's Hospital. I did a fellowship in child psychiatry at Children's Hospital in Washington. That's most of my educational background.

I attended the Howard University College of Medicine, a black institution, or shall I say, an institution where there is a majority of black people. The school's focus was on medicine, but because there are so many black people in Washington, there was more of an interest, perhaps, in the health and well-being of blacks at Howard than there would be at predominantly white medical institutions. Beyond that, when I started psychiatric training, I was motivated to look very deeply into the mental health problems of black people, but that was not the focus of our training. Our programs were predominantly white training programs. Black people were dealt with in terms of, "Well, they are not of a sufficient level of intelligence to discuss their problems." The modality of treatment was generally drug therapy. That was unacceptable to me.

As I was getting deeply into sitting and talking with black patients, I kept running into the dynamic of racism in their lives. It was a very, very negative force that I felt was contributing in a major way to their psychiatric problems. Certainly, this point of view was not part of Freudian psychoanalytic theory, the theory upon which most of my training was based. But I was just determined that by being a psychiatric physician, I was going to understand all of the behavioral and emotional problems that black people were presented with. I was going to shape and mold myself into a very effective medical psychiatric instrument to help black people with their problems.

I had to go from where the training left off and do a tremendous amount of work, thinking and trying to help solve the problems that black people face. I hate to say it, but that's a good twenty-plus years ago, and from what I've seen, things have not changed much. There are not any major centers that are focusing on the mental health problems of black and other nonwhite peoples. So I think certainly I'm one of the pioneers in that area.

I knew what I was interested in. I was interested in unraveling the causes of behavioral and emotional problems of black people. I have been interested in that for a long time. Going back to my childhood, I remember asking my grandmother, "Why are black people lynched?" I wanted to know answers to questions like that, and I didn't want to go through any changes to get them. But when you have a question in your mind, you just have to respect that question enough to go to the library, do the thinking, and do the work to seek and find the answer. I was determined to get an answer to some of these problems.

I was a black person determined, like my grandparents and my parents before me, to make a contribution to the development of black people. I have been on that course from I guess the time I was born, but in terms of formal training in psychiatry, which was the course that I had to go through, the answers were not there. Still, I learned the ideas that were in that body of training. I pursued them so that I could go in the direction that I know I was supposed to go. So it wasn't any big brain-change for me. It was just knowing the course I had to go on. I knew I might have to go through certain tunnels or over certain kinds of passages in pursuit of it.

When I was doing a fellowship in child psychiatry, around 1967, I met a gentleman, Mr. Neely Fuller, who lives in Washington, D.C. He's a guard at the Bureau of Engraving. I met him at a Black Power Committee meeting. He had been writing his ideas about racism for quite some time, since the Korean War. He was the first person that I'd ever met who said that racism was not about economics. See, when I was in college, I studied a lot of Marxism, a tremendous amount of Marxism. I read all of Marx. I thought Marxism was the answer. I soon found out, this was before I met Mr. Fuller, that Marxism did not have the answers to the issues around race. I knew that there was an answer somewhere, but they were not contained in the body of Marxism or other economic theory.

Neely Fuller said racism was not about economics, that it was, pure and simple, about people who classify themselves as white and who seek to maintain control and dominate people who are classified as nonwhite. He pursued that line of thinking, that whites were not doing that purely for profit motivation— they were doing it out of some kind of internal necessity. They just *have* to dominate. So I spent a lot of time talking with him and looking over his ideas, but I still kept asking, "Why?"

Neely Fuller was saying that people who classify themselves as white, all over the globe, were about the business of maintaining white supremacy domination and maintaining racism. He had catalogued the behavior patterns of the white collective in all areas of people activity: economics, education, entertainment, labor, law, politics, religion, sex, and war. He had looked at the kinds of moves they made on the chessboard, so to speak—that's my terminology, not his. He had also developed strategies for countering racism. He looked at racism as a major injustice on the planet. According to Fuller, whites, out of necessity, have to engage in racist behavior, so those were the moves he wrote about. He also wrote about the moves black and other nonwhite people needed to make in the same nine areas of activity, if they were going to neutralize or checkmate white supremacy behavior and bring justice and peace to the planet.

So I listened to his ideas. I was a psychiatrist at that time, so the deeper "why" behind human behavior was just intriguing to me. We would debate and scream and yell and talk, all in the course of thinking through ideas. I just kept wondering, why, why, why, and still why?

One day it just came to me. The question "Why?" really turns on the brain computer. If you raise the question, you're really challenging the brain to come up with data about cause and effect. I just put my "why" in the back of my mind. I was standing in my kitchen one day, and it just came together: If you take the global white collective, you see that they are a tiny minority of people. They are genetic recessive to black, brown, red, and yellow people. That's where the expression "one drop of black blood makes you black" comes from, because white plus any color—black, brown, red, or yellow—produces a colored person.

The bottom line was that whites are vulnerable, since they are a tiny, tiny minority on the planet. They are vulnerable to genetic annihilation. So I said, "I see! This is the underlying reason for white supremacy or the behavior that we call racism."

We blacks have dealt with racism—white supremacy—as a moral issue. In other words, a person was seen as being immoral or not Christian if they practiced racism. I don't look at it that way. I say "white supremacy" is a preferable term to "racism." White supremacy, I maintain, is the behaviors that are necessary—the patterns of perception, logic, thought, speech, action, and emotional response—that are necessary to allow for white genetic survival. Or, one can say, white supremacy are those behaviors—conscious, subconscious, unconscious—the goal of which is the prevention of white genetic annihilation on the planet.

Let's say, for example, white-skinned people go to the continent of Afrika, and they see the remains of a very ancient, fantastic civilization. And they decide that they are going to attempt to destroy the connection between that great civilization and skin blackness. They are then going to say that somehow they, the whites, produced that civilization. That's white supremacy. That's a pattern of perception and logic that produces the goal objective of white supremacy. White supremacy is due to the necessity to assure white genetic survival or to prevent white genetic annihilation. It is an attempt to say black people are genetically inferior, when it is people whose skins are white who are the ones in the vulnerable genetic situation. Black people cannot be genetically annihilated. The white collective can be genetically annihilated. I say that skin whiteness is a genetic mutation. Black people can produce white people. White people can only produce white people. Whites are mutants of black people.

All of those behaviors, the distortions in the Bible, they are all done to bolster up, in the white psyche, this concept of superiority. They are done so that

FRANCES CRESS WELSING

there can be justification for the imposed inferiorization of black and other non-white people. In that way, whites can survive genetically.

I go around the country asking white people, "Do you want your children to be white? Do you want your grandchildren to be white? Would you mind white genetic annihilation?" It's not a hostile thing, it's just questioning. And I have never met a white person who said that they did not mind being genetically annihilated. Some whites, when you confront them with something like that, they say "Oh, I don't mind." Then I say, "Well, do you want your children to be black?" Then that stops them. "Do you want your great grandchildren to be colored?" That stops the denial. If a white person ever told me, "I don't mind having nonwhite grandchildren. I don't mind having nonwhite children," I would put them on a lie detector. If they proved they were not lying, then they wouldn't feel the imperative to engage in white supremacy behavior or the behavior we end up calling racism.

If a white person says they want their children and grandchildren to be white, then they *have* to engage in the behaviors, consciously or unconsciously, that are going to allow that to take place. That means that black, brown, red, and yellow people must be subjugated, blacks in particular, because black has the greatest genetic potential to annihilate white. Do you see what I'm saying?

So this is, as far as I'm concerned, a major turning point in time when people are supposed to be into analysis of this problem. Black people are no longer supposed to be engaged in emotional protest, begging and pleading for justice from people who classify themselves as white. We are now supposed to be operating strictly on the basis of analysis and governing our behavior accordingly.

Once one begins to understand that the white collective globally is in fear of its genetic annihilation, one realizes that whites commit suicide, genetic suicide—genocide on themselves—when they help us. If they help us, then they allow themselves to be genetically annihilated. If we look back at their behavior over the last hundred years or two hundred years, no matter how many white persons have said racist behavior is not right, you find that they still have to behave in a way that is not right. They're trying to survive genetically, whether they consciously understand it or not. There are people in the white collective who understand what the issues are, but they cannot help us.

By the same token, under the conditions of white supremacy, any white person who has intimate sexual relations with a nonwhite person is furthering the psychological destruction of nonwhites. Nonwhite people become massively confused behind that, because they do not understand that white supremacy exists on the planet locally and globally. Nonwhite people don't understand the necessity for white supremacy domination, but white people understand that

they have to dominate. So when a white person is in bed with a nonwhite person, because of the long history of conditioning that tells them nonwhites are inferior, the nonwhite person will be programmed to love white people.

See, nonwhite people have been programmed to worship a white image, i.e., God, Jesus. If Jesus, who is portrayed as white, is the son of God, that means, in their brain computer, that God himself, or herself, is white. Do you see what I'm saying? This has all been brought about by controlling images within the white supremacy system so that nonwhite people worship white images.

The highest desire, under white supremacy programming, is to be loved and validated by a white person. So the white person who is acting counter to white genetic survival by engaging in sexual activity with the nonwhite person is actually achieving a greater goal: the goal of domination. The nonwhite person's mind has been turned against their own interests.

Now somebody may say, "How can you say that?" I say it because it is true. I used to say to people that I could tell if a black person was sleeping with a white person. I can see it in their eyes, hear it in their discussions when they get down to critical issues about race. The nonwhite person has to turn against the interests of other nonwhite persons to protect the interests of the white person they're in bed with. That means the white person is the dominant person, no matter who's on top or bottom in the act of sexual intercourse. The white person demands the nonwhite person choose white over nonwhite. That's the bottom line. So to that extent, the nonwhite person does not marry the white person, the white person marries the nonwhite person. The black man can't even speak to a white woman unless she says he can speak to her. Do you see what I'm saying? Otherwise, she could say, "If you speak to me, I'll yell rape, and you'll be dead."

These relationships are all controlled by the behavior system of white supremacy. This system gives the illusion to the nonwhite person that somehow they have overcome racism, that a white person loves them. They are just psychologically confused. If you ask the white person involved with a nonwhite person if white supremacy should be stopped, that's another ballpark because the white person is interested in the black person loving them more than they love themselves. If you didn't have white supremacy, you wouldn't have that. If a white person wants to help in the war against white supremacy, then they have to stay out of bed, altogether, with nonwhite people. They have to stop luring nonwhite people into bed with them and confusing them about this greater issue of injustice.

If you conquer a people and oppress them, then you are forcing them to disrespect themselves. If you mistreat them, if you develop all kinds of negative images about them and project negative images about them, then you are teaching those people to hate themselves and to love that which is dominant. That is all a part of white supremacy. If I have been taught to hate myself, I won't defend myself. No matter what is done to me, I will go along with the oppressors' agenda.

For example, let's look at two television programs, "Webster" and "Different Strokes." Those programs were projecting the genetic malformation, or genetic inferiority, of black people, black males in particular. Black people sat and looked at these shows and applauded! You have a genetically and constitutionally impaired black male playing opposite a great, big, tall, white male. The only reason black people can watch those programs is that they have been taught, at very, very deep levels of their brain computers' circuitry, that they are genetically inferior.

At the surface level, if you ask how many black people think they're genetically inferior to white people, out of a hundred black people in an audience, a hundred will say, "I don't." If you ask them, "Well, do you watch 'Webster' or 'Different Strokes'?" They'll say, "Yes," but the only way you can watch these shows is if you believe in the genetic inferiority of nonwhite or black people. You're not going to have a white male dwarf playing opposite a great, big, tall, black male. You're not going to have that, because the dominating one is an absolutely critical image.

When that television image of a dwarfed black male is in the brain computer, the behavior comes out accordingly. The black male is seen as childish and inadequate compared to the white male who is seen as powerful and adequate. Having ground in those images for hundreds of years, those images are now in place. It's going to take a tremendous amount of consciousness-scrubbing on the part of black and other nonwhite people to get rid of them.

To the white collective I say that it's unjust, what is being done. Whether it's conscious or unconscious, it doesn't matter, it really is unjust. It's horrible. But again, if I use the analogy of the chessboard, where the object of the game is for the white king to checkmate the black king, then producing a "Different Strokes" or a "Webster" or a "Fantasy Island"—that's just like the white king saying checkmate to the black king or the nonwhite king, whoever is on the black side of the chessboard.

Black and nonwhite people have to rise to the occasion and play the black side of the chessboard. No matter how many names we're called, we've got to rise to the occasion and be champions. Right now, we don't even understand that the chess game is on the board.

So I use that metaphor because white supremacy culture is always playing games of competition. Football, tennis, basketball—all their games are games of competition, where one side of the court is supposed to bring together all of the intelligence, all of the physical ability, and everything else to help their team be victorious. You also have to study what the other team is doing and all the plays they make. Study their coaching patterns. Study who the players are. You have to develop your pieces, your men, so that they are capable and able to analyze and play, to develop offenses and defenses, and know which game is on the table.

So that's one thing: to study. But we black people are—we have to face it—like ninety-nine percent washed out in terms of self-respect, meaning that any time you have people who don't want to be themselves and want to be somebody else, it's a major, major injustice. But that's the game that's on the table.

We have to realize that we do not believe in ourselves. I often ask an audience of black people, "How many people would like to have a Mercedes?" Everybody's hand will go up because it's a beautiful car. Then I ask, "How many people think the black person sitting next to you could *make* a Mercedes?" Nobody's hand goes up. That's a test of how many black people think they're genetically inferior, in terms of intelligence, to white people. Black people don't understand what is really being asked. It's not a trick question. It's a question that brings out the truth about the conditioning of black people under white supremacy domination.

We don't believe the people who built the pyramids—the first people on the planet, people who have had three-and-a-half million years of existence—were black people. That we are descended from the mothers and fathers of all the people on the planet, the founders of civilization. The founders of science, philosophy, religion, culture. The circle has come fully around. The people who started it all are now at the very bottom. We are going to have to understand that cosmic time flow. We are now at the very bottom, and we don't even know that we did those things. To me, really, it's like a cosmic challenge. We have to rise to the occasion.

This whole question of parenting, within the framework of white supremacy, is a very important political issue. It's political, meaning it's about power relations. If I can control and structure what you call "family," then I can control and structure you. If I can destroy your family and make you call a single-parent situation a family when it's really a survival unit—and make you accept it as your reality of family—then I can have control over you for the rest of forever.

Black people are going to have to understand that a family is a mother and a father, or a father and a mother, of sufficient high levels of maturity who can shape and mold strong, emotionally mature offspring. If you don't have that, then it means war is being waged against you in a most critical area of life, namely, the family structure and family activity. We have—what, nearly fifty percent of our children being born to teenagers, and everybody else being born in sin-

gle-family situations? That's just the white king checkmating the black king on the chessboard.

What we are going to have to understand is that we have to have highly mature people becoming parents. That is, if we as a people are going to prosper and go forward. Under the present conditions of white supremacy, a black woman should not have any children until she's thirty years old. Then, she should have no more than two, and no closer together than—I used to say two, now I'm going to say four years apart. A black man should be thirty-five years old before he becomes a father.

If people want to fall on the floor and crack up when I say this, they can fall on the floor and crack up. What am I talking about? I'm not talking about "I'm in love and I want to do it." I'm not talking about that. Or I'm not talking about some fifteen-year-old telling me, "Dr. Welsing, I can too be a mother." They can't, because the family is the first school. The second school is when the child enters kindergarten. We have all these little black children today entering what they call the first school, when in reality it's the second school. They squirm around and can't sit still. They can't learn. They're not bad children, it's just that their first school failed them.

White supremacy has made that happen. If white supremacy is going to survive, it has to attack the black male because it is he who can cause white genetic annihilation. You cripple the black male, take him out of the family, don't give him a job, don't give him opportunity, set up that situation of a single-parent mother with a lot of children who is trying to get welfare payments to survive. You build an inadequate level of emotional nurturance among black children. When you have that, you produce teenagers who want to have sex, who are obsessed with sex, because they are trying to get their emotional needs met. You create a vicious cycle.

So we're back to the chessboard, trying to master playing the black side of the chessboard. When that situation happens, then the move we have to make is that black women have to refrain from having children until they're thirty, and have no more than two, no closer than four years apart. Then we can build a strong people. We may have to say, "No *sex* until you're thirty." We may have to get that strong, because it's not a question about what you or I want. We may *want* to use drugs, but do we use drugs because we feel we *want* to use drugs, or do we go back to the chessboard and say, "What moves do we have to make on this chessboard if we are going to have justice and the elimination of white supremacy on this planet?" If we are going to have justice and eliminate white supremacy, then we're not going to use drugs. We're not going to play around with sex. The production and development of the human being is going to

become the highest task that we can engage in. That is, if we're going to win on the black side of the chessboard.

This is what I'm saying: the formation of personality development is based upon "lap time." How much mature lap time a child gets is absolutely essential. Black people are going to have to understand that. This goes along with the non-begging approach. We have been massively programmed into the begging approach for the elimination of injustice—"Please, white people, don't be unkind to us, give us justice." That means we only have to have the intellect sufficient to beg. *They* have to utilize the intellect to determine how they are going to help us, if indeed they are. If we say we're not going to beg anymore, that we are going to play our side of the chessboard, we will need to analyze what it is that we will need to win and then develop what it is we need.

When we think about what we need, in terms of the development of our people, then the answer is strong mothers and strong fathers. Ninety-nine percent of the males who are sitting in prison didn't have fathers. A little boy who doesn't have a father holding his hand, teaching him how to be a functional constructive person as a male human being, is a victim of white supremacy. The war for white genetic survival on planet earth is making those conditions develop.

Instead of getting mad and saying this is immoral, we have to analyze these conditions and realize, "Oh, they're playing the game of white genetic survival. They are trying to cancel out the black male." Well, what moves do we need to make, in the areas where black people live, that will say, "No, we're not going to have the black male canceled out. We're going to insist that he be all that he can be, that he is not just a sex machine, not just an impregnator. He is going to be a full-fledged man. He's descended from the father of all the people on the planet, but he has been reduced to nothing. We're going to insist that the black man regain his proper place so he doesn't just have to be about making babies."

Now, making babies is not to be belittled. If a dynamic is coming toward you to reduce your manhood, to reduce your masculinity, and you don't consciously understand exactly the nature of that force, then you will react by trying to prove that you are a man. So how do you prove it? By having a string of babies. The unconscious reaction of having manhood taken away is to react by producing a string of babies.

If one wants to go from the time we were brought from Afrika—or we can go back two thousand years when the Greeks and the Romans went into Afrika—if you experience your power being taken away, then you see that you might start attacking your own image. You come to understand the reasons behind the very high level of black-on-black homicide and black males killing each other, forming gangs, or getting angry because they feel a sense of powerlessness and don't understand who's really taking their power away. So they attack their own image, or they sell drugs to their own image, or they just react by producing babies. If you feel power being taken away, you feel really reduced. You start feeling like you want to have sex with a three-year-old baby. All these things are tied together.

I'm talking about elevating our understanding of what is actually happening to us, about elevating it to a level of analysis and conceptualization rather than just reacting. Master chess players don't react. They make their moves based on in-depth analysis of the game. They sit there as coolly as they can and make as precise moves as they can possibly make relative to the game that's on the table. If you're playing the black side of the chessboard, you want to checkmate the opening move the white player has made on the chessboard. The white move is white supremacy and injustice.

We've got to go back to a fundamental analysis, even in the so-called women's movement, which is white female activity within the framework of a system of white supremacy. That's how come black women are excluded from it. I don't care how many black and white women run around together, the bottom line is that black women will be excluded from the women's movement because the game is still about white supremacy, globally and locally. That means the white collective is about the business of its own genetic survival through economics, education, entertainment, labor, law, politics, religion, sex, and war. So their behavior is supposed to follow just like that, falling negatively upon the heads of people who are classified as black and nonwhite. Now, just because they haven't taken the analysis to that level—and probably would deny it if the question were put out there—that's okay. They can deny what they want. It's up to us to analyze their behavior and say, "Well, if you have a system, then every activity that goes on within the system plays to the tune of what the goal objectives of that system are."

Black women have to get into loving and respecting themselves. If they are in love with and respect themselves, they will respect black males; and if black males are in love with and respect themselves, they will respect black females. Then you will have the black king and the black queen on the black side of the chessboard playing in harmony with the other chess pieces. Then they can checkmate the moves made by those on the white side of the chessboard.

Now if we don't get that straight, it'll just be another chess game that's lost and another chess tournament that we fail to win. We have been losing chess tournaments in this area of the world for the last three hundred-plus years. We have been losing chess tournaments on the world stage for over two thousand years because we don't understand the game that's being played. I predict that until we understand, we will keep on losing.

I mean, sure, individual black people will drive around in a Mercedes. Individual black people will have a yacht. But if we will look at the whole people, we see marriages falling apart, children on welfare and in foster care. We will see people who are the most undereducated on the planet. We will see people in Afrika who are starving and facing white supremacy oppression, especially in southern Afrika.

Right here in the U.S., Dr. Martin Luther King, Jr., was a great political scientist who had a thesis. He believed that if black people moved toward white people with love, that would bring about the desired objective of justice. He talked about morality, immorality, and injustice. What Dr. King found out was that when he moved with love, he was assassinated. He had been given the Nobel Peace Prize, he was moving with love, he was killed. So when one analyzes that great social experiment, one concludes that Dr. King did not fully understand the nature of white supremacy. He conducted an experiment on the thesis that the problem was about love. He was killed, meaning that love wasn't what it was about.

So I come along, and I say this problem is about white supremacy and white genetic survival on a planet in which whites are a tiny minority and genetically recessive to everybody. If all the nonwhite people went toward the white people with love, what would happen? There would be white genetic annihilation. If everybody was in love and not paying any attention to skin color, then all of the people on the planet would be black. That's why Dr. Martin Luther King, Jr., died.

Critical to this discussion is the issue of melanin. I gave a paper back in 1972 at the National Medical Association in Kansas City. The paper was titled "Melanin: The Neurochemical Basis for Soul." Melanin is a pigment of the nervous system. It causes skin, hair, and eyes to have color. Melanocytes are the cells in the body that produce melanin. The melanocytes are described as second only to the cells that we use to think with in terms of their sophistication and importance in the nervous system, second only to the beta cells in the cerebral cortex. I think a lot of the things we see black people doing, displaying rhythm, emotional refinement—like the old people used to say, "The blacker the berry, the sweeter the juice. If it ain't got no soul, it ain't got no use"—can be attributed to this pigment, this black pigment that I believe is perhaps the most fantastic stuff on the planet. It allows for the special spiritual qualities and emotional refinements black people have.

Of course, the importance of melanin has been debased. It has been debased because the white collective does not have much melanin pigment in their skin. Albinos are totally deficient in melanin pigment. Having white skin is albinism. The specific cause of albinism is the absence of an enzyme called tyrosinase, which is absent from white people's skin melanocytes. Black people have plenty of tyrosinase in their skin melanocytes, thus their melanocytes can produce lots of melanin pigment. Because white people don't have much of it, they deny its importance. Then they go out and get suntanned, to try to force those cells to eke out any melanin pigment they can possibly eke out, even if they get skin cancer in the process. In the meantime, they also teach black people to debase melanin. So black people say, "Don't marry anybody darker than yourself. Try to marry as 'white' as you can—so that we can get rid of our melanin." All the while, white people are trying desperately to get it.

Without going into a very deep discussion of this, I will say that I believe melanin is the neurochemical basis of what we call "soul," the neurochemical basis for the sixth or seventh or eighth sense we have. There have been at least seven, if not more, international conferences on the pigment cell. White people are in laboratories right now studying this fantastic, incredible cell in the nervous system. But if white supremacy is going to survive, it has to debase the genetic ability to produce melanin pigmentation, which can cause white genetic annihilation.

Melanin is sort of like a hydrogen bomb at the genetic level. It's like the secret weapon that nonwhite people have that can genetically annihilate the global white collective that is interested in surviving genetically. To survive genetically as whites, they had to line up the colors in terms of darkness. You know, the saying, "If you're black, stay back; brown, stick around; yellow, mellow; white, right." So the colors are respected, at the surface level, inversely proportional to the ability to produce melanin.

If you are in the classification of nonwhite under white supremacy, the lighter you are the more mobility you have, the more acceptable you are. You notice that most of the nonwhite people in the movies look almost white, even though, in the final analysis, if they're nonwhite, then they have to be in some degrading role. They're either Aunt Jemimah or a whore, or something like that.

At the deeper, subconscious levels of knowledge, I maintain that the more skin pigment you have, the more powerful you are considered to be by the white supremacy culture. I say that this is why, in white supremacy systems, judges wear black. Ministers wear black. When you get married, you put on black tails. The highest form of dress is to wear black. A white female always wants to have her basic black dress, and she says that her ideal male is "tall, dark, and handsome."

We do not understand the issues of white genetic survival, of preventing white genetic annihilation. We just fall into the pattern that if you're lighter, you're going to have more opportunity than if you're blacker. And it's not just black people, it's all over. It's in Asia. It's in South America. It's in Central America. Wherever white people have come into contact with nonwhite people, they start by lining up the colors. The lesser the level of melanin skin pigmentation, the lesser the threat you present to white genetic annihilation; therefore, the greater the level of your social mobility. A very black-skinned man sends shivers of fear down the spine of the white genetic survival system and culture, so we need to understand the meaning of the colors, or the keys to the colors, and not fall into that trap.

We must try to line ourselves up on the side of the chessboard where blacks and other nonwhites are playing for justice and peace on the planet. We must get out of the debasing patterns of color discrimination within the entire nonwhite group. That's a lot of work.

When we look at another crucial situation, it's like all roads lead to Rome, or out of white supremacy comes white supremacy. If you have a systemic white supremacy dynamic, then you are going to have to effeminize the black or other nonwhite males. See, a nonwhite female, like a black woman, is not a threat to white genetic annihilation. She cannot force intercourse. A male can. So the black male, the nonwhite male, is the threat, the black male in particular. If he is the threat to white genetic survival, then that's the goal objective on the table, to effeminize him.

If a black male person becomes bisexualized or homosexualized, if he has been made to give up his masculinity in terms of sexual functioning, then the threat he poses to white genetic annihilation is perceived as less. Total effeminization is ultimately the homosexualizing of the male. Now, how does that happen? If you take the male out of the home, and if the female is angry and upset with males, then you can lead a people in the direction of producing passivity, effeminization, bisexuality, and homosexuality in their male offspring. It's like a continuum. We did not have epidemic levels of male homosexuality in Afrika. It is a European-created phenomenon. Somebody may say that homosexuality was the dominant form of sexual relations in Greece and Rome. I say, absolutely.

I decode homosexuality. I do not deal with it as a moral issue. I look at homosexuality to see what exactly is the symbolic meaning of the behavior. If the male has his penis in the mouth of another male or in the anus of a male, then he is taking semen—male substance—into his GI tract, his gastrointestinal tract. The gastrointestinal tract is the tract that nourishes the body. I say that this behavior indicates a sense of absence of male substance, or a sensed deficiency of male adequacy: "I have doubts about my masculinity. If I feel insecure about my masculinity, I will engage in putting more semen into my body." The behavior becomes obsessive, so it demands multiple, multiple, multiple sexual contacts.

Now, let's look at Afrika—the gigantic continent of Afrika—and then at North Afrika and the Mediterranean, then Greece and Rome, and finally at tiny little Europe. Looking over the Mediterranean, those white males saw these black men on this great big huge continent who could genetically annihilate them. What were these pale white males going to feel but deficient in male substance? So their form of demonstrating their sense of deficiency of male substance was to engage in homosexual behavior, meaning that they didn't feel adequate as men so they wanted to increase their sense of masculinity in a symbolic sense. So they had a historical pattern of male inadequacy behavior.

They realized their circumstances and decided to develop massive weapons of destruction and go around conquering everybody else, which does not prove power, it just proves that one is smart and cunning. It doesn't change the reality of genetic power. So the white male posture, from Alexander to present times, is—now we are going to dominate the whole world. The nonwhite people, non-white men in particular, did not understand males who functioned from a sense of genetic inadequacy. But, in the white male brain computer, the need to make all kinds of weapons, which are symbolic extensions of the genitals, and dominate was the driving force. Finally, the nonwhite males were brought into submission.

The nonwhite males in Afrika did not have homosexuality in the first place. After they are conquered and reduced to passivity and taken out of the home, you begin to see a pattern of homosexuality and bisexuality within the black population. At this point in time, we have epidemic levels of black male bisexuality and homosexuality.

I say that it needs to be looked at as a political phenomenon. It is fallout from white supremacy domination and the need for the tiny white minority on the planet to survive genetically by reducing black men, who are the most genetically powerful men on planet earth, to bisexuality and homosexuality. In that way, they will not be a threat to white supremacy. That's done through the mechanism of controlling the structure of the family.

If you can produce a major disturbance in the relationship between the male and the female, the mother and the father, then you're going to eventually produce patterns of female homosexuality too. We black people now also have a rise in female homosexuality. Now some people might stand up and say, "Oh, Dr. Welsing, that's not true," or "I *choose* to be homosexual." Nobody chooses their pattern of sexuality. It is produced by specific patterns within the family. Once you begin to disturb the patterns of relationships or disturb patterns of mutual respect—female respect for male, male respect for female—then you're going to produce these patterns of distortion. This does not become clear until one decodes all the way back to the foundations of Western civilization and finds out

that we are dealing with a collective that feels vulnerable in terms of its genetic and numerical make-up.

Further, I think there's a very high level of homosexuality amongst white males and white females, a high level of distortion within the white family structure itself. Because the white male feels vulnerable as a male, when he compares himself with the majority males on the planet, he has to engage in compensatory "I-feel-inadequate-but-I'm-going-to-posture-superiority-within-my-own-family" behavior. So he starts degrading the white female, starts putting down the white female, debasing her and making her not feel of value. When a woman is disrespected in the eyes of men, does that push her toward patterns of homosexuality? I would say yes. Also, when the white female is demeaned by the white male, she takes it out on the white male child, thus negating his masculinity.

All of this comes from a fundamental dynamic of white genetic and numerical vulnerability, of not feeling whole. White people do not feel whole. They don't look at themselves in the mirror and say, "I admire and respect myself." They look in the mirror and say, "Oh, my goodness, I'm so pale. Let me get out in the sun" or "Let me run to the suntanning parlor" or "Let's compare tan lines." There's a fundamental disrespect of the white body, naked and unadorned. From that degrading and debasing of self comes all the negativity that is attached to people with skin color.

If you degrade your appearance, you will degrade the act that produces you. You will degrade the genitals that produce you. Then you will end up with pornography, or with sexism. If a white female says her ideal male is tall, dark, and handsome, can she be allowed to go out on her own? In a system of white supremacy, no. If she's not controlled, she will then contribute to white genetic annihilation, so you have to keep control over her because she might choose a black male, a nonwhite male, over a white male. I say that's the origin of sexism. These are not isolated occurrences.

One can even examine capitalism or the focus on money and profit. If I felt whole as a human being, I would not have to just keep trying to pile up paper money and plaster it to myself. You know how Adam and Eve in the Garden of Eden—portrayed as white people, of course—placed fig leaves over their genitals out of shame for their bodies? I say paper money is that fig leaf. It is what the white collective uses to cover its body shame; thus, the symbolic association of money with tree leaves and the expression "Money does not grow on trees." They do not say, "Here I am, a human being on the planet, and I'm naked and unadorned and I feel total respect for myself."

White people's shame about their bodies goes way, way back in time. My thesis is that white are mutants of black people. Afrikans put them out because

they had a genetic disturbance and chased them up into Europe. I even say that's the meaning of the Adam and Eve story in the Bible. Black people walked around naked before white people returned to Afrika. They felt their bodies were beautiful. They respected their bodies. White people had shame for their bodies. They sought to cover their bodies many ways. They have an expression, "Clothes make the person," not the body.

This whole issue of white body shame explains why, when President Nixon was disgraced and removed from power, we had this phenomenon where white males would run around with no clothes on. They called it "streaking." That behavior was a symbolic phenomenon. The head of the white state had been pulled down and disgraced. White males all over the country were pulling off their clothes and running around naked. We haven't seen that phenomenon since. It came during that period. It went away as quickly as it came after that whole period came to a close. It was the association of the white body with shame.

The Adam and Eve story is a symbolic story about early white people. Adam and Eve were in the Garden of Eden. They ate the forbidden fruit. They became ashamed of their nakedness and were chased out of the Garden of Eden. It's like in medicine: All the people in Afrika are black people, but if black people started producing albino mutants at some point—that is, if they started evidencing a genetic abnormality—the first thing a doctor would ask the mothers is, "Did you eat something different?" So, to account for this white skin coming into being, they had to say Adam and Eve ate something strange—the forbidden fruit, the apple—then they became ashamed of their bodies and left the Garden of Eden. I say it's really a story of how whites came to be located in Europe.

Just like in the present day: If somebody produces a genetic abnormality, they don't keep it at home, do they? They put it where? Outside, or in an institution. When black people started producing these mutants, they were not left in the group, they were chased out. We have the story of the founding of the state of Rome, where Romulus and Remus had to nurse from wolves, meaning they didn't have what? No mother or father. The black mother and father in Afrika put the albino mutants out and chased them away.

I think the initiation ritual in the Greek-letter organizations about "crossing the burning sand" refers to those "original" white people who, in ancient, ancient time, were forced out of Afrika, across the desert, and up into Europe. As albinos, they would have had to move north anyway, to get out of the sun. That's what I think.

Then history cycles around, and white people do what? They go and get black people out of Afrika, bring them to America, and introduce what was called the "slavery period." Black mothers and fathers were forced to nurse white babies and not take care of their own black babies. They were made to leave their black babies at home or leave them in the field. They were made to come into the big house and suckle and nurse white babies, forced to take care of white people because whites remembered, deep down, that Afrikans had put them out of Afrika because they had white skins. That they had lived in caves and run around Europe for centuries as uncivilized and barbaric savages. That's why we find ourselves circling back around now, with blacks reduced to the lowest state of existence. Now we have hundreds of thousands of black children in foster care, on welfare, and far too many black families completely broken up. Our black babies were sort of put out in the cold, not getting the care and attention they needed.

When you come up with any new idea, I think initially people respond with, "Uh, oh, what is she talking about? She must be a candidate for a psychiatric hospital herself." I'm sure all of that has been said. However, I am not interested in just putting out new ideas. The question is whether these ideas help us to understand present-day problems. I say that they do. With these ideas, we can begin to make steps toward solving problems that everybody else has thrown up their hands about.

Sometimes people ask me if I plan to change my theory. I say, why? You don't throw out something that works. You don't throw out something that helps you understand what is going on. I will be the first person to throw it out when it doesn't help explain what is happening.

There are things going on right in our own homes, but we can't see them. For example, I think it should be mandatory for parents to start discussing and understanding something I call "dependency deprivation." Dependency deprivation occurs when we fail to give all of the necessary emotional attention to our children. I say this attention is the foundation of personality strength. Yet, a major problem is happening amongst black people. With the white supremacy dynamic raining down on black people's heads all the time, fracturing the structure of the black family, our children fail to get all the necessary emotional attention and care, or lap time, they need. They don't come to depend on their mothers or fathers. I say we will create a internal revolution within the black population when we begin to understand the critical importance of dependency deprivation.

You have to understand white supremacy exactly and specifically. Understand how it engenders massive levels of dependency deprivation within the black community. That's why we have teenage pregnancy. That's why we have narcotics addiction and alcoholism. That's why we have massive depression.

That's why we really have failed in male–female relations—because people who are mistreated as children move to the next level of intimate interaction, which is husband-wife relations, and then mistreat each other. A man who has been repeatedly left by his mother, even by her going to work, is going to up and leave his wife, saying, "I was hurt, you abandoned me. Now I'm going to abandon you," and vice versa.

We're going to have to understand that white supremacy has produced major distortions in terms of the level of care given to black children. That is why I say become parents when you are thirty and thirty-five years old and follow the rest of my formula. After white supremacy is eliminated and we have a foundation for the just treatment of human beings, then maybe family patterns can be different. Maybe people can have and take care of up to eight children. We don't have those conditions today, so we're going to have to make compensatory moves.

We've got to understand the critical role of mothering. That's why you see Afrikan statues of mother and child that show such a high level of nurturing and patience—it's the foundation for personality development, for a just society. We've also got to understand the importance of the father's presence as providing support for the family so the mother can carry out this nurturing pattern. This is absolutely critical.

If we don't do it, if we allow our teenagers to keep on having children, then we're going to have all these victims of dependency deprivation among us. We're going to have to put a stop to it. The white collective cannot produce a solution to this problem. They'll say, Well, we were dependency deprived when our black mothers put us out, and you want us to come up with the answer? No, we black people are going to have to come up with answers and solutions for ourselves.

We have to keep in mind those pictures of Afrikan women with babies tied to their backs, or of those Somalian mothers holding their babies, while they are starving to death. Will those babies, if they survive, grow up with dependency deprivation? The answer is no.

There may be some students of psychology who want to leap right into some of the things I am saying, but first things first. I would say whatever training program they're in, they need first to learn what their instructors are teaching, and then pass whatever tests are based on that. Don't waste your energy fighting it. Learn it, then realize that you're going to have to get into a completely different school of thought to understand the social system and the global and local societies that have developed around the concept of white genetic survival. The distortions that concept produces within the white collective, and certainly the distortions it is producing as far as black and other nonwhite people are con-

cerned, represent a whole new arena of investigation. This is an area in which black people are going to have to become the experts. I certainly will do everything I can to help.

When I see young people, I tell them that we have a magnificent planet. We have a magnificent universe. To all young people—I give the challenge to white young people too—I say get into a more sophisticated understanding of who you are. Try to reshape and mold your thinking and behavior so that you can contribute to justice in the universe. Most certainly I say this to black and other nonwhite young people, the vast majority of people on the planet, who are the victims of white supremacy. It is incumbent upon them to pull themselves up and contribute to this struggle for justice and peace.

Justice, at this present time, means the elimination of white supremacy on the planet. It means not falling victim to the bullets of destruction that are called drugs, the bullets that are some person motivating you to become a member of a gang or to fight and kill one another. That's just divide and conquer. Drugs are divide and conquer. If you sell drugs to your friends, to your sisters and brothers, you help kill them. You have to avoid these obstacles that are coming from the opposite side of the court, that are causing you to lose the game. Get smart. Stop singing songs about degrading yourselves. Stop singing songs that degrade the magnificence of your humanity. Struggle to free yourself from sex obsession and degrading sex.

I would also tell young people how to get rid of white supremacy by practicing justice. That's like saying, how does a black piece checkmate the white king on the chessboard?: by studying the game. Neely Fuller has produced a book he calls a "textbook" for victims of white supremacy.[1] I encourage everyone who can get a copy of that book to do so and read it. He has done an outstanding job of opening up an area of insight. It is really a manual for playing the black side of the chessboard. As far as literature is concerned, I say read everything. Read as many newspapers every day as you can. Go to the library, and read as much as you can. Read everything, but read with an understanding that the critical issue is this issue of color. Don't try to brush it aside just because it pops up everywhere. There are not a lot of people who are studying the whole dynamic of white supremacy. They can be counted on one hand, so there's not, at this point in time, a great body of literature. The great body of literature has to be produced.

I've had individuals ask me why those persons classified as white listen to my lectures. Some of it may just be curiosity. It's almost as though they have their antenna up more because they are vulnerable to genetic annihilation. In most things that occur on the planet, they are the first to take an interest. They

are primed to think, "We've got to survive genetically. We could be genetically annihilated." So they take a high level of interest in most things, while people who have a greater sense of genetic security are kind of relaxing. These white-skinned people are always hopping around, jumping and moving and leaping and racing, climbing Mount Everest and going to the depths of the ocean, while we say, "Just relax. Cool it. Enjoy the sunshine." I would certainly hope that there will be an increasing number of people who classify themselves as white who will decide that they want to bring justice to the planet. But so far we've only had one John Brown.[2]

[1] Fuller, Neely, Jr., *The United Independent Compensatory Code/System/Concept: A Textbook/Workbook for Thought, Speech, and Action for Victims of Racism (White Supremacy)* (Washington, DC: Author, 1969).

[2] John Brown (1800–1859), American abolitionist, was executed for leading a raid at Harper's Ferry, West Virginia, the purpose of which was to capture arms to be used in the fight against slavery.

WILLIAM LARUE DILLARD

MINISTER, AUTHOR, TEACHER

William LaRue Dillard is one of the ablest biblical scholars in the country, but he does not approach the field from the typical Eurocentric perspective. His book, Biblical Ancestry Voyage, brings to light the true racial make-up of the characters in the Bible. His revelation that the large majority of different groups—as well as significant individuals such as Abraham, Moses, David, Solomon, Mary, Jesus, and many, many more—were actually black people sends chills down the spine of those who would perpetuate false information. Dr. Dillard paints the true face on the people of the Bible.

Coming to the ministry was for me a divine call from God. I had been involved in aeronautics. I love jets and planes, and I have enjoyed tinkering around with them since my Air Force service career. Subsequent to that career, the divine call of God came into my life. It was a spontaneous action to go forth and preach the Gospel. This was back in 1957. From that time, it was a definite. I mean, there was no doubt about it. A definite call was lodged in my spirit and in my heart that God wanted me to carry His Word.

I believe in the divine intervention of the Lord. Of course, during the time of my calling I was young. I was in the church, loving God, reading, meditating and studying His Word, and with that foundation, one hears. I heard it in my spirit. The Lord called me to preach His Word. Reading the Bible narratives and discovering how He called others, naturally that's in the mind, but there are great differences in the call for each one of us. With me, it was a deep unction, a surge of God's presence upon my life to preach the Word of God. Not knowing much about the Bible, and knowing very little of anything else, I immediately talked with my pastor. He shared with me some knowledge of what it was all about, and told me that I was to pray. Knowing that, I thank God now as I look back thirty-five years ago. That knowledge has helped me through many of the hurdles that have come; through many of the things that would be set before me and cause my footstep to turn and go another way, despite this divine call and mandate to share the Gospel.

More than thirty years ago, during my tenure in the seminary, while studying ancient Hebrew and Greek, the words to which we were introduced, the people, etcetera, inspired me to write. When I came upon the fact that the names of the persons I was reading in the Bible were not Hebrew, a curiosity arose in my heart. It was then I started writing various papers. This curiosity was intensified by the answer one German professor gave me when I asked him, "Who are these people?" He was vague in giving me an answer, so it drove me to do further research.

I abandoned it for many years. I think it was a little more than thirteen or fourteen years ago that I renewed my search to look at the characters in the Bible. As a student of theology and Christology, I felt that if I didn't know who these people were whom I was reading about in my Bible, then the lay person could not know. I wanted to know. As I began my research I knew I wanted to be able to share this with people.

This was not a part of my seminary training. I make mention of this in my book, *Biblical Ancestry Voyage;* that there is and has been a great distortion in the translation of the Bible. When we read the terminology describing various persons like the Kushites, the Jebusites, the Hittites, the Hivites, and all the rest of them, we see that they are somewhat camouflaged as other ethnic groups and not clearly pointed out. When one comes upon that in the Hebrew language, it doesn't jibe with what you see in the translation of the text. That gives me some concern. There needed to be an uncovering of those facts. That was my effort in bringing together *Biblical Ancestry Voyage.*

Studying semantics and doing word study I began to get the inkling of a sense that some of these people were black. As I studied and researched further back, I began studying the findings of various historians, findings from the educational community at large, artifacts, as well as various statues and things. Scholars were making reference as to what these people looked like, their features, their structures, and other things. That really heightened my interest. I found out that these folks had other names, that their names went back to Ham and his descendants, as well as to the Arabs and others. So, of course, I wanted to know more.

Then again, during the turbulent sixties, there were many of our young people who were abandoning the Christian religion and declaring that the Bible we believe in, the Christianity to which we hold firm, is a white man's religion, that it came from Europe. That disturbed me because I knew theology and Christology went much too far back, long before Europe was born, for that to be true. It existed while Europe was still in an idolatrous state. Then I had a need to know even more. I had to bring that information forward.

Those driving forces kept me going as I traveled from country after country, through many countries in Afrika, and throughout Europe. I would always visit the libraries and study both the history and the antiquity. When things began to come together in my own heart and mind, I said, "Oh, yes, we need to really inform the populace about the realness and the truth of this Holy Book."

In studying the Bible chapter by chapter, verse by verse, from Genesis on, of course we know about the destruction of humankind on planet earth. Eight individuals were left, the Bible declares, including Mr. and Mrs. Noah; their three sons, Japheth, Shem, Ham; and their sons' wives. They were the ones who repopulated the earth. The Bible says, "From them were the whole earth overspread."

I wanted to know who these fellows were. So I went to the Bible, beginning in Genesis, chapter ten. I began to run references on the names and also the lineage of each one of Noah's sons. I more or less centered my attention upon Ham because of the rich meaning of his name. I discovered the name "Ham" originally meant "black," "salty," "chocolate," "sunburned." I came upon his offspring: Phut, Mizraim, Canaan, and Kush. I did a word study on the meaning of their names, where they originated, and who their descendants were. Kush was the father of the Ethiopians; Mizraim, the father of the Egyptians; Phut, the father of the Libyans and the Cyrenians; and, of course, Canaan, the father of the Canaanites. I ran the reference right from the Bible, using history to support my research along with other writings of theologians.

When one reads the names Hittite, Hivite, and Jebusite, one is reading about black folk. More specifically, one is primarily reading about the Canaanites, or the Egyptians. Egypt, of course, was a black nation, as were Libya and Cyrene. These people are descended from those sons of Ham. Prior to the flood, it was just one people, one nation, and one language. Following that time, because of the mishaps, because of sin, and because of disobedience, this division occurred. As we follow the lineage of Noah's sons as to where they went, the Japhites, the Hamites, and the Semites—the children of Shem—became differentiated.

When one reads these names in the Bible, right away a red flag should go up. Who were they? Were they all bad guys or were they good guys, too? Were they a part of the Jewish religion or were they all just idol-worshippers? I think that's what *Biblical Ancestry Voyage* has sought to do.

Now, the area we are talking about is the whole Mesopotamia Valley, the valley of the Nile. We are talking about that entire area, which during that epoch was known as the Land of Ham and which is now East Afrika. I believe, based on my scholarly findings, that this is where the birth of humankind took place, because of what it says in the Bible and especially in Genesis, chapter two. Geographically, it speaks about four contributory rivers and names those rivers. When one studies geography, one sees that nowhere else on planet earth, in the old world or the present world, will one ever come upon any four contributory rivers running together other than in that locality known as East Afrika or Ethiopia. If that is the case, the Bible definitely talks about the Garden of Eden being located there.

Why, pray tell me, would we have believed years ago that the birth of civilization was in Europe? If we are going to believe in the scripture and follow this scripture as it explains the location geographically, one can see the fact clearly. There is no doubt that East Afrika is where the Garden of Eden is located.

One great thing that brought it into the living rooms of many Americans during the Gulf War was when we saw by television the various Arab nations. No one has never asked what they looked like or where they came from. When we start reading the Bible, I try to point out in my book when I deal with Abraham, we should ask, Who was Abraham? What did he look like? Where did those Arabs come from? The answer, of course, is they came from his wives and from Ishmael, his first son. God gave Ishmael twelve sons, and from those twelve sons came twelve nations, who were and are the Arab nations. The same brothers we warred with. In reading our Bible all these years, no one never told us that. They gave us a distorted picture. We didn't know who those guys were, we just knew everybody was bad.

When I use the term "Jewish," I'm not talking about the nation or their nationality, I am focusing on their religion. There were many people, a mixed multitude, who comprised the Jewish religion.

God started dealing with man in Ethiopia and then later at the Tower of Babel or Babylon, and again in the nation led by Nimrod, who was another young black man, the son of Kush. I definitely believe that the religion of humankind began there in Ethiopia, as well as in Egypt.

The people of Egypt had many gods. God called Abraham out of the land of Ur, or the land of the Chaldeans, a black nation of people. When we see the paintings and pictures of Abraham and many other characters in the Bible, we see them with light or white skin, with maybe blue eyes, or long, brown flowing hair. But, my God, when one studies the people of that epoch and their beginnings and learns who they were, based on the findings of our theology, that image just does not jibe.

The Semites and the Hamites were similar in color, black-skinned, just like Moses. Moses did not look like Charlton Heston. Moses could not have looked like that. He was a Hebrew. He was a black-skinned Hebrew, as his mother and father, Amram and Jochebed, were. Moses had black skin and kinky hair. That is the reason even the Pharoah, Pharoah Seti I, thought he was just another Egyptian.

Moses was adopted by Pharoah's daughter, Thermuthis, and reared in the palace. Later, Pharoah even adopted him as his son. He rose to be second in command of all Egypt. Pharaoh didn't know he was a Hebrew. This lets us know the Jews or Hebrews of that epoch were black. The only way one knew the difference between them and the Egyptians was by their language or dialect. As far as looking at them, one could not tell the difference.

WILLIAM LARUE DILLARD

Even today, as I travel in Ethiopia and, of course, in Egypt as well as in Israel, when I run across many Israelites and others, I can't tell whether they are black Americans or black Afrikans. We saw them bringing that great number of Ethiopians out of Ethiopia. They had been down there for almost two thousand years, in fact, about five years before the birth of Jesus Christ, or 4 B.C. We saw it on our television. The Israeli government said, "Yes, these are our Hebrew brothers." If you look at them, they look just like you or I, with black skin and kinky or woolly hair. Some of them have straight hair, depending on the geographical area from which they came.

What I believe we need to focus on is the fact of that epoch of Moses: Hebrews as well as Hamites were the same in color pigmentation, hair, and other characteristics. One could not tell them apart. That didn't really change until about 332 B.C., when Alexander the Great led his army into Egypt, subjugated it, and held Egypt for about three hundred years. Then one sees a change because of miscegenation and the mixing of the bloods of various persons. The Bible definitely speaks about it.

What I'm saying is, from the beginning of humankind, man's skin pigmentation—and I'm just going back to the time of Noah and his sons and thereafter, because the first generation of humankind was wiped out in the worldwide flood—I definitely believe those folks in that Ark were black, black-skinned. At least Shem and Ham, because, from my studies, all of which I don't understand, there is an allusion to Japheth being of a lighter skin. The Aramaic word that is used in reference to his name suggests this.

Upon the destruction of the Tower of Babel, the Japhites followed Japheth and all of his crowd up into the Cimmaron area, up into Asia Minor. When one studies the historicity of them from the Tower of Babel, one finds references to white skin, blonde or brown hair and all of that. As far as the Semites and the Hamites are concerned, however, they were a blend of one. They migrated via the same routes, the Hamites being the first to populate what became known as the Holy Land through Ham's son, Canaan. They populated the land and called it Canaanland.

So when we start talking about all those great cities in the Bible, we are talking about the cities of black folk. When we are talking about Jericho, we are talking about Hebron, the land of the Chaldeans. Altogether, we are talking about Jerusalem. Jerusalem was not a Hebrew name. Jerusalem was a city founded by Jubas, who, in Genesis, chapter 10, is identified as the son of Canaan. Jerusalem was named after him. The Jebusites were his descendants.

One does not start to see any white-skinned Hebrews until well after 332 B.C., after Alexander the Great's subjugation of Egypt. That is when, of

course, miscegenation took place. The Jews started directing their daughters and sons to marry the lighter-skinned Jews. When we see them now, we think that's the way they looked way back when Ham, Shem, and Japheth were around, but not so.

Abraham's son was Isaac. It was Isaac's son, Jacob, who wrestled with the angel who wouldn't turn him loose until God blessed him. God blessed him by changing his name from Jacob to Israel. Thus, his descendants came to be known as Israelites.

In later years, long after Solomon's reign—David and Solomon both reigned for forty years each, as sovereign kings over one nation—we see the dividing of the Kingdom of Israel and the Kingdom of Judah. There became two reigns, but we are dealing with the same people. We call one the Israelites and the other the Judeans. Jesus came through the lineage of the tribe of Judah. Judah, of course, was the fourth born son of Abraham and his black wives.

I use the term "miscegenation," to refer to the mixing of the blood between the Jews. I use the term loosely, but specifically I am talking about religion and, of course, the Hamite people. Maybe I should say the Semites and Hamites. Because of miscegenation, they were one people, living side by side, after God directed Joshua to subjugate Canaanland and take over that land from all the black nations who were then sovereign rulers of them.

When one reads about the nations of Jericho, Hebron, Sidon, Tyre, one is reading about the black Canaanites who were there long before Europe was even civilized. When God promised that land to the Israelites, because of their obedience and walking in His paths, he told Moses to lead them to it. Then later, Joshua led them into it. They subjugated the land.

Joshua destroyed most of the Canaanites. The Canaanites became extinct during that epoch. The other black nations, like Ethiopia, have always been sovereign. No one other than Ethiopians has ever ruled over Ethiopia. As I said, Alexander the Great subjugated Egypt and ruled over it as well as some of the other lands such as Libya and Cyrenia, but not Ethiopia. We don't see a change until we come to the New Testament. The New Testament focuses on Europeans, with the Jews being missionaries and carrying the gospel, the Biblical theology, and Christology to all people.

Let me deal with the lineage of Jesus and try to clear it up. For years, in our Sunday school and in our Bible studies, the Biblical lineage has been spoken of as being rather dull. First, let me go back first to the Old Testament. God directed Joshua to lead the Israelites, to subjugate the land of Canaan, which was populated by black people who worshipped the god of Astoreth, the god of Baal, the god of Uz. They had many gods but not the true and living God.

There's one particular story in Joshua, chapter 2, that tells us what happened when the Israelites subjugated Jericho. It was Joshua who led, but there was one woman involved, one beautiful, black temple princess by the name of Rahab. She was, in fact, a prostitute. When she hid Joshua's spies, she believed they were sent by the omniscient, all-creating God. She did somthing that brought about redemption.

She confessed to the living God before the spies. As a result, she and her family were the only ones who were spared when Joshua led the battle against Jericho. I'm sure all of us know that he marched around Jericho seven times and the walls came tumbling down. God had given him those instructions. They had to destroy everyone and leave no one alive. Rahab and her family were left alive because she hid the spies.

It is significant to know that Rahab went with them when they went on down into Jerusalem and subjugated it. She married a man, a Jewish prince by the name of Salmon. Salmon, a black-skinned Hebrew, married Rahab, a black Canaanite woman.

God brought, through their union, a son. They named that boy Boaz. Boaz later found a Moabite woman by the name of Ruth, a beautiful black woman. Boaz and Ruth got married. God gave them a son. They named him Obed. Obed brought forth a son. He named him Jesse. Jesse had eight sons, black sons now, including David, who was the youngest son. David was married to many wives, of course, but specifically to Bathsheba, the Hittite black woman. They had a particular son by the name of Solomon, and one may follow that lineage right on down through the scriptures.

What I'm pointing out is the lineage you read about in Matthew, chapter 1, the lineage you read in Luke, chapter 3, as well as Ruth, chapter 4, and Genesis chapter 5. That lineage is that of the tribe of Judah. It runs right on down to Mary, the black Madonna who birthed Jesus. Jezebel, the black Jezebel, is in that same lineage.

The black Canaanites were marrying the black Hebrews. You mean to tell me that Jesus is going to come out with white skin, blue eyes, and long blonde flowing hair or brown hair even? Of course not. I believe that when we see the lineage as it is written, it tells the whole story. Not only does it bring us up to Jesus, but it takes us all the way back to Adam.

My research in doing *Biblical Ancestry Voyage* caused me to discover that all of the countries honored and worshipped the black Madonna, black Mary, and her black baby. They did it for years until the rise of white supremacy in the fourteenth century. In fact, there's only one nation that continues to this day to honor the black Madonna and her black baby, and that is the nation of

Poland. They never stopped. With the rise of white supremacy, when they found all of the statues and everything depicting the black Madonna, they burned and destroyed them. Poland never did. I think it would be interesting for any scholars or students who would want to dig a little deeper to study the history of Poland and their religion. One can visit a Polish temple today and see there that in their paintings, their shrines, and their stained glass windows they still honor the black Madonna. Russia has two Madonnas, a black and a white one.

Before the rise of white supremacy, this blackness was not a problem. It never had been in the Bible. Only because of Europe and its prejudice, because of the slave masters of this country and their brainwashing, and because of Bible translators who distorted the holy scriptures, did it become a problem. There is nothing wrong with the primary text in Hebrew, Greek, and Aramaic, in which the Bible is written. There is nothing wrong with these, but there's something wrong with a translation out of those languages into our tongue that does not tell the absolute truth about who the persons in the Bible are and how God dealt with them, which would reveal what they looked like at that time. I think that's what *Biblical Ancestry Voyage* does.

Europeans, for many years, taught all of their subjects that civilization began in Europe, that Europe was the cradle of civilization. The Greeks, the Romans, they carried universal sway over the world with their great power, like Alexander the Great, with all his troops marching off all over the map gaining conquests. Then they went down into Egypt and Afrika. By the way, Egypt was always known from the Bible as the Land of Ham, the black land. When the Europeans started discovering all of these statues, the Sphinx and all the rest, they found on these statues that they had wide flat noses, thick lips, and almond-shaped eyes. In fact, they became so enraged that they demanded the destruction of those statues. That's why you see today, in many of our books and encyclopedias and other literature, statues that are faceless. They didn't want people to understand and know they had been studying black people.

Imagine it, when we think of all of our arts, sciences, mathematics—you name it—these came from blacks. When we read of the great philosophers—Plato, Socrates, Aristotle, and all of them—they received their learning from black people. Even the Hebrews or the Jews didn't have an alphabet themselves. They borrowed theirs from the Babylonians and the Canaanites. That is the reason the calendar we use today is a calendar that is a reversal of the calendar that was being used by the Jews of the epoch following their delivery from slavery around 1526 B.C. When one talks about Abib, which is the first month to the

Jews, it is made clear in Leviticus, chapter 23, and in Exodus, chapter 12, that the names you find in the Bible are not Hebrew names. Those calendar months are Babylonian and Canaanite words, the words of black people. We didn't know it then but, praise God, we know it now.

Some people may be upset with what I am revealing, but I simply try to follow the biblical blueprint, the premise and the words of Jesus in John, chapter eight, verse 32. Jesus said, "And you shall know the truth. And the truth shall set you free." When I tell the truth—explaining, expounding, and exposing the word of God, what the Bible says about who is who—it doesn't matter whether I'm a black or white or brown or a yellow scholar.

If whites are going to exegete the Bible in its original contextual setting, they're going to have to say the same thing in order to tell the truth. If they say that what I'm saying is racist or bigoted or whatever, then I say, now wait a minute, what do you mean by that? Do you think I'm trying to highlight blacks and put down whites? If that is the case, then you misunderstand me. All I'm trying to do is to correct those ills and wrongs and misnomers of the past that have been done. The thing God is using me to do is just to share from the background of my scholarship what He has released in my spirit. I think when any serious-minded person studies the Bible, she or he will see it.

By the way, *Biblical Ancestry Voyage* isn't a book that's just highlighting black people and telling how good they were. Let me tell you something; many in those black nations were despicable people. They did some awesome things. I mean, just terrible things when it came to humanity and dealing with them. My book is not just saying, "Well, look, you all, at all of these black folks. They were all good guys." No, some were awful, terrible.

When we think of all the Herods we've read about in the New Testament, we must know that all of the Herods were black. They got their start from Esau and his three black wives, who were the ancestors of the Edomite race. All of the Herods—from Herod the Great, Herod Antipas, and Herod Anchelaus—all of the Herods that you read about were black, and look at what they did. Look at the destruction: killing little babies, two years of age and younger, just because they heard there was a newborn king. These were black people.

What we must let people know is that the Bible is not just a book about all good people. The Bible talks about the good and the bad. The Bible talks about the obedient and the disobedient. As it was then, it is now. When we talk about the righteous men God used—Abraham, Isaac, Jacob, Moses, all of them—hey, they did a lot of things going against the will of the omniscient God. Incest, having more than one wife—that wasn't God's direction, but those acts were accepted in their culture.

If that person wants to know who they are reading about, then don't they need to know where those people came from, what they looked like? The only way one can know that is by going back to the beginning, studying their names, and their descent, finding out where they came from, because the names of areas and the names of persons meant something significant. It wasn't like the way we just throw names on people today. Back then, names really meant something, something spiritual, especially if it had to do with God's people.

Of course, names meant something spiritually to those idol-worshippers too. They named their youngsters after the gods they worshipped, whether it was Astoreth or Baalim or Baalioms or Uza or whoever it was. It was still something significant, spiritual.

The information in my book is so striking, it is going to have an impact on those who read it. First, I believe this impact should rest in the hearts of the young as well as oldsters once their minds are turned toward people of antiquity. The young Afrikan Americans, I think, will be helped in their sense of self-worth and self-esteem as to who they are. As they come to know the rich, illustrious, intelligent history of their beginnings, it's going to help from that standpoint. It's going to help across the other line with Caucasians and others as it turns around the myths and distorted truths in messages that have been going out over the years that said, if you're black, you're inferior and you always have been—you're nobody, you're nothing, you're just what we've made you, and what we've given you. Many whites really believe that because they've been taught that way— that they are better and that we are less, that we were cursed, and so by the curse we are supposed to always be servants, no good, slaves, the whole bit. I think my book will help to educate and turn things around.

Second, I believe it will cause many to look at this Christian religion and say, "Well, wait a minute, I have been against the Christian religion because I thought it was a European religion, started by Europeans. They brought the slaves over here and brainwashed them in this religion." It's no more than about two hundred years old as far as this country goes, a few more hundred years old as far as Great Britain goes, and so on. Now, because of the study of this, readers can actually see that Christianity goes way back to antiquity, to the very beginning. They can see that the first nation mentioned in the Bible is Ethiopia, in Genesis, chapter two. The second nation mentioned in Genesis, chapter two, is Assyria. The third nation, Egypt. Then Babylonia and right on down the line. Once one discovers who these people were, one will have say, "Ah-ha, so all that we have today, all of our technological advancement in the sciences has came from a people who we thought, all of our years, were inferior, ignorant, no good,

couldn't learn, despicable." That's going to have to change. It's going to turn around the minds of young and old.

I believe they're going to start looking at and reading this Bible, the Qur'an, and other literature to bring about more understanding of the religions as well as understanding why we put such great stress and focus on Christianity. I believe this book is designed to do that. Sure, it's going to meet with a lot of resistance. We don't like change. Who's going to fight education, really learning the truth, but he who does not want to believe?

I get a question from many whites, "What about white people? Are they mentioned in the Bible?" I say, of course they are, you just don't find them in the Old Testament that much. In fact, a colleague, Dr. Cain Hope Felder, who teaches New Testament at Howard University and who wrote the book *Troubling Biblical Waters*, declares there are no white-skinned persons in the Old Testament scripture.[1] However, I definitely believe that the Gentiles are the descendants of Japheth who migrated to the north country—the Cimmaron, Asia Minor, up in that area. Subsequently, one doesn't read much about them until you come to the New Testament scriptures.

In the Old Testament, in II Kings, chapter five, we read where Elisha, the prophet of God, brought about a curse on Gehazi because he took money from Naaman and hid it for himself. Naaman's leprosy was cleansed by Elisha. Elisha brought about a curse on Gehazi and said, "From now on, the leprosy of Naaman shall cleave to you, and to your seed forever." There are several types of leprosy, but some types cause changes in the pigmentation of skin. In II Kings, chapter five, verse twenty-seven, that's where we see the first curse in the Bible that speaks of changing the pigmentation of the skin. Other than that, the only time we hear about whites is in the New Testament when the Bible talks about the Romans, the Greeks, the Turks, etcetera, who are Gentiles and descendants of Japheth. They are rising now, but remember all those thousands of years before. In writing *Biblical Ancestry Voyage*, what the Lord directed my mind to do is to read a passage of scripture. Then I would exegete that scripture. Exegete, meaning to explain, expose, and put it in a contextual setting, to share what it meant, what it was and what it is from the original language. That's what *Biblical Ancestry Voyage* sought to do. When people read what I have to say, what historians, geologists and other theologians have contributed, they will see that it is based on passages of scripture and that it tells the truth about what we read in the Bible.

I wrote *Biblical Ancestry Voyage* out of my background of biblical research and scholarship. I believe the holy book of God, the Bible, was written by holy men of God who were led, inspired, and directed by the holy God Himself, using their talents, the members of their bodies, their tongues, their minds, their instruments to write down the word of God without error. That's why I do believe the Bible is the unadulterated, inerrant word of God, from Genesis to Revelations.

The Qur'an—I respect it, I've read it, I know about it, I've studied about it. I've read the Apocryphal books that some wanted to bring in and make a part of the Bible. When I see what they are saying, I say, "Oh no, this would just be another novel, another book with all kinds of mistakes." This book, the Bible, does not contradict itself. I certainly hold firm to it.

Some of the later versions of the Bible began to extract any reference to Jesus being black. I think that is a distortion. So now, to really tell the truth one has to exegete from the original Hebrew and Greek languages, and, of course, the Aramaic language, in which the entire Book of Daniel in the Old Testament is written. Of course, Jesus spoke in the Aramaic tongue. So to exegete that, when one has to interpret and exegete that as it is. One must tell the truth. I personally believe whites do not want their constituents to really understand that Jesus was a black man.

Please understand, in my scholarship, in my background, in my Christianity, in my stance, I teach and believe that the Bible teaches Jesus was one hundred percent human, one hundred percent divine. I definitely believe Jesus was God, incarnate in human flesh. I believe to have seen Jesus was to see God, because God is a spirit. I definitely believe, even now, that Jesus is just as much alive today as He was before He died.

To tell the truth about the Bible, we're going to ave to take out the distortions and bring out the truth about what Jesus looked like, who he was, and who he descended from. Whites know it. They have great scholars. They know the truth. I believe that's the reason some are suggesting that the Book of Daniel be changed. Daniel, chapter nine, and John's prophecy in Revelations, chapter one, verse fifteen, talk about "woolly hair" as an anthropomorphic figure of God. God let Daniel see Him, in his dream, as having colored arms and feet and woolly hair. John, on the Isle of Patmos, saw the same vision. A vision is a sensory perception that comes from the divineness of God. He puts it in the mind and heart of his servants and causes them to see and write about it. Turn this around? I believe that would be taking from or adding to the divine word of God. The judgment of the Lord God is against that.

In closing, I want to pass on some words of encouragement, words of our Lord Jesus Christ. They are found in Paul's writing, in II Corinthians, chapter four. These words give me the strength when I pass through those valleys and times of depression, when I pass through seasons of drought where I feel downtrodden and put against. Listen to these words, then I would just like to elaborate. It says: "We are troubled on every side, yet not distressed; we are perplexed, but not in despair; persecuted, but not forsaken; cast down, but not destroyed; always bearing about in the body the dying of the Lord Jesus, that the life also of Jesus might be made manifest in our body. For we which live always are delivered unto death, even for Jesus's sake."

We know that our Lord Jesus Christ was put upon, spit upon, beaten, talked about, demeaned, and all of that. Ultimately, he was crucified on a cross. He, being our Savior and Life-Giver, has extended eternal life to us. Just as He went through all of those things, certainly we must go through our times of testing and trials and persecutions—the lack of a job, the lack of being accepted, of being put down and called all kinds of names, of having doors shut in our face—because of the pigmentation of our skin. Just as they did to our Savior.

I definitely believe there is a turnabout coming, for the Bible declares to us in prophecy, "The first shall be last and the last shall be first." Even though I say that, I understand that I'm talking from the standpoint of my knowledge of the Bible that blacks were first and once held in high esteem. We once ruled the earth.

I believe that we started descending with the death of Hannibal, a great black general. You and I, we studied about him in school, but no one ever told us he was a black man. They never told us he was black, and he did all these great things—leading those troops and elephants over the Alps and destroying the Romans. We never knew that. Eisenhower, MacArthur, they used some of the same tactics used by a black man by the name of Hannibal. That's when black supremacy started falling, at Hannibal's demise and ultimate death.

I believe there is a turnabout coming. As we see in the great diversity of a melting pot, especially in southern California, but I believe it's going to be worldwide. It is that way worldwide already. It's just that America has not felt it yet. I believe that, as a prophet in Psalms says, "Weeping may endure for a night, but joy cometh in the morning."

We want to keep our faith strong, our self-image and self-worth and self-esteem lifted high, knowing that what we are presently passing through will not always be this way. We are headed into another dimension and another direction that's not just in the sweet by-and-by. I believe it's right here on planet earth before this earth comes to a conclusion. My motto in life is, "What God guides, He provides." Amen.

⚡⚡⚡⚡⚡

1 Felder, Cain Hope, *Troubling Biblical Waters: Race, Class, and Family* (Maryknoll, NY: Orbis Books, 1989).

ASA G. HILLIARD, III

EDUCATIONAL PSYCHOLOGIST, EDUCATOR, AUTHOR, LECTURER

Everyone goes through some sort of educational system. The accuracy of the education is predicated by the type of curriculum to which one is exposed. Dr. Asa Hilliard, one of the innovators of an Afrikan-based education, has helped to create a movement that is changing the scope of education around the country. His ground-breaking work in the development of the African American Baseline Essays for the Portland (Oregon) Public Schools, has been a model for further development in this area, and a centerpiece in the development of Afrikan-centered curricula. Dr. Hilliard also conducts educational tours of the Nile Valley.

I was born in Galveston, Texas. My family was centered in Bay City, Texas. They originally came from Georgia. After slavery, my grandfather was freed. He changed his name, invented a new name for himself and moved to Texas. So they settled in an area near Oakland, Texas, called Hackbury. From there my grandfather moved to Bay City. My dad grew up there, and I was born in Galveston. I'm mainly Texan, I guess you'd say.

As far as specific work, my dad was a high school principal and his father was a high school principal. A lot of the family were teachers. I was pulled in the direction of education, but I decided early on that the last thing I wanted to be was a teacher. That changed after I got to college and found that I really couldn't deny that yearning that I had and I decided to go into teaching. But in another sense, though at a deeper level, not so much counting the specific job, I always leaned in the direction of what my father used to call "race things" and "the freedom struggle," because that's part of what he did in his own way. So did his uncles and brothers. I caught the fever fairly early.

We talked a lot about freedom and liberation in our family, but not a lot about Afrika. I remember as far back as I can remember, I think it would have been in junior high school, I was basically offended by the way I saw Afrika portrayed in film. Whenever I would read about Afrika, I knew there was something that was absolutely wrong about that. I didn't know where I could go to get it corrected.

After we moved to Denver, I remember that we had a small group of children and one teacher who identified very closely with Afrika. In fact, we formed an Afrikan dance troupe. I remember the pride I felt. It was like striking a blow to assert in the teeth of all the negative things that were being said about Afrika.

We cared and we identified with Afrika. We used to perform for something called the Show Wagon. One of my prized pictures right now is the picture of that dance troupe. That goes way back to the forties now.

Much of the activity in support of my interest was, I guess, unguided until I began to seek things out around the high school level and finally at the college level. That's when I was able to do more independent reading, come into contact with many Afrikan students, and begin to learn about people who knew about Afrika. From that point on, I was kind of on a greased slide.

After much thought and investigation, I decided, from early on, to concentrate an enormous amount of time on curricula. What I found: the primary problem in the curriculum in the schools is either neglect, distortion, or falsehood with respect to the experience of people of Afrikan descent. Not just people of Afrikan descent but people of color across the board. It's acute with people of Afrikan descent. There are things that help to explain who we are that are never presented in the curriculum. As a result, when we do appear, we appear as fragments. We appear out of context. We appear inaccurately. The strongest statement I can make is that we have a truth problem or a validity problem in terms of curriculum.

The problem is sometimes defined by other people as, let's say, a self-esteem problem. Of course, we want to support children's self-esteem, but we want to do it in a way that takes us off the topic. To talk about self-esteem as the only reason for looking at the curriculum makes us ignore the fact that we've had this extreme neglect and, in some cases, acute dishonesty in the curriculum for almost four hundred years, especially for the last two hundred years. In fact, it was so acute, Leon Lidwack, who was president of the Organization of American Historians, once told a national meeting of his colleagues that, "No group of people, no group of scholars were more deeply implicated in the miseducation of Americans and Afrikan Americans than were historians." He said that without a challenge.

This is a serious, serious problem of validity. That's what we're dealing with. It's not a problem, of course, if we have valid curriculum. I would expect that it would contribute to self-esteem, mainly because the negative images that are transmitted about Afrikan people contribute to a lowering of self-esteem. When we provide the truthful images, then it will be clear to our children exactly who they are.

Another example of a misinterpretation of the curriculum goal is the argument that the reason for curriculum change, or the reason that we argue for curriculum change, is that it will raise academic achievement. That's a typically confused kind of thinking, because you are talking about two separate topics, really. The topic of whether the curriculum is telling the truth or not is one thing. You want the truth told whether academic achievement goes up or down. The curriculum problem cannot be responded to by changing the subject on how to get children's academic achievement up.

Now, if you want to get academic achievement up, we know how to do that too. We also want that. In fact, you know, most people I associate with expect the highest academic achievement of Afrikan American students and all students. There's no reason for any child to fail. But you don't expect taking a class in American history to raise the kids' academic achievement. You teach that for another reason. You shouldn't expect a class in Afrikan history to raise academic achievement for black students all by itself. If you want achievement raised, there are certain things a good teacher knows that will cause that to happen.

This is really a topic that deserves an awful lot of time because I think we are hoodwinked in this society into believing that teaching our children is a problem. If we don't believe it, other people believe it. They believe if you see children who are Afrikan, who are poor, you have an automatic problem on the part of the child, as far as learning is concerned. That's totally untrue.

A couple of things could be discussed. One, we have a long record prior to the time of colonization and slavery of being very successful in educating our children. We also have a long record in this country, since colonization and slavery, of building the institutions that give the best examples of teaching. Institutions like Morehouse College, and an institution here in Los Angeles, the Marcus Garvey School. These are institutions that are built by Afrikan people to teach Afrikan children.

I recently wrote about Dr. Abdulalim Abdullah Shabazz at Clark Atlanta University. I talk about him every time I get a chance, because here is a man who is directly or indirectly responsible for training over half the black Ph.D.'s in mathematics in America. His contribution was made during a six-year period in a master's degree program he led when he was chairman of the math department at Clark Atlanta. He had a lot of students who were, in many cases, deficient in math and deficient in English. He had a one-item admissions test that asked the question, "Do you want to learn math?" If they answered that question, "Yes," then they were admitted to the master's degree program in mathematics. The result was that he trained over one hundred master's degree recipients who went on to become the group that earned their doctorates in mathematics, and taught others who earned doctorates.

That doesn't sound as if we have a problem teaching, it sounds as if other people have a problem teaching. The rest of the country has a problem, but he didn't have the problem. I can show you many pockets of excellence rooted in the Afrikan community here in the United States, even under segregation, slavery, and stuff like that.

I spoke about four years ago to the Council of Chief State School Officers, in Whitefish Montana. I made a speech about what they were calling "at-risk children," a term I really don't like at all, but for the purposes of the discussion, we'll use it. I wrote an article saying the risk was in the system, not in the child. What we needed to do was to get the chiefs behind the development of videotapes about successful schools that were educating Afrikan children and others. They bought it. They created a project through their agency, the Agency for Instructional Technology, and put close to one million dollars into this film project. We've just completed it. It's called "Every Child Can Succeed." We used in the film eight schools around the country that have children from low-income areas, high-performing children. There are actually six schools; two of them are transition schools that look as if they're going to be successful very quickly.

We had in that group two schools one hundred-percent Afrikan American. One was in Pittsburgh. That school, for the past almost twenty years, has been at the top or near the top in mathematics achievement in the city, in spite of the fact that all its children live in the lowest income area in the Hill District of Pittsburgh. Here you have these two black schools at the top of the academic achievement level in Pittsburgh, unnoticed by anybody until we created these films. Occasionally, somebody would do a little newspaper article on them.

We went to Dallas and got the Charles Rice School, which is an all-black school in the East Oakcliff neighborhood. The school was knocking the pants off everybody in the local Mathematics Olympiad. Its trophy cases are full of mathematics trophies. You walk in, and you think you're looking at a basketball trophy case, but it's almost all mathematics.

I have made it my business, in the last twenty-five to thirty years or so, to find places like this where educators do not puzzle about what to do with our children. We know that it is absolutely no mystery how to successfully teach children of Afrikan descent, or anybody else whose education is, as Ron Edmonds said, "of importance to us."[1] If a child's education isn't of importance to us, we find excuses not to teach them.

We found nine things that were common in high-achieving schools. I don't know if I can remember all nine of them right now, but they're noted in the videotape. After we made the video, we re-visited those eight schools again to see what they were doing alike. Remember, none of these schools knew about the other. One's up in Canada, a couple are in Seattle, the others are in Maine, Texas,

Asa G. Hilliard, III

California, and Pennsylvania. They had no knowledge of each other before, yet, they were all doing similar things.

One of the things we found was that there was a no-nonsense principal in every school who set the tone in the building and set the objectives for the school. Instructional leadership means the principal kept the faculty focused on the instructional program of the school. That's what they spent a lot of their time talking about at faculty meetings. That's what the reward system was focused on, and so forth. So in good schools, the conversation is about the instructional program. By the same token, in poor schools, you don't have much conversation about the instructional program. There's more conversation about the children, their families, their diet, about dope in the neighborhood. They'll talk about anything except the instructional program.

A second thing we saw was an emphasis on staff development. They had a very particular kind of staff development. When you say that, people say, "Well, I've heard that before." But when you go into these high-performing schools, what you find is that most of the teacher training is done in the school building where the teachers are. That faculty gets together. They make the decision on what they need to improve on. They set up the staff development process themselves in the school. This is staff development, or teacher training, done at the school. Many times they are in the classroom with the children, while one teacher demonstrates and another observes, imitating then criticizing each other. That kind of staff development, or you might call it problem-solving staff development, that's something else they did.

They also look at reading scores. They say, "Look, we're not teaching what we know our kids can achieve. What is it that's holding us back?" They do trial and error until they figure out a way to get those scores up where they belong. There's a special character to the staff development that's different from just sending two teachers from the building off to a conference or to a meeting of fifty people downtown somewhere to listen to some lecture on a topic that's irrelevant to the problem of the school.

We found that parent involvement is very high in the schools that were, what I call, excellent schools or, as I prefer to call them, "power schools." Parent involvement is very high. Parent involvement usually comes after the school has begun to improve. In other words, parents become involved because they are attracted to the positive things that are going on in the school, rather than parents becoming involved in order to get the school going. It's hard to get parents to believe you're serious unless they see some results, and that's what we saw in these schools.

The goals of these schools are set very high. Teachers don't look at the children to see how they're dressed or whether their parents are married or whether the income is high before they set their goals. They set the goals for those children just like they're teaching millionaires' children. They set them high. For example, one program offers college-level algebra problems to children in the kindergarten through sixth grades. That's an example of what I'm talking about. It goes on and on.

There's also a book available to accompany the video. It has fifty chapters, fifty very carefully selected articles. One is the best I've ever read, by Dr. Barbara Sizemore, who was superintendent of schools in Washington, D.C., and is presently dean of the School of Education at DePaul University in Chicago. She has done the best research on high-performing schools of anybody I know. It's the kind of chapter a principal or teachers could pick up—it's almost like a recipe of things that are clear about these power schools. For people who are looking for practical ideas, it is probably the best single article I know on that topic. There's been no time in my professional career where I haven't been concerned about the curriculum. From the time I was in school myself, I was concerned about the fact that there were things missing from the curriculum. Like Dr. John Henrik Clarke, I knew there were some missing pages in world history, but it was a long time before I could actually pursue my interest in that area.

I really got actively involved in curriculum change after I came back from Afrika. I taught for a couple years, went back, got my advanced degree, and taught at San Francisco State for a year. In 1963, I went to Afrika to live for six years. I had lots of time to read many of the things I had wanted to read all along and a few things I wanted to re-read. When I came back, I had discovered some of those "missing pages." I began to try to bring them into my own teaching first of all. Through sharing and networking, I tried to figure out strategies for disseminating more of this information. My first opportunity to do something in a major way came when I got involved in a school district up in Portland, Oregon, which put major resources into curriculum research and allowed us to bring in dozens of people who had studied the areas I was interested in very carefully. That was really, I guess, the place that gave us the greatest leverage, because we were actually able to produce documents that some people now know as the *Portland Baseline Essays*. Some people erroneously refer to it as the "Portland Curriculum." It's not a curriculum. Actually, it's just a book with six chapters. Each chapter, on one of the academic areas we thought important, was put together by several specialists. Each chapter tries to answer a question, like, "What have Afrikan people done in mathematics?" "What have Afrikan people done in art?"—from the beginning of time up to the 1990s.

Once those materials were produced, they became a type of catalyst and an example to other school districts and educators. Many things happened that

were not exactly the same but were stimulated by the Portland example in other school districts. We did a lot of things like that in several other school districts.

I think the next major event was a workshop we did in Atlanta on the infusion of Afrikan and Afrikan American content into the school curriculum. A book came out of that after the first annual meeting. We've had three now, and we'll have others. What we did was bring together all of these isolated educators who had been working, in many cases, on the same problems. We had incredible people there like Théophile Obenga, Cheikh Anta Diop's partner. We had Sheila Walker, an anthropologist from the University of California at Berkeley. We had Robert Ferris Thompson out of Yale University. We had Dr. John Henrik Clarke and many others who came to that conference. Most people who went said it was a high point of their professional careers because it was serious business around the clock. There was no playing. Most of the organizers didn't get to see any of Atlanta because we felt that every presentation had to be of keynote quality. There are people I meet from all over the country even today who tell me that the activities they are now following through on in their school districts and at colleges and universities were stimulated out of those conferences they attended in Atlanta.

But there are so many different critics and so many different points of attack—it's hard to have a global response to them all. In the first place, there's nothing about what we do that says people have to stop teaching what they're teaching. They can go ahead and teach what they're teaching. I don't mind a Eurocentric curriculum. If it's Eurocentric and true, that's what I would expect to come out of any place where you had a lot of people who were of European descent—just as you would expect, if you have a lot of people of Afrikan descent, to have things that are shaped more in their direction.

For example, you go on any Black college campus in America—the character of the curriculum, even when they are not trying to do an Afrikan-centered curriculum—there's going to be quite a few of those faculty members who will bring up literature that's specifically aimed at Afrikan people. What I object to is the idea that I would be prevented from bringing my missing pages, so to speak. If there's a contest between the content of one center and the content of another center, that contest ought to be played out in an open arena. In other words, you shouldn't have people meeting in a smoke-filled room to decide what's right and what's wrong. I think you ought to put all the evidence before the students. That's in the tradition of what we call scholarship and democracy.

Most of the critics I know about, and I've seen a lot of the criticism, they are more propagandistic than they are scholarly. They characterize our curriculum efforts, but they don't critique it. When they do critique it, they do it in private. Let me give you an example of what I mean when I say people characterize. Most people have never seen the *Portland Baseline Essays*, but they use them, especially the science essay, as "whipping boys." They want to criticize the work because one of the two authors didn't have a doctorate, although I don't know what difference that makes, because there are a lot of writers who don't have doctorates. You shouldn't criticize the person, you should criticize the content. You have to say that what this person said was false; not discuss whether he got his degree from the University of Chicago or not.

I know the news media operates on sound bytes. I just saw the other day where some guy got about five words of something I was supposed to have said somewhere, and I can't even remember ever using the words. It was quoted in one of the major newspapers on the East Coast. What I see on television and in print is that writers and others have their stories already written, then they start looking for catchy phrases. They report on catchy phrases, which means we don't have an opportunity to give voice. It's not academic critique.

In one case, someone said that our science essay states that Afrikans were flying around in hang gliders off the pyramids or something. I went back to the essay, and that's not in the essay. What is in the essay is a quotation by some people from NASA and the museums in Cairo who reported that they had found a model among some Egyptian artifacts that they thought was a bird. They spotted on one of these so-called birds a dihedral fin and said, "That's weird, birds don't have dihedral fins." So they went through a process of analysis to determine what it was. This is all reported in the *Journal of Afrikan Civilizations*. They took it to NASA. They took it to all kinds of places. The upshot of the story is that when they enlarged the scale model and tried to throw it through the air, it flew like a glider. All the person who wrote the essay was doing was quoting that reported event. He was not saying people were flying around. He didn't go any further than that. It was distorted by those who wanted to characterize it as something else in a propagandistic fashion. It's hard to respond to propaganda.

That's one thing, but look at this. If we're going to take everything out of the curriculum that doesn't contribute to high academic achievement, then let's take out American history, okay? Why should we teach American history if it doesn't produce high academic achievement? You teach American history for other reasons. Therefore, you teach Afrikan history for the same reason you teach American history or world history. The record of human experience is valuable in and of itself as we attempt to understand ourselves as a people and project our future. Why should Afrikan people be the only ones on earth who have no history or no respect for their history in the school curriculum? To me, that's just bogus. I don't really have anything more to say about it.

I found many European Americans understand the necessity for history to the extent that they will go ahead and support some of our efforts. In fact, in my experience, European Americans have been some of the ones in some of these school districts who have been pushing our agenda.

I like the title of the book we did on curriculum, *The Infusion of African and African American Content in the School Curriculum.* That was a very carefully selected title. It's the same title we used for our curriculum conference. What it says is that there's a body of knowledge and information we need to master, and some of it needs to go into the school curriculum to modify the interpretation of human events that are now being interpreted without benefit of this information. You notice I did not call it an Afrikan-centered curriculum. I am strongly Afrikan-centered. The reason I didn't call it an Afrikan-centered curriculum was because, by definition, public schools serve all kinds of ethnic groups. Policy is under the control of all kinds of ethnic groups. More importantly, if you're going to teach an Afrikan-centered curriculum, which to me is nothing more than ethnic education that should be offered to Afrikan children, it has to come from people who are prepared to do it. See what I'm saying?

What I mean by "prepared" is if you're going to have somebody teach the history of Afrikan people in mathematics or the history of Afrikan people in history, for example, or history generally, you want someone who will show commitment to the community, who will sustain the research effort necessary to pick up the information. I really think there's only going to be a limited capability on the part of the public schools to fill positions with people who are prepared at that level. They're going to have to do a limited job of infusion. That means making sure blacks are not insulted in the curriculum, making sure that as accurately as possible, we are represented in the curriculum.

There's another level of knowledge that goes beyond infusion. I think that has to be the responsibility of the Afrikan community itself, primarily because that's where we address our special priorities. That cannot be done in the public schools.

Let's factor the black colleges into this discussion. My son graduated from Morehouse College. I've been around the horn of Afrika, but I've never worked at a black college, directly. I've been on campuses for years. I've just completed a study of twenty-five black colleges. I had to visit and look at their staff development programs and what they do. I have more information than I had before. I know some institutions I thought I knew better. I know some I've never seen before fairly well now.

It's hard for people in California to understand what a black college is, particularly a Morehouse. What you're talking about is a total socialization and education environment. If you go to UCLA—in the first place, it's big—they probably don't care about any student other than in a very routine way. Morehouse is about nurturance.

You've got people at Morehouse like Professor Emeritus Henry McBay, who has probably taught more Black physicians chemistry than any other person on earth. He is *the* premier chemistry teacher. He's an institution. His thing is taking students who don't know and making them know. What do you think it means when every Thursday two thousand young black men, all with a similar purpose, convene in an assembly and one day Robert Mugabe is there, the next week Carl Rowan, Jesse Jackson the next week, Ivan Van Sertima the next. Can you imagine the impact this has on those young men? Reverend Lawrence Carter of the Morehouse Chapel has this group of students he trains. I don't know what name he gives them, but they manage the programs of the Chapel. Every Sunday, they have these programs that are part spiritual, part academic. He organizes conferences that are just incredible. All this, and Morehouse is right across the street from Spelman, which is for sisters, where exactly the same kind of thing happens.

I just attended the Spelman-Morehouse Commencement Weekend. It's like no other experience on earth! Clark Atlanta University is right there, adjacent to both. Morris Brown College is right there. You have an incredible intellectual environment of black people packed tightly together—you can't reproduce that anywhere else on earth!

To me, if I had the choice personally to pick between teaching at UCLA or Morehouse, at the undergraduate level, there would be no contest, absolutely no contest—I would go to Morehouse. A person would have to just not know what was really being done at Morehouse, and not know how well they do the academic thing.

Everybody knows, too, that most black colleges don't have graduate schools. But you also ought to know that most of the black people who finish graduate school come out of black colleges. They have a higher persistence rate. But let's not stop there.

Somewhere in the mid- to late '60s, I became acquainted with people who enhanced my information about Afrika, especially classical Afrikan civilizations. I knew that at some point I had to do more work to share this information. I tried to figure out a way to do that, mainly through slide presentations and lectures and so forth. But it occurred to me that it would be much more powerful to be able to examine concretely whatever is left of that civilization where it is right now. The way to do that would be through a study tour. So my wife and I designed a study tour and tried to locate people who were really serious about study in Afrikan civilization. We're not interested in folk who wanted to collect ashtrays and float on the Nile and do all that. We have developed a very hard working tour. We get up early and go to bed late. We felt being on the site, visiting the museums and the monuments, by getting some sense of the space, geography, time perspective, and so forth would help to make more real what Afrika was like in the past.

Why is that important? To me, whole people have a sense of themselves in the time perspective and in the space perspective. That is to say, if as a people we think of ourselves as beginning with slavery, then we have chopped off ninety percent of the history of Afrikan people. It is very important to replace that history. Even starting with Kemet, or Egypt, as people call it, is to have ninety percent of our history chopped off because there was much, much more before that. But it's the place where our records begin, at least the best records of what Afrikan people have done when they were approaching their perfection as a society.

Those records are kept best in the northeast corner of the Afrikan continent. For that reason, we do what European people do. They claim Greece and Rome, which is certainly open to question, but at least they claim it. A person who lives in England and claims Greece as their ancestral culture is totally off-base. That person was a part of a land area that had not even developed at the time of Christ. Julius Caesar, who visited the British Isles, talked about them as if they were savages. Nevertheless, almost any one from England, when they are trying to tell their story, they don't begin it with the time of Christ. They begin it with the time of Homer or even the pre-Hellenic civilizations. They say that is really the best period of European development. Even when it is inaccurate to do so, they find it necessary to call on this antiquity. I think that same thing is true of people anywhere in the world, and it's certainly clear that the Europeans understand the meaning of antiquity, even if we do not.

The European went to war on our knowledge of ourselves. They cut it off at slavery and don't even give us a good picture of slavery or of the things that have happened since slavery. We find it necessary to try to piece those things back together again in order to get some sense of wholeness, in order to be able to explain how we got where we are and have a foundation for taking the next step.

Where you find this problem magnified, and where there is a huge level of influence, is in the entertainment world. Many of our people who are in that profession don't understand the field they are working in. It is very clear for Europeans. They understand what Hollywood does. They understand what Detroit does, what Motown does. They are very clear about it. For example, one of the reasons the world accepted Israel is because the Jews prepared the way for it through Hollywood. Through all of those years of Cecil B. deMille's spectacular films like "The Robe," "The Ten Commandments," "Ben Hur," and all that. Those images were created so perfectly most people believe in them as if they were the real history of the world. It's only a short step from that preparation to the political activity people take.

I remember Hollywood did a film on the Mafia, and the Italian community was up in arms over it. Why? Because they know it isn't just entertainment. The images people get affect what they believe to be true and affect how they act toward other people. There is no such thing as "neutral entertainment." One of the worst problems we have is when our people begin to believe they are merely artists and nothing more. Artists are, in every case, totally political, even if they don't do anything, because there is a political consequence of not doing anything. To take up space with nothing other than entertainment is to prevent someone else from taking that same space who might have moved the agenda of Afrikan people ahead.

I'll give you one more example. I saw the film "Shaka Zulu." I checked with a lot of actors who were involved in it. Somebody got paid to propagandize for the South Afrikan government. Some black people got paid because Harmony Gold, the company that did the film, is subsidized by the South Afrikan government. Someone ought to be educated enough to ask the question: What would South Afrika's interest be in projecting those kind of images about black people?

If you know the true story of Shaka Zulu and compare that story to the one told in the only film that we've seen about Shaka Zulu, then you can see that, at key points, the South African government succeeded in selling to the world a picture of Afrikan people that would undermine the confidence we in the rest of the world might have in those people. To sell a picture of Shaka Zulu as an Afrikan male who slaps his mother—that never appeared in any of the stories anyone else told other than the "official" South Afrikan story. So here is a Hollywood-type thing that will have long-range consequences. It will affect the image Afrikan Americans have of Afrika. It will affect the image Europeans all over the world will have of Afrika. Someone is responsible for that. It seems to me, given the condition of Afrikan people all over the world, that to have an opportunity to operate a camera, a microphone, and fail to use that opportunity to do what can be done for the benefit of one's people is nothing short of treason.

Here again, many people in various professions, many parents, don't know where to start. Any Afrikan American or any Afrikan anywhere ought to see as a primary obligation their identification with some study group. In other words, there ought to be a period of your life that you set aside to study those areas that public education will never touch. This is a growing phenomenon in the United States, at least. There's been, in the last ten years, just an incredible proliferation in the number of study groups, which means people who used to watch TV all the time or go to the baseball game or go fishing have found a way to take some of that time and invest it in the discovery of things about themselves. It takes time to do those kinds of things. I find that such group activity, when the group has the right agenda, is the primary vehicle to help people.

Sometimes it gets lonely. Men and women who are trying to do all these things and who don't necessarily have the information resources or the network resources can have that information provided to them by study groups. A study group, an activist group of some kind, an independent school, can serve as a catalyst for self-education, for socialization for the children, and so forth. It is a major self-help and self-improvement effort that I recommend to almost anybody who is getting ready to rear children.

Clearly, the parents are the children's first and primary teachers all the way, throughout life. No matter what anybody else says, the parents have the major role by what they do or don't do. To be prepared for that role, we should be obligated to invest in this training of ourselves. There are a lot of things parents need to know. If they belong to the right network, they will come into contact with many of these things.

For example, our parents ought to know that there are some special things about raising Afrikan children. In a study of children in Afrika, in Uganda actually, and also children of Afrikan ancestry in America, done twenty-five or thirty years ago, it was found that these children were what they call precocious. In other words, when they were given tests of normal development, both intellectual and physical, these children outscored other children everywhere in the world. They were just at the top of their form, even though these children had never seen anything like the test material. These children were so bright, the child development researchers went back to study them several years later. The first study was done by a lady named Marcele Geber, and many years later, almost twenty years later, Mary Ainsworth went back and reviewed some of the literature and did more studies. Studies were done this time in Pretoria, South Afrika, and in Senegal, so the continent was triangulated. They found that no matter where they got their Afrikan children, they were precocious, way ahead of the norm.

Then they began to do studies like that in the United States and found out that the same was true of Afrikan American children. Okay, now they get interested. What's causing this? You've got two choices: You could make an argument that there's a genetic explanation or a cultural explanation. Naturally, if the findings show that we're ahead, they go to the cultural explanation. They said it might have something to do with how black parents raise their children, and indeed it did. Cultural patterns led to accelerated development, which the Afrikans called normal development on the part of Afrikan children. Things like holding the baby close to the mother, with skin-to-skin contact, nursing the baby on mother's milk, talking to the baby, keeping the baby in the mother's presence, never giving the baby over to strangers—a whole host of things like that. What's interesting about this is that Europeans studied these child-rearing practices, and now they are beginning to copy them as they teach other people about child development.

It seems to me, if Europeans find what Afrikans do with their children that attractive, we Afrikan Americans ought to find it at least as attractive as they did, and probably even more so. There's a focus of attention black parents ought to have, not only on our history and culture as a group, but on information about child development that's specific to Afrikan American children.

Amos Wilson's book *The Developmental Psychology of the Black Child* is probably the best single book for black parents.[2] Janice Hale–Benson's book *Black Children: Their Roots, Culture, and Learning Style* is another.[3] These two books probably contain most of the culturally specific information about black child development that you can get in any kind of popular form. Other than that, you've got to go to the academic journals and begin to read the literature in another way. It seems to me that most of us have been reading Dr. Spock and Barry Brazelton and all these other people. We ought to know that there are some people who have spent a lot of time looking at what's good and special just for us.

Whether a child goes to a private school, or a public school, or even an Afrikan-centered school, it's absolutely essential that parents provide a rites of passage program for their children. Nathan Hare writes about them in his book, *Bringing the Black Boy to Manhood*.[4] There are also similar descriptions of programs for young girls. What I'm saying is you can go to school and learn your times tables, you can learn how to conjugate verbs, those are all things everybody all over the world wants to learn. But there are still some other things our children are supposed to know that they can only get through a long-range, systematic, sustained program of education. Rites of passage programs can be organized either in the school or outside the school, in tutorial Saturday schools, summer camp sessions, or elsewhere. It's very important that parents and communities organize these systems to deliver special Afrikan content to the child, so that our children grow up with the appropriate degree of consciousness and what I call a sense of reality.

It's amazing how many things Afrikan people have done that European people have studied and now copy for their own children. We haven't done the same thing. The rites of passage is one of those things we should do now.

I think one of the things we have to do first is find a way to be comfortable with the diversity we are going to find among children. That really doesn't have as much to do with the children as it does with the parents. One of those areas where you find misconceptions in families is the various speeds at which children learn. It's rare that any two children achieve at exactly the same rate in everything. I have four children, all different. They are all over the place in terms of what they are interested in, their academic achievement, their best subjects, and so forth.

On the other hand, if there is a child who has some impairment, or you suspect an impairment, it is absolutely essential that appropriate assessments be made, not the typical school assessments. School people are almost totally incapable of making an assessment, except in the most severe cases of retardation or learning disabilities. I'd say in ninety-eight percent of the cases, there probably is not even the hint of an impairment. Just because two children don't achieve at the same rate doesn't mean the one who is not achieving is impaired. A lot of things are tied in, like interest and motivation.

In most cases, what parents can do to help their children do better in school is to spend time with them. One thing we have stopped doing as Afrikan people is interacting with our children. Some people have called it dialoguing with the children. Most of us slip into a communication process with our kids that you just have to describe as a monologue. We don't ask them questions, try to hear what they think, or try to find out the reasons for their thoughts. What kids get from us most of the time are instructions: "Do this," "Don't do that," "Watch out for this," "Watch out for that." That's a monologue. What has to happen if you want to activate and release that child's intelligence is that you have to invite the child to engage in questioning, in critique. We parents have to organize our communication with our children, and we have to remember to do it. We know how to do it, but we slip into some awfully bad habits.

I'm not quite sure what the reasons are for those bad habits, but they are very prominent among our people. You know, we say things to our kids, like "Shut up," "Be quiet," "Sit down." That may give you control over the child's behavior, but doesn't give the child's mind anything. If a child's mind is going to grow, it's got to have something to chew on. It's got to turn over things, try them out, and not be directed from moment to moment. Nurturing that independent critical orientation is a part of what a parent has to do for a child.

Having an extended family can help in this process. In other words, our world view taught us that there was something like a blood relationship between people who live close together. That's the Afrikan way. That's the way it is in traditional Afrika today, just like it was thousands of years ago. It used to be that way with Afrikan people in the United States. Wherever we went, there was always some person who got called "cousin," "brother-in-law," "brother," "uncle," "sister,"—who had no blood relationship whatsoever, who, after just a very brief period of time, was treated in exactly the same way as a blood relative. Many of us know that for a fact.

We see these structures deteriorating in the Afrikan community today, partly because we are not socialized the way we used to be socialized. We tend, more and more, to be socialized as nuclear European-type families, as individuals. As that happens, it is hard for children to count on those extended family resources. Again, that's interesting. Europeans have studied the Afrikan family, and now they talk about the extended family and are trying very hard to create that same kind of condition for themselves. But we had the ultimate in family structure.

When I was small, my extended family worked the way others did. When my dad couldn't afford certain kinds of things, his brothers took care of us. I mean, even down to the clothes on my back. My father, he had all these children. The uncle who had money knew he didn't have to be asked to help him out. When I went to Houston, my Uncle Sid would have us over to his house for two or three days, or a week during our annual visit to my father's. He would always suit us up. We knew we were going to get complete outfits or clothes for the year. Sid had his own children, but he also knew his brother's children were needy at that point. He just took over.

I had another uncle, Uncle Robie. My father was a little bit prudish and skittish about things having to do with sex. He didn't feel as comfortable telling us the facts of life, so that brother did that. Uncle Robie said, "Well, it's time for us to sit down and talk. There's certain things you need to know." Over and over, most of us can go back into our experience and find those places of significant, meaningful assistance and the incorporation of people into the extended family. That is less true now.

Robert Hill's study, "Informal Adoption Among Black Families," was done about twenty years ago, but he found something very interesting.[5] He found that, back then, when Afrikan American women had babies out of wedlock, they almost never gave them up for adoption. European American women who had babies out of wedlock almost always gave the babies up for adoption. In the social science literature, you will be hard-pressed to find a statistic with a gap like that.

What was happening? Look at the family structure of Afrikan Americans and the family structures of European Americans. The European American family was rejecting their pregnant young daughters. They were ashamed. They would send them off to someplace like a home for unwed mothers. They'd put them out of the house and things like that.

In the Afrikan American family, after they screamed and yelled and talked about the girl like everything and got that off their chest, the next step was, "You bring that baby home." Nine times out of ten, the adoption process Hill was talking about was an informal adoption where the grandmother or some aunt took the child when they knew the mother couldn't handle or raise it. We never let children just be out there.

Here's something else that is really important about this: the poorest families among Afrikan families were the ones who were adopting the most children. In other words, if you look closely at our community, the ones who have kept the faith, in terms of culture, more often than not have been those among of us who are the poorest. As we get money, we begin to become more like Europeans. We adopt the values European people have. We give up the extended family. We are less likely, if we make fifty thousand dollars a year, to adopt a child. If you make one hundred thousand, you've got too many things to take care of, too many places to go, and so forth. My fear and concern, because we no longer make the investment in providing the right kind of socialization, is that our children are not going to grow with those values in mind.

It's harder to find extended families among black people today. We romanticize about it, but when you come down to it, it's not there the same way it was twenty years ago. If we're not careful, we'll look like everybody else in another ten to twenty years.

In a single-parent family, you have a different situation. In my opinion, it's best if you have the resources of two people. Economically, it's better. Ultimately, what really counts with the children is what the mother or father or mother and father are doing with and saying to the children.

I'm a product of a broken home, they say. I didn't know it was broken until I got to a sociology class. My father and mother divorced when I was about two or three years old. I was raised in one city with my mother during the academic year and with my father during the summer. We wished our parents had been together, but both of them were very mature, and neither one ever put the other down. They explained to us that whatever their problems were, and we never did understand what the problems were, they had found a way to work together to help us to grow.

When I look back, in a house with a single mother with all these children and with my mother struggling trying to raise us, at no point did I ever feel we were slighted in any way because of what my mother was saying and doing. When I was with my father, it was the same way. It isn't the split, per se, that makes single parenting hard, it's the fact that the income is split and more stress is placed on the one parent. The mother has to spend more time working, less time communicating. She's more likely to become frustrated and less patient with the children. That's where the problem comes. It's not the split.

Naturally, I think it's best if both parents are around. It's always better to have two people than one. Just like I think it's better if the grandmother is there. It's better to have three people than two. It's better to have the uncle around, and so forth.

Before my brother died, we were just as happy as we could be in San Francisco. There were just times when my children needed to see my brother. He was as great an uncle as anybody could possibly be. The children still talk about him. They remember Uncle Tom. He was the person who was always there. I remember one New Year's Eve when he came to the house and saw Pat and me going out. The children were going to be there, and he had his girlfriend with him. He came after we left, picked up the children and took them out because he didn't want them to be in the house by themselves on New Year's Eve. He spoiled his date just to make sure those children were taken care of. That's the kind of thing I'm talking about. It takes that kind of networking, if you can get it. If you can't, it doesn't mean the mother is a failure. It doesn't mean the children aren't going to grow up right. It means the mother has to keep her wits about her, to say, "Now that I'm in the situation, many of the problems that are going to come about are economic. I have to resist the temptation to become frustrated and make sure I send clear messages to my children."

My mother laid part of the responsibility for parenting on me. I was the oldest child, so I grew up with the sense I had to make sure everything was alright for those who came after me. In effect, I raised my younger brothers and sisters. That was a way my mother handled the situation.

The things that worked for us in the past would work for us now if we thought about them very seriously. The things that worked for us in the past were around in many communities. Afrikan families belonged to the church. In Denver, we had the YMCA; that was a big family thing. It doesn't really matter what it is, there needs to be things families belong to. If you don't belong to any of those things, you can still create it.

When our children were young in Colorado, we were broke. We didn't belong to a number of organizations because we couldn't pay the dues. So what we decided to do was to have a picnic at our house every holiday. Everybody knew they could count on it. I mean, no matter what holiday—Labor Day, Christmas, any holiday, when people normally did big things—we'd have a big pot- luck picnic at 3143 Clayton Street. We had a little bitty house and this great, big, giant yard. We could have two or three hundred people out back, and we frequently did. The only rule was that you had to bring food for your family, which you then shared with everybody else. The other rule was you had to bring your children. You couldn't leave them with a baby sitter. In other words, we deliberately designed it to provide a place where families could get together, and the children could get to know each other. This would all take place where we had oversight over what was happening with the children.

We just had a whole series of activities. There'd be volleyball out in the alley. There'd be bid whist in the living room, two or three bid whist games going. Somebody would be dancing out on the patio, somebody else sitting over in the corner talking, playing checkers, or whatever. Come and go when you want. Stay all night if you want.

This went on for a number of years. It was our attempt to invent another way of replacing some of the socialization activities that had gone by the wayside. It didn't cost us any money. I'm not trying to pass it off as a panacea, I'm just saying it takes something systematic. It takes something that has been calculated to fill in the gaps we are going to find as we live in an increasingly anti-family society.

One of the side effects children see and experience at this kind of gathering, because they do act up, is discipline. Contrary to what they may say or anybody may believe, kids want to know what's expected of them. They want to be held accountable. With all the adults around, discipline was acted out in various ways.

The worst thing for a child is disorder. They don't like living in situations where they don't know what to expect. They want to know what their parents' values are, even if they don't always follow those values. They want to know they are going to be handled consistently, that the parent isn't going to be erratic when they do something wrong.

The line should not be drawn between the question of whether to discipline or not to discipline. Discipline should always be there. The line should be between torture and discipline. Some parents do not disciple their children. Just because they pick up a bottle and throw it at them, that's not discipline. The child may not even understand the frustration that caused the action, or if cruel and unusual punishment is being meted out.

I happen to be one parent who still believes in spanking. I'm probably not like many of the liberal educators I share many ideas with, but when mine came along, I gave them a little warm-up on the rear end when they misbehaved. I guess that would be called child abuse right now, but my mother abused me that way, and I didn't know it was child abuse.

I mean, I really only had to spank my kids once or twice, because the thought that they get a spanking was enough to get their attention. That's all it's really about anyway, getting the intellectual attention of the child. Once you get that attention, you can communicate in ways so that they internalize the values you really want them to internalize. I would draw a distinction between what I see many parents do, which is just true torture. I see Afrikan parents doing something now they've never done before. People who are in social welfare services tell me about Afrikan children showing up with cigarette burns on them, black eyes and things like that. That was never a part of Afrikan families. Child abuse was so rare. That kind of person would be brought up on charges, but we see more and more of it now.

That's where I draw the line, but there was never a day where my mother didn't hold the line on discipline. I didn't have any holidays, or breaks, when I could say, "Okay, I've been good for five days, so for the weekend I can do what I want." No, no, no. That discipline was consistent. My mother still lives, and I'm very happy she's here. She still has the same value system. Even though I'm a grown man, if I'm going to do something that is outside her range of acceptance, I'm certainly going to respect her enough that she will not know anything about it.

All of this is important in preventing deviant behavior or one of the biggest negative social problems we have, which is gang behavior. The one thing that will produce gang behavior, as I understand it, is the severe stress and threat to their safety people perceive out there, the need to be protected. If you are out there by yourself, you could be hurt. That's one thing, but it is almost secondary to the main reason I believe gangs exist. I believe gangs exist because our community has abandoned our children in the socialization process.

Ask the young men who are in the gangs how many of them were involved in a systematic, sustained program of socialization under adult supervision over a period of time. Were they in whatever boys clubs we run? Were they a part of churches or community agencies where adults were constantly trying to help them take a look at the things they are supposed to do? My guess is, in most cases, you'll find the single ingredient that was missing was us. We abandoned them. When I say "we"—I think we really have to be up front about this—I'm talking as much about Afrikan American male adults as anybody else. Women do a little better than men.

Too few of the men budget time away from their work and entertainment to devote toward meeting their obligation, not just to their own children, but to the thousands of young boys who are growing up raising themselves. If these young boys raise themselves, how can you blame them for what they become? There is somebody out there on the street who will do for them what we fail to do for them. I really believe, in large part, that's part of the reason so many of them drift away. I mean, you will always have gangs anyway, but I think we could rescue many of our young boys if we did what we were supposed to do as men. We are not doing it right now.

One thing we can do immediately is become more aware of what our children are watching on television. It can have a terrible effect on them. They begin to act as if things that are on TV are more real than things in the real world. They develop a pattern of paying attention that doesn't fit with what is required in school. For example, on TV, you can turn on a program and go from foreplay to climax in a half hour, everything. The story gets a beginning, a middle, and an end, and it's finished in a half-hour. If you have a two-hour program, they just have four of those kind of episodes to make up the two hours. TV works in half-hour time blocks; life doesn't work in half-hour time blocks. If you are going to read a book, you might have to sit for three hours to get through a good chunk of it, to make you feel like you've done some work. So it changes the structure of your attention pattern.

That's one of the things TV does that affects learning. Then there's the kind of excitement TV generates. A kid goes back to a math textbook and says, "Well, I'm not getting all this, you know, but murder and violence and everything keep my adrenaline flowing. I'm not going to give math the kind of attention I'll give to TV." So it's extremely bad.

Well, why are the children doing this? I've seen some numbers and the numbers tell me not only are the children watching TV, but their parents are watching TV. Parents watch more TV than children. In many cases, it's because the parents are watching it that the children are watching it. It goes like this: something like 22,000 hours of television will be watched by white children during the school years. That's the average. There are 11,000 hours of public school from first grade to twelfth grade. When you compare white children to black children, you see that black children watch more TV than and get more messages from what they watch than white kids do. It has more of an effect on black kids. That's what the research shows. Not only are black children watching more TV than white children, but black parents watch more TV than their children are watching. Clearly, as a group, we've invested too much time and attention in a medium we don't even control. We are just spectators. We don't create the programs. They weren't really created with us in mind.

But there we are, like puppets, like robots being manipulated and sold stuff we don't even need. And they know the programs we watch. Those are the programs with all the beer commercials, the cigarette commercials, and everything like that. They know they can sell to our community, that their advertising has a more devastating effect on us.

Television doesn't have to be that way. There are also some fantastic things on TV. Some of your educational programs and entertainment programs, selectively used, can be valuable. There is nothing wrong with television when used properly. We have television in my house, and we try to use it appropriately. We don't always make it work exactly the way it's supposed to work every time, but I don't think parents ought to avoid TV. I think they have to be selective and support good programming.

See, if almost all of us learn by watching models, what models are available to us? It turns out that, for the Afrikan child, the most prevalent model is whatever's on TV. Now what gets sent to him? There's a guy named Rambo. The child gets to model after him. There's Superman, brought back now, which was invented during the Nazi era, by the way. We had Superman over here, and Adolf Hitler had Superman too, and they usually had blond hair, blue eyes, and so forth. Our children get J. J. thrown at them, that's supposed to represent you. What is J. J. doing, really, that's important? We get "The Jeffersons." If you grow up and become somewhat enhanced, in terms of money and class, then you become totally ridiculous, a clown. That's what the message of "The Jeffersons" is. Compare "The Jeffersons" to "Dynasty," for example. There is no comparison.

So this child is sitting down in front of the TV screen, trying to figure out what image to imitate? If they happen to see somebody who is worth imitating, they may only see that person for ten or fifteen minutes a week. They don't really get a sense of what that person does. The most information our children get, they get from television. We already know what the quality of those models are. Our children are really being harmed.

But parents can bring in some alternatives by doing some work themselves. Their reading can enlighten them to create some other models their children will not get in school. Let me suggest some things. Of course, if a parent can only get time to read one book, they ought to read *The Destruction of Black Civilization* by Chancellor Williams.[6] That book is important because it gives us a comprehensive story of our people from approximately 4,000 years before Christ, up to the present. That's effectively the recorded time of the human family. It's extremely important.

There are other books that go into experiences that have happened in the West. I think parents ought to read *They Came Before Columbus* by Ivan Van

Sertima, just so our children can go to school knowing we didn't come here first with Columbus. We were here long before Columbus, and even long before Christ. We were very much present in the New World, and we had an effect on things around here. It wasn't just we were here and dropped an arrow, a hat, or something like that. We actually affected the culture of this continent before the time of Christ. I think our children ought to be made aware of that as they arm themselves to go to school, in cultural terms.

There's another little book no one really seems to know much about it, because it tells such a complete story about a group of people called Maroons. I think the Maroons should serve as models for black people today. They were Afrikan slaves who got away during slavery and who went down to Florida to hang out with the Indians. For almost a hundred years they had a little nation going down there in Florida, before they went out into the Midwest and finally down into Mexico. The name of a book about them is *The Exiles of Florida* by Joshua Giddings.[7] Our children go through twelve years of school and don't even know what a Maroon is, let alone read a story that reads like a novel about them, and that's what this book is.

One of the very easy-reading books parents should also get is Joel A. Rogers's *World's Great Men of Color*.[8] In it, he takes a lot of individuals who have had very exciting lives but who are never portrayed in school, men and women, and brings them to life. That's very important. The last thing I recommend would be the *Journal of Afrikan Civilizations*.[9] If parents can get every volume, then they'll have an incredible resource. They have some of the work of the best scholars from all over the world and the most recent information about the Afrikan and Afrikan American experience.

That's more a cultural list. Let me suggest some educational materials. The first one, and clearly a superior book, is the one written in 1933, by Carter Woodson: *The Miseducation of the Negro*.[10] I really think it's important for parents to be able to step outside of where we stand right now and view what's happening to us as a people. Carter Woodson, who founded Black History Week—Black History Month now—clearly states what our problem was, and it is in that book.

Aside from that, there is a book called *Education for Critical Consciousness* by Paulo Freire, who is a Brazilian writer.[11] The reason I mention it is because, when I say something about helping children to think critically, that's what we want our children to do. This book offers a model of how we can go about getting that done. Freire was trying to teach adults how to read, but the way he went about doing that is how we ought to go about educating our children.

Any parent who is getting ready to have a baby ought to read the book *Magical Child* by Joseph Pearce.[12] It has a section on Afrikan child-rearing that should be recommended to the world. We might as well look at it and see what they found out about our babies. It tells parents how to act before the baby is born, that they can do things to hurt their baby before the baby is born by the intake of drugs, diet, patterns of stress, and things like that. It talks about what needs to happen in the first few years of life.

Let me not forget a book I had the good fortune to be a part of: *The Teachings of Ptah Hotep—The Oldest Book in the World*, along with co-author Larry Obadele Williams and Nia Damali. Many of us who study Afrika get into it to refute European lies about Afrika, that Afrikans were swinging by their tails from trees and such. We began to study Afrika to show that's not true, and so we go back to the beginning of time and get real happy when we find out Afrikans were doing important things like building pyramids, at least a couple thousand years before Europeans even got organized as nations.

But, many of us don't do the next thing, which is to forget Europeans and ask the question: What did Afrikan people think? When you ask that question, no matter when you ask it, you're off on some of the most exciting kinds of excursions you can go on.

For example, if you ask that question about music, the answers are endless. If you ask that question about religion, you get some real interesting answers. You could find the oldest teacher in the world, that's who this person, Ptah Hotep, is. He lived around 2300 B.C. What would he be teaching? This guy is teaching the son of the pharaoh, which is another way of teaching the public. He has thirty-seven things he tells this young pharaoh to be. You study these things to try to understand what the ancient Egyptians were thinking. Then you get this incredible feeling of joy, knowing that at one point Afrikan people had a deeply spiritual and positive way of looking at the world that is fulfilling right now. I can read Ptah Hotep and want to teach my children the things he taught the young pharaoh. They are good lessons for living now.

Why not read Afrikan people in their own words and let them speak for themselves? That's why we got off into this book. I wish I could do "The Eloquent Peasant."[13] This man, who was so bright and gifted, was arguing about justice to the Egyptian magistrate. In the course of arguing about justice, he gives a theory of justice that's as good as anything you'll see at any law school anywhere. If people could read and hear the ancient Afrikans talking for themselves, it would be uplifting. It would allow us to identify with Afrika in a much deeper way than we've been able to do before.

There was an old Bible verse that my mother emphasized when I was growing up. I still live by it and think of it all the time. It's one of the few verses I can remember completely: II Timothy 2:15. It says, "Study to show yourself approved unto God, not unto man, a workman that need not be ashamed, rightly dividing the word of truth." We need to have a massive mobilization of Afrikan people around the world. We need to see what the future looks like for us in the next thirty to forty years. We need to take a long view. In fact, we need to think about the next two hundred years. Where do we want Afrikan people to be twenty years from now? If you get an answer to that question that's anywhere near correct, it will tell you what you have to do now to get ready for that. I'm concerned that we are not now doing what we need to do to get ready for the world I think we would like to have if we thought about it. I just really hope we begin to mobilize our thoughts and ultimately our resources toward creating a new future for Afrikan people, that we revise and revitalize the continent so we will be safe wherever we live in the world.

❧❧❧❧❧

[1] Ronald Edmonds (1935–1983) was an Afrikan American teacher and Harvard-trained educational researcher whose concept of "Effective Schools" has been heralded by educators as a culturally effective and relevant means of reforming education for Afrikan American and other children of color placed at risk of failure.

[2] Wilson, Amos N., *The Developmental Psychology of the Black Child* (New York: Africana Research Publications, 1978).

[3] Hale–Benson, Janice, *Black Children: Their Roots, Culture, and Learning Style* (Provo, UT: Brigham Young University Press, 1982).

[4] Hare, Nathan, & Hare, Julia, *Bringing the Black Boy to Manhood* (San Francisco: Black Think Tank, 1985).

[5] Hill, Robert, "Informal Adoption Among Black Families" (New York: National Urban League, 1977).

[6] Williams, Chancellor, *The Destruction of Black Civilization: Great Issues of a Race, 4500 B.C. to 2000 A.D.* (Chicago, IL: Third World Press, 1987).

[7] Giddings, Joshua, *The Exiles of Florida* (New York: Arno Press, 1969).

[8] Rogers, Joel A., *World's Great Men of Color* (New York: Macmillan, 1972).

[9] See *Journal of African Civilizations*, in this text under Annotated Bibliographies, Ivan Van Sertima.

[10] Woodson, Carter G., *The Miseducation of the Negro* (Trenton, NJ: Africa World Press, 1990).

[11] Freire, Paulo, *Education for Critical Consciousness* (New York: Continuum, 1993).

[12] Pearce, Joseph C., *Magical Child: Rediscovering Nature's Plan for our Children* (New York: Dutton, 1977).

[13] Lichtheim, Miriam (Ed.), "The Eloquent Peasant," in *Ancient Egyptian Literature: A Book of Readings* (Berkley: University of California Press), Vol. I, p. 169.

ROBERT A. HILL

HISTORIAN, EDUCATOR, AUTHOR, EDITOR

Professor Robert A. Hill, Jamaican Afrikan historian, is a world-renowned
expert on Marcus Garvey and his movement. He is also editor of the
Marcus Garvey Papers. He has also provided one of the most scholarly
examinations of the history and culture of Rastafarianism. In that latter
work, the veneer of romanticism is removed and the struggle of Rastafari
people, their religion, and the evolution of their world music is revealed.

I came across a document dated June 1865, written by an anonymous
unknown Jamaican man. It was a poster found in the seaport town of Lucea,
which is in the northwest part of the island, the town just before you get to
Negrill. Lucea was a very important port for the shipment of bananas out of
Jamaica late in the nineteenth century. It's a beautiful seaport town. This man
apparently nailed up his poster on the wharf gate of Lucea. Its title declared,
"Nearly a Year Since I Saw the Vision." It goes on to note that, in his vision,
black people come from America with a special teaching for Jamaicans. That
Jamaicans must heed the teaching and give up the ways of what today we would
call Babylon. Then he states that this communication came directly from the
vision.

My feeling is the Rastafari experience begins with a series of visionary
experiences that take place in the 1860s, in Jamaica, indicating some kind of
coming together for a social base or a social movement to carry and embody this
vision. The vision may go back even earlier than the 1860s, but that poster marks
the first time we see a document explicitly referring to Jamaicans as Afrikan people and one that says black people will be coming from America with a message
Jamaicans must heed, that they must listen to the voice of the black American.
It's an exciting prospect because it tells us something we did not know before,
the degree to which there was indeed a pan-Afrikan perspective among black
people in Jamaica in the mid-point of the nineteenth century. Today, we think of
it as a twentieth-century phenomenon.

In 1917, Robert Athlyi Rogers from the island of Anguilla, in the Leeward
Islands, had a similar vision. He said an angel came to him telling him to preach
the doctrine of Afrikanity. Robert Athlyi Rogers was also later the author of a
book called *The Holy Piby*, which I will talk about later.

A series, therefore, of successive visionary experiences in different parts of
the black world all centered around a pan-Afrikan unity theme, the identity of

tion, waiting for a social movement to embody them and carry them forward into social and political struggle.

Two years after his Imperial Majesty Haile Selassie I was crowned Emperor of Ethiopia, they developed, in St. Thomas, Jamaica, a militant land-occupation movement that also preached the doctrine that black people should pay no taxes. This movement of land and liberty connected with the doctrine of Ethiopian spiritual sovereignty in 1932. They are what precipitated what we today call Rastafarianism.

Before it took root in Jamaica, the preliminary teachings had been circulating in South Afrika; in Newark, New Jersey; in Detroit; in Colon, Panama; in Costa Rica; in many places of the black world. Different black communities were making specific and important contributions to the idea of the coming of Ethiopia's sovereignty in the spiritual sense.

After the emergence of Rastafari, the movement moved out from Jamaica to spread now throughout the black world to Afrika, Europe, Latin America, North America, the Caribbean. Wherever you look, you will encounter the presence of the Rastafari today. My work is primarily concerned with the development of the Rastafari movement, its antecedents and how they took root in Jamaica. Right now, I'm concentrating on the period from 1865 to about 1984–85 and on the evolution, development, and origins of the movement in Jamaica.

In theory, the spiritual and the philosophical ground was prepared for this movement in many parts of the black world. Why should it have emerged specifically in Jamaica and not Panama, or Florida, or South Afrika? My feeling is, without the social movement from below to give embodiment to these visionary ideas, it would just simply have continued to circulate. It needed some concrete embodiment. This is how it happened in Jamaica.

Selassie was crowned emperor of Ethiopia in November of 1930. This land and liberty movement of the peasantry in St. Thomas was preaching that the land belonged to black people and that black people should not pay any taxes to the colonial government. Along came a group of men from Kingston. They had been trying to preach the doctrine of Selassie in Kingston but were not making much headway.

They had heard about this movement in St. Thomas and went there. What they said was, "You don't have to pay taxes because our king is not that boy Stuart." They were talking about King George of England. They called him "that boy Stuart." "He is not our King," they said. "Our king resides in Ethiopia." By disrecognizing the throne of England, the black peasantry of St. Thomas was, at least theoretically, open to challenge the colonial order in Jamaica.

Rasta brethren from Kingston went one step further. They said, in any comparison of the king of England and the king of Ethiopia, "Our King is mightier than all of them." The reason they gave was, "Our King is both King and God." They turned the peoples' attention to those texts in the Bible, particularly Revelations, that prophesize the coming of a Conquering Lion of Judah. They believed that this individual was the returned Messiah.

The peasantry responded by saying, "We don't wish to pay any taxes to the British crown. Our king is not only a king, but is the returned Messiah." That is the moment for the igniting of the Rastafarian ethos and the Rastafarian project.

The British colonial authorities, the police, and the military tried to crush the movement brutally. In trying to crush it, they only forced it to spread further. It spread from eastern St. Thomas into central Jamaica and the towns of Kingston, Montego Bay, Port Antonio, and other parishes. From about 1934–35, when the brutal suppression of the Rastafarian movement commenced, to the period of the early 1950s, you had a very isolated yet still a very important presence of Rastafari in Jamaica.

In the late 1940s, Rasta brethren and sistren began to preach the doctrine of a return to Ethiopia. That's when the movement's second phase of existence began. In the late 1940s, they petitioned the governor and the British Crown, demanding the right to return to their ancestral homeland, the country of Ethiopia. At this time, thousands of Jamaicans and other West Indians were embarking for migration to England. This began to stir up hopes and ideas. The time was now feasible to embark on a return to Afrika.

Side by side, with this incredible wave of migration to Britain, in the beginning of the late 1940s, we have these eloquent petitions being prepared. Many of their signers were semi-literate, but still they produced eloquent petitions from numerous brethren and sistren. We have the actual petitions. You should look at the difficult way in which they are written. They are asking and demanding for the right to return to Afrika.

The second phase of the movement culminates with the crushing of Reverend Claudius Henry's movement. Henry returned to Jamaica from Beaumont, Texas, where he had been a convert of the Prince of Ethiopia, Prince Cholalozees, who was working in Beaumont, Texas. His movement was called the "Seventh Emmanuel Brethren." It was based on the Coptic teaching. He was very adamant that it was the right of black people to return to Ethiopia. He pursued that cause very militantly, taking up arms and preparing people to actually carry out offensive operations if they were impeded in their quest. The government, through informers, learned about his activity. They came down on him and charged him with treason and sedition. He was given ten years in prison. It's the crushing of Reverend Henry's movement that put the movement in a profound crisis. That was in 1960–61.

The movement doesn't really emerge out of that crisis until the arrival of the emperor himself in Jamaica, in 1966. His coming opened up the movement to a whole new phase of thinking. The culture, particularly the music, reflected this reawakened movement. That phase, from 1966 to the late 1970s, is very culturally rich and expansive. It is the phase in which the politics and official culture of Jamaica increasingly begins to reflect Rastafarian precepts, ideas, and cultural assertions.

Politicians begin to use the linguistic communication of Rastafari: "brethren," "peace and love," "I man," and "groundation." All of these terms emerging from the Rastafarian root got taken up by official, mainstream Jamaican culture. This is also the period in which the movement begins to internationalize itself.

A number of brethren and sistren decided to try to control how the movement was being shaped. You see a concerted effort to "churchify" Rastafarianism, to establish sectarian teachings, limit who can participate, and set down organizational discipline for those members of what was called "the House." You have competing houses now. You have the Twelve Tribes, Prince Emmanuel's International Afrikan Congress, the Theocratic Order of Nyabingi of Black Heart, and others.

What you have in the present period in Jamaica, and throughout the international sphere, is the evolution of Rasta into orders, which is very different from the free-wheeling open movement you had during the 1950s and 1960s. What you now have are people who are laying down serious, organizational discipline. The doctrine has now become almost rigid and codified. Strict sanctions are passed on people who veer away from the teaching. It is during this period, I think, that we are about to see the time is ripe for certain changes, a pendulum swing. It's very difficult to sit down and reason with many brethren today because you have to join Rasta. You have to be part of that groundation.

When Selassie I was crowned Emperor, and incidentally he wasn't called "Emperor" by people in Jamaica, he was called "King,"—King of Kings, Lord of Lords, Conquering Lion of the Tribe of Judah—his coronation had some very important highlights. One of them, the most notable, being the fact that the King of England sent, as his official representative his cousin, the Duke of Gloucester. When the Duke of Gloucester was at the coronation, he knelt down before Selassie and handed him the gift he had brought with him from England.

The gift was originally something that had been stolen from Ethiopia and carried to England. He was returning it. His kneeling down before the crowned

Photo credit: UCLA Photographic Studio

Robert A. Hill

emperor of Ethiopia signified a reversal of the relationship between Afrika and white Europe. It signified an acknowledgment of who was truly supreme among crowned heads.

People began to identify, at first, with the emperor of Ethiopia, basically as the embodiment of a prophecy now fulfilled, namely, "A prince shall come out of Egypt. Ethiopia shall stretch forth her hands unto God." The coronation, in November of 1930, signified the coming into finality of that prophecy from the Psalms.

The doctrine of Ethiopia's divinity had been around for a long time. We find it in 1901, when a Brooklyn man named W. L. Hunter wrote a very fascinating treatise titled "Jesus Christ Had Negro Blood in His Veins." He tried to show the continuity between Ethiopia and the theme of redemption as it was written in the Bible. We find it in a book published in 1919 by James M. Webb, a black preacher from Seattle; and in a book published in Chicago titled *The Black Man Shall Be the Coming Universal King*. We find it that same year in a Jamaican living in Detroit who wrote a treatise which I have spent a lot of time working on. It's called "The Revealed Secret of the Hamitic Race." A follow-up to it is titled "Who Are the Real Jews?"

Throughout all of these statements runs the theme of Ethiopia's centrality in the Bible. Ethiopia was seen as the foundation of Christian belief, a foundation that had been usurped by Europeans. Within this doctrine of Ethiopia's divinity, two competing doctrines emerged. On the one hand, you have the conservative ideologists who are preaching that black people are simply asking for acknowledgment of their place in the Bible. Then you have a very radical and militant opposing ideology to the conservative ideology that seeks to have black people and Ethiopia recognized as being part of the Christian tradition.

These people who emerged in opposition to the conservative wing say it's more than that. They say black people are the real Jews. They articulate this militant, radical new doctrine, which I call the Afro-Israelite doctrine, that indeed, the people who claim to be Jews are not the real Jews. The real Jews are Ethiopians. They base that teaching on their own radical interpretation of the Bible.

When Haile Selassie I is crowned Emperor, many black people are fully cognizant of both the doctrine and the prophecy and the debates between what you might call the conventional Ethiopianists and the radical Afro-Israelites. The crowning of Haile Selassie I took the black world to another level.

In the course of Emperor Haile Selassie's reign, the fascist Italian leader Mussolini invaded and conquered Ethiopia. That roused a level of solidarity among black people throughout Afrika, America, Europe, and the Caribbean, the likes of which we have not seen since the early years of the Garvey movement in the early 1920s. We would not see it again probably until the campaign against apartheid in South Afrika.

An incredible wave of protest against Mussolini's invasion arose, even here in Los Angeles. Black people in Los Angeles came together to form a black army. They wrote petitions saying they were ready to go to Ethiopia with arms and fight. All over the black world, people wanted to enlist to go to defend Ethiopia against Italy's fascist armies.

The attack against Ethiopia was further confirmation that Europe understood they had to deal with the movement of black supremacy that's outlined in one of the early Rastafari bibles called the *Royal Parchment Scroll of Black Supremacy*. Mussolini's attack against Ethiopia simply was further confirmation that Europe would not allow this "king," who represented black supremacy, to carry out the worldwide unification program of black people. This had also been prophesied by a European, a man who wrote under the pseudonym, "Phylos." He claimed there was a worldwide conspiracy among blacks, under the direction, chairmanship, or coordination, if you will, of Emperor Haile Selassie, that took the name "Nyabingi"—death to white and black oppressors. This preaching about this so-called Nyabingi conspiracy took the form of an article, published in Germany or Hungary in 1935. It was actually part of Mussolini's fascist propaganda against Ethiopia and against black people, which asserted that they were part of a global conspiracy to overthrow the dominion of whites. Phylos's article was translated into English and reprinted in Jamaica under the title "The Black Peril." That's what set the idea of Nyabingi loose in Jamaica. All of that is really what solidifies Rasta as not just Jamaican, although it has Jamaican roots. What happens in Jamaica is representative of the fate of the entire black world.

One thing we have to remain conscious of is that there also was a musical development coinciding with this movement. Drumming is this basis of the music. There are many people like Garth White in Jamaica and the Rasta elders, who know much more in detail about the evolution of the music. I would say the roots of the music come from Kumina. Kumina is a Congo cult that had been developed in the same parish of St. Thomas where Rasta took root. The language of Rasta, which is a secret, mystical language, came from this cult of Kumina. Kumina incorporates both dance, spirit possession, language, music, and drumming.

The Rastafarian brethren who were proselytizing the doctrine really didn't have any avenue to express their beliefs except on the streets. They held regular street services based on Rasta adaptations of Methodist music, Methodist hymns, what are called the "sankeys." It's interesting—as a Jamaican who grew up listening and hearing different kinds of Jamaican music, my ear instinctively picks up on the fact that Peter Tosh's music is a Rasta adaptation of Methodist hymns.[1] From Kumina drumming to the utilization of Methodist Sankey hymns to a more militant version of Rasta music, we are only now beginning to understand.

There was a group, which was very difficult to find information about, called the "Angelic House." These were brethren who had come to Kingston in from the country parts to attend the International African Congress convention of 1958. Many of them stayed on in Kingston. They preached that Rasta was too close, that it was corrupted by the surrounding Christian Evangelical movement. They preached that Rasta needed to purify itself of these contaminations. They are the ones who brought the Burru drums and the militant Nyabingi drumming into Kingston in the late 1950s. We're still trying to locate individuals who can describe to us the activities of the Angelic House.

You had a second group of militant brethren at that time called Youth Black Faith. Youth Black Faith were the individuals who really radicalized the doctrine and prepared the way. They would have nothing to do, incidentally, with Reverend Henry. The most important figure in that group was Ras Shadrach— Ras Shadrach Meshach and Abednego. It is out of the combination of Angelic House and Youth Black Faith that a third phase of the music evolved. That is the period of "ska," and the ska drum. That is the period of the groundation of Rasta in the western part of Kingston, Trench Town, Denham Town, and in eastern Kingston. After the visit in 1966 of Emperor Haile Selassie I to Jamaica, ska and "rock steady" music changed into reggae. During the ska or rock steady era, you didn't have any singers who were putting forward righteous lyrics. The music went dread after 1966. That is when you see the rise of the vocalists and the vocal stylists who advocate the perspective of Ethiopia and the doctrine of Selassie I.

Let me explain a little about the work I am now doing. It is crucial for understanding Rasta. It is a long work based on the three major scriptural texts of Rastafarian teaching: *The Holy Piby*, published in 1924 and written by Robert Athlyi Rogers; *The Royal Parchment Scroll of Black Supremacy*, written in 1927 by Reverend Fitz Balintine Petersburg: and *The Promised Key*, written by someone who adopted the name of G. G. Mirage. That group of three texts, when you read them back to back, take us right up to the early 1930s and show us how the teaching evolved into Rastafarianism.

Over the years we have accumulated more and more of the spiritual teachings that emerged out of the Garvey movement and beyond. We decided it would be a shame just to publish these three texts, though they are the basic texts of Rastafari teachings. *The Promised Key* stops in 1934–35. What about the years after that? What about the 1960s? What about the 1980s? So we decided to go back to the drawing board. We laid out what we had and, based on what we obtained from other researchers who were very willing to share with us, we put together a much larger book of about four or five times the size of the original work. It begins with that extraordinary poster from 1865, "Nearly a Year Since I Saw the Vision," which was signed, "A Son of Africa." Can you imagine that? In 1865, a man in Jamaica calling himself a son of Afrika, calling on black Jamaicans to be prepared for the visit of these black Americans and to heed their doctrine?

We incorporated in the book as well the prayers of the great shepherd, Alexander Bedward, the shepherd of August Town, who is really the exponent of a modern day Myal culture. Myal was an Afrikan religious movement that developed in Jamaica in the eighteenth century. It took many forms. One form was anti-witchcraft exorcisms. The other was these tremendous religious revivals among Afrikan slaves on the plantations. Bedward's movement, calling upon blacks to establish and migrate to a celestial black kingdom, was crushed by the colonial regime in Jamaica. This shows us the foundation of this visionary mystical communication and communing with a black divinity.

My book encompasses a great deal of the pristine religious texts of the Rastafarian faith, both its antecedents in Myal culture, straight through to the black world's Ethiopianism and the Afro-Israelite tradition of the 1920s, right up to the middle 1980s. When this book comes out and people have it, they will see the evolution of this world phenomena of redemption within the framework of an Ethiopian doctrine for which the expression is today called Rastafarianism.

✕✕✕✕✕✕

[1] Peter Tosh was one of the original members of reggae superstar Bob Marley's group, The Wailers.

DEBORAH MAÁT MOORE
MATHEMATICIAN, EDUCATOR, AUTHOR

One of the oldest myths in the world is that Afrikan people had nothing to do with the creation or early use of mathematics. The meticulous work of Professor Deborah Maát Moore clearly illustrates how the major forms of mathematics had their foundation in Afrika. Her work, which points us to the documents where the proof is open to the world, has increased the achievement of mathematics among American Afrikan children.

I am originally from Detroit, Michigan; born and raised there. I began to embrace an Afrikan consciousness when I got to college. I was exposed to the literature in my Black Studies classes and was taken under the wings of older students who were graduate students. They introduced me to organizations like the Association for Black Psychologists and other organizations like that. They introduced me to volunteer work within the Afrikan American community. I became more conscious as a result of that and especially when I began to work for Europeans.

Gradually, I began to develop the mind-set that it was time for me to step out on my own. When I saw the control that whites had over Afrikan Americans, that's what made me more conscious beyond a shadow of a doubt—when I saw that we had to go to them for everything, especially for a job.

I began to specialize in mathematics while at Wayne State University as a sophomore. I was formerly a psychology major. I took all of the classes that I could take. I reached the highest level in mathematics classes as an undergraduate. After that, I began to think that I would like to get into something more technical. I always wanted to be a writer and a scientist. I recognized that when I was ten years old.

However, it wasn't until I got into Wayne State University that I began thinking I wanted to be an engineer. First, I was going to be an engineer because my grandfather was the first black engineer hired by the city of Detroit. I guess it was just that family thing. I really was in engineering first. I entered the College of Engineering, but the way that I was taught there turned me off toward engineering. After that, I just changed my major to mathematics because of my love for science.

In the area of science at the college level, my training was very poor. I had a very good science teacher at the elementary level who was a European. He taught me things about photosynthesis that I still remember today. At the college level and the high school level, there was nothing that whites did to really turn me on to science. I stayed in mathematics because mathematics was an exact science, and I liked exact sciences. I love facts and figures. I felt stronger in a field with facts and figures.

Eventually, I had to research the Afrikan origin of mathematics, which was not very difficult because Afrikans left their records behind. Pharaohs ordered scribes to record their history. So the recorders of history and the first civilization left behind a math book. That math book was called the *Ahmose Papyrus* after the Afrikan gentlemen who wrote it.

The person who acquired that papyrus after Ahmose died was a Scotsman named Henry Rhind. Thieves stole the papyrus from Ahmose's tomb and sold it to Rhind. It's now called the *Rhind Mathematical Papyrus.* That is the oldest book that we have on mathematics. It was found in Afrika, in Egypt, with the mummy of Ahmose. We're talking about at least 1650; 1700 B.C. We're talking about at least 3,500 years ago.

It was a profound papyrus that was very, very complex. When I say complex, I mean in its scope. It contained arithmetic, geometry and trigonometry problems written in the language of *MDW NTR,* or *Medew Neter,* "divine speech." It contained problems that showed how the ancient Afrikan people dealt with π (pi), and how they figured the earliest value for π from a circle inscribed in a square. It had mathematics problems that indicated the sine and the cosine of a triangle. It had geometric series. It had a division table. It had first-degree mathematical equations, what we now call linear equations. It had fractions that they reduced down to the lowest terms. It had area problems for determining the volumes and areas of pyramids, those types of things. There's a problem in the papyrus in which Ahmose talks about finding the lengths of sides of similar triangles. Those are triangles that share the same side and the same base. We are still talking about a period between 1600 and 1700 B.C.

It's amazing. When we look at algebra, geometry, trigonometry, calculus, physics—all of these forms of math were created in Afrika. There's a problem in which Ahmose says, "find the lengths of the side of the *seked.*" *Seked* was their term for "tangent." The tangent is the cosine over the sine. So we've got that trigonometry problem. That's trigonometry. In another problem, he finds the area of a triangle—that's geometry. Then you've got arithmetic. He says something about multiplying or making two fractions complete. In that problem, he adds two fractions, then multiplies them. He calls that "completion." We would call it subtraction. Then there's a problem that deals with geometrical series, what we call the Fibonacci Series, where the third term is the sum of the first two preceding terms. And so it goes, on and on and on.

We see the beginnings of calculus in Ahmose's *Papyrus,* but it's integral calculus, not differential calculus. Differential calculus is modern-day calculus. It's the calculus that deals specifically with finding speed or how fast a particular object is going. That's important for travel. Europeans were heavily into differential calculus because they are travelers. They wanted to know how fast one can go from the earth to the moon or from the United States to Europe. They are always dealing with speed.

The ancient Kemetic people worked with integral calculus, which deals with areas and volumes. They found those areas by adding up the sum of the rectangles under a particular curve. Those types of problems, integral calculus problems, were very important for building. Our people were builders.

When we look at the pyramids, at Rameses's statues, and all the other magnificent structures, we see that a lot of measurements were done. I think the epitome of mathematics is measurement, applying mathematics to structures like this. The pyramids and those huge Egyptian statues had to be measured accurately. When you measure them accurately, they look better. Who wants a lopsided building? The Egyptians wanted extreme accuracy. With the pyramids they used the Kemetic Theorem—that is, $(c^2 = a^2 + b^2)$. They also dealt with the volume formula to determine the volume or the amount of space inside a pyramid before the capstone is put on.

I recently translated a document called the *Berlin Papyrus.* I personally think it's older than any papyrus that we've found, including the *Ahmose Papyrus,* the *Moscow Papyrus,* and the *Kahun Papyrus,* because of the condition of the papyrus. I also found that, with the *Berlin Papyrus,* I had to restore a number of the symbols in the *MDW NTR,* another indicator that the papyrus was very old.

The *Berlin Papyrus* contains the so-called Pythagorean Theorem, which was developed far before Pythagoras. The brother who wrote it writes, "The quantity two, I make three-quarters of the quantity, one of the other. What is the quantity?" That was the introduction of the problem. Then he says, "Always take the square of one side." We do that when we solve for the Kemetic Theorem, which involves a ninety-degree triangle. We take the square root of two sides, then take the longest side and square it. Then we take the other side and square that. Then we square the third side.

In order for me to work with this material accurately, I had to learn the *MDW NTR* so I could understand what our people were talking about. Something in me said, "Don't trust these Europeans." I did, to an extent, but I found out that they made errors. They said, "Oh, the black people, the scribes made the errors." I did not find any errors in the *MDW NTR.* I found errors in white's interpretation of the *MDW NTR*. That's why I went back and reinterpreted the *MDW NTR* for myself and even restored parts of it that were worn away.

It took me about six years to become competent in the *MDW NTR*, and I haven't totally mastered it, but I've mastered it well enough in mathematics. I found that learning the *MDW NTR* of mathematics has helped me understand the *MDW NTR* in the other literature; its presentation of the story of the "Excellent Follower." I found that it took me at least five to six years to really understand and translate all of these documents.

The *MDW NTR* gave me a better perspective on language. See, English is one-dimensional, *MDW NTR* is three-dimensional and infinite. When I say English is one-dimensional, I mean it's based on phonics. Look at the twenty-six letters of the alphabet. You know them by pronouncing them. You say, "a," "b," "c," and so on. With the *MDW NTR*, you have the phonics because some of the *MDW NTR*'s hieroglyphic symbols are based on sound. They are also based on what you see. They're based on sound and sight and concepts and ideas because every one of those symbols translates to an idea.

For example, we see the symbol of the Khepera beetle over and over again in the *MDW NTR*. The Khepera is the Egyptian symbol for transformation. We find that when we're dealing with an algebra equation, the left side of the equation is being transformed to the right side. That is symbolized by the Khepera beetle. We have the symbol for eternity, which was their equivalent for infinite. In the *Berlin Papyrus*, where the brother says, "Forever take the square of one side to eternity," we see a picture of the sun, which represents time. The sun is endless, as far as we know.

The symbols stood for sound. The symbols were visual. The symbols were concepts. They were ideas. What's the idea when you see an owl? An owl is a symbol for trust, wisdom, and intelligence. We see that over and over and over again.

The language of the Egyptians was very profound. It was a very romantic language. The language itself was righteous. If there was something bad in the language, it was telling us not to be bad, not to be evil—or it was telling a story about a person who was evil and who maybe overcame his evil. It's hard to say something bad in the *MDW NTR*.

In a sense, the *MDW NTR* is metaphysical. A lot of positive things happen to you when you start reading it. I've talked to a number of people about that. I can't explain it. I don't know what it is. I know that it's very cleansing for me. When I read or write the *MDW NTR*, it cleanses me. It takes anything that's bad out of my system, any bad thought. It's definitely a spiritual language. It has a spiritual nature.

DEBORAH MAÁT MOORE

However, I have only run across one instance when the *MDW NTR* relates to a particular deity in the math literature. In the other literature, I don't know, but in the mathematics, there was a problem where a brother was talking about going to the South, I think Nubia, to shoot buzzards or vultures in order to make some clothes. I think he said—but I'm not sure—that he was going where the goddess Stt, or Satis was, in Idahet, which at that time was a location in Nubia. That is the only reference to a deity I've found.

We see the symbols for God in some of the mathematics writings because the symbols for God was the flag and the club, and also a brother praying with his hands up. The highest symbol in the number system is a million, and it is a symbol of a man praying to God. So in a sense, we do see instances of God in the numbers.

Looking at other areas where mathematics was practiced during ancient times, there was Babylonian mathematics, Mesopotamian mathematics, and Sumerian mathematics. Some say they came along at the same period in time as Nile Valley mathematics. Their earliest writings are not as early as ours in mathematics. I have not studied them that much, however. I know of the Ishango Bone, found in Zaire, in Central Afrika. That's further down to the South. I have been told that is where mathematics actually began and where the earliest numbers were found. There were a number of tallies on that particular bone, which goes back twenty-five thousand years. You've got the mathematics on one side on this bone, which was really a fishing harpoon. They used it to kill fish. On one side, there are even numbers; on the other side, odd prime numbers. Prime numbers are numbers that only two numbers can be divided into, namely, the number itself and one.

We have the Ishango Bone, which is twenty-five thousand years old, and then after that, according to Dr. Josef ben–Jochannan, we have a calendar that is at least ten thousand years old. I believe that calendar is either from Nubia or Kemet. I myself have studied another calendar that is written in *MDW NTR*, which is dated from at least 4100 or 4200 B.C. There's nothing in the Mesopotamian or Babylonian literature to show that they had calendars based on numbers that early.

One of the most astounding things is that the math that was practiced by our ancient ancestors is very applicable today. Students need to know that the reason we're still doing square roots is because of these black people that lived at least thousands of years before. They need to know that first-degree equations, like two times plus three times is equal to twenty-four, were worked on by people of color, thousands and thousands of years ago.

Now, what does that do to the mind of children? It helps them to be motivated for mathematics, because the ancient Afrikan culture was a very colorful culture. They need to know that the foundation of modern math was based on the foundation that was laid out at least five to seven thousand years ago. Right now, they're being taught mathematics in a vacuum. They're being taught without a foundation. They don't understand it. They don't think there is a math philosophy. They don't know why they're doing the math.

When they study the foundation of math, the Afrikan contribution to math, they know why they're doing it. With knowledge of the Afrikan contributions to math, they see how the ancient Afrikan people applied it to their everyday life. They had mathematical problems on how they constructed the pyramids; mathematical problems on how they made clothes. If they see examples of math being applied to their everyday life back then, that gives them the understanding that they can use math for this, we can use math for that. It gives the students a foundation. It helps them become motivated to learn math.

One of the problems we face is that only twenty percent, maybe fifty percent of the mathematics professors in college know this foundation. Many know it, but they just don't tell it. There are a number of professors who have done research studies on Egyptian math. It's in the research papers. Many of them simply don't include it in their daily lesson. I did run across a European at Wayne State University who recommended my book for the Detroit Public Schools. He is teaching a class on number theory in which he uses examples and concepts from the so-called *Rhind Mathematical Papyrus.*

The title of my book is *The African Roots of Mathematics.* It can be purchased through the Association for the Study of Classical Afrikan Civilizations, or it can be purchased through the Shrine of the Black Madonna bookstore in Detroit, Michigan. I recently finished a *Teachers' Resource Guide* that contains a report on why blacks fail math and what can be done about it. It contains twenty-one sample lesson plans to let high school, elementary school, middle school, and college teachers know how they can connect the foundation for math, back to ancient Afrika, with modern math to help students become motivated and to help them understand the philosophy. It helps them go on to achieve and value math.

Now, the reason we don't do well in math is because of a number of reasons. The primary reason is how it's taught to us. It's taught to us by people who really don't love us. In order for students to learn science and math, which is sensitive and challenging, they have to be taught by people who respect them and love them. If our children and adults are taught by people who don't love them and respect them, then it doesn't sink in.

Second, it's being taught from a Eurocentric frame of reference. Look at the math books, they have a picture of Lebnitz, who was a German. They have a picture of Sir Isaac Newton, who was from England. They say, "Well, these people invented calculus." You don't see black people. You don't see people of color in these math books. That makes our students feel that they didn't have a part in the math, so why should they learn it?

Japanese students achieve because of one reason or another. Maybe they identify with the Europeans. I think they do. They want to identify with whites. However, our students, young and old, are not learning, young and old, because of the disrespectful way that we're treated by math teachers. Also, some books are inaccurate. We ran across books in one school system in which there were fifteen different errors in three middle school books, which were recently approved by a school district. I won't embarrass that school district, but it's just a shame. Those errors have got to confuse the students.

Also, we don't learn math because we don't challenge ourselves. We cop out and don't stick with it when we should. We have to see it as being a challenge. We can't let math whip us. We have to use it as a challenge and go on to learn to be true women and true men. This is what our ancestors wanted us to be. We have to walk in their shadows and walk in the ways of our people from the Nile Valley, from Ghana, from Mali, and from other parts of Afrika. They used math to build their civilizations, and they left it for us. If we don't sit and do the math, then we're punking out.

How do we do that? Number one, parents have to let their children see them sitting down at the dinner table, at the living room table, struggling with math. Even if they get the answers wrong, at least when that child comes in they see that mother and that father struggling with math. That parent doesn't have to say anything. The child is learning from their example.

Second, parents have to get involved with the school systems. They have to go and meet their child's math teacher. They have to talk to the teachers of their students. They have to find out what chapter the class is on, how their child is doing in math. They have to make sure the teacher lets them know when their student is not doing well and why. They have to challenge the teachers and get involved in the school system.

Parents cannot pass on their legacy of not doing well in math to their children. The child perceives it as, "Well, my mother couldn't do it, so I can't do it; or, Oh, I've never been able to do math." That passes along a negative legacy. That legacy is copping out. We've got to stop doing that.

Examples have to be used. Most of us use George Washington Carver in science. Yes, he was a genius, but there were other geniuses besides George Washington Carver. We've got to go further back, back to the Moors in Spain who built Muslim temples and schools based on quadratic equations. After

1492, all those Moors were put out of Spain. They drove them back. The slave trade totally suppressed any type of scientific development among Afrikan people for maybe about one hundred years. Sure, we had a genius like Benjamin Banneker, but in more recent times, black men and women have contributed their math knowledge to corporations. All their mathematical knowledge and inventions went toward helping the white culture. You didn't hear about them unless you went to those corporations or unless you did some extra studies to find out. Where are the black mathematicians? Oh, they're at Michigan Bell. They're at one particular industry. They're at Xerox. They're kept hidden.

So now, we have someone like Ivan Van Sertima, who is documenting the Afrikan contribution to mathematical science and physics. We're seeing a rebirth in the knowledge of Afrikan mathematics and science. This is our renaissance. Young students are purchasing books written by Afrikan scholars. They're going to find out that George Washington Carver was a genius, but that there were other geniuses like Ahmose and the Afrikan scribe who wrote what is now called the *Moscow Mathematical Papyrus*, and other people who did great things. There are great math teachers, like Dr. Abdulalim Abdullah Shabazz at Clark Atlanta University.[1] I heard of him for the first time this year. I've never studied under him, but I would really like to do that.

My personal goal and mission in mathematics is to affect the world and leave a legacy behind which shows that Afrikan people invented mathematics, that Afrikan people are capable of doing mathematics, and are capable of being mathematicians. My legacy is to increase the consciousness of the importance of mathematics among people of color first. Other people secondly, but people of color first.

My mission is also to bring us back to our former greatness because we were the great mathematicians. We were the great physicists. Maybe we built those pyramids on Mars, because Europeans don't have it in their history. So we may have gotten up there somehow. One of the satellite missions photographed pyramids on Mars. They also photographed a sphinx on Mars with the same structure as the pyramids here on Earth.

For anyone who wants to do some research on the pyramids on Mars, there's a European who has a book out on them. The name of the book is *Monuments of Mars.*[2] The author, Richard C. Hoagland, also has a video on the topic.

Overall, my mission is to create a revolution. That revolution is in the field of mathematics and science, but particularly mathematics. Obviously, math is the engine that fuels science. I want to increase the awareness of mathematics throughout the world, not just in America, but throughout the world.

This is already happening. I was astounded and speechless—I didn't know what to say—when I saw the reality of our children from the Marcus Garvey School, in Los Angeles, solving calculus problems at five and twelve years old. It was just astounding. I was just very, very proud. Extremely proud. When they started figuring those problems in *MDW NTR*, I just had to sit down. I didn't know how to take it, but, to me, they were geniuses. They showed us that we can produce geniuses. The mathematics, the knowledge of math, the ability to do math, is still within us. Our ancestors' genes still come through. That genius is an unbroken chain.

In the very near future, I'm opening up a mathematics academy on the east side of the city of Detroit. The students are going to deal with nothing but mathematics and computers. We're going to learn Afrikan-centered math and the Afrikan contribution to mathematics the right way. I think that's something that is needed badly all over the country. We'll see how it goes in Detroit. I think it's going to go well. I'm going to put my all into it. I want it to be a world-renowned institute. It's going to be called the Ahmose Mathematical Academy. We're simply going to do mathematics, mathematics, and more mathematics—and computers. The math is going to be related to the computers, because students are going to write about what they learned from the mathematics.

I would say to the young people: Read your history. Read about who really invented mathematics. Do the reading and the research to find out that Afrikan people invented mathematics. Stay with the math, no matter how difficult it is. Stay with it, and don't let it get you down. It's there for you. We are a mathematical people. Mathematics is patterns. It's numbers. It's rhythm. We're a rhythmic people. We deal with timing. We're natural mathematicians. We have it within us. The genes from our ancestors are still within us, and we can be great again.

---

[1] Dr. Shabazz teaches mathematics and is graduate programs coordinator in the mathematics department at Clark Atlanta University. He is directly or indirectly responsible for training over half the black Ph.D.'s in mathematics in America.

[2] Hoagland, Richard C., *Monuments of Mars: A City on the Edge of Forever* (Berkley: North Atlantic Books, 1996).
Note: On August 7, 1996, the front page headline of the *Los Angeles Times* read, "Rock May Bear Signs of Ancient Life on Mars".

NA'IM AKBAR
PSYCHOLOGIST, THEORIST, EDUCATOR, AUTHOR, LECTURER

Na'im Akbar, an Islamic Afrikan behaviroal scientist, is one of the most dynamic American Afrikan psychologists in the country. His concepts, as one of the creators of Afrikan psychology, address the holistic behavioral and spiritual needs for people of Afrikan descent and negates the European-oriented, singular behaviroal approach espoused by Sigmund Freud, Carl Jung, and others. The author of several books on this topic, he is an active, much-sought-after lecturer and educator.

L et me extend my greetings of peace to the whole Afrikan community, and to the human community everywhere, of which we are the fathers.

I'm originally from Tallahassee, Florida. I returned several years ago, having left immediately after finishing high school. I was actually born, reared, and finished high school right here in the area where I am currently living. Of course, I moved around quite a bit. I spent ten years in Michigan, five years in Atlanta, two years in Chicago, two years in Virginia, and I currently travel around the country on a regular basis. I find Tallahassee to be a very livable community, primarily ideal for raising a family. As a foundation for a family setting, it's one of the nicer cities I've found in the country. It's a base, and out of that base I can reach the entire world. All I have to do is catch a plane, and I can go anywhere.

My religious orientation is Islam. I was led to it by Elijah Muhammad. I was not looking for a religious answer at the time. I'd been raised as a fairly devout Christian Methodist Episcopal. I had developed a fairly strong spiritual orientation out of my Christian upbringing. When I joined the Nation of Islam, I was not really looking for religious answers. I was looking for solutions to the problems of Afrikan American people with a spiritual base.

Coming through the sixties, I was involved in many protest movements at the university. I had observed many efforts to try to institutionalize positive developments that would begin to make a difference for our people. I knew that we needed institutions to change our condition as a people. In the late sixties and early seventies, there was absolutely nothing I could find anywhere that could compare with the very broad institutional development Elijah Muhammad was doing. He was developing schools, businesses, banks, publishing companies, truck distribution centers, international trade, farmland— everything that everybody else was talking about, he was doing. All the nation-

alists and all the other groups, the Republic of New Afrika, the Student Nonviolent Coordinating Committee, even the civil rights organizations were talking about the need for the very structures and institutions Elijah Muhammad had in place. The only problem was that many of the institutions of the Nation of Islam were poorly run. He was relying upon people who had minimal skills to keep them operating. They had the commitment, the sincerity, and the attitude that permitted them to make a difference.

In addition to that, I found that the Nation of Islam, under Elijah Muhammad, was actually healing all the problems that everybody else was concerned about. Here I was, a master social scientist—or at least I thought I was—a Ph.D. psychologist, supposedly equipped to help eliminate drug addiction, resolve personal problems such as depression, criminality, marital difficulties, and so forth, and I found that all of the problems everybody was talking about, Elijah Muhammad was curing.

Actually, I joined the Nation of Islam out of genuine curiosity. I wanted to know what this man was doing that was making such a difference. I got trapped, in a sense, because I found a set of concepts and a lifestyle that answered the questions that I had as a Black man committed to our people. I found the Nation to be a genuine curative process for myself and for Afrikan American people as a whole. I continue to see that process, whether you accept the Nation or not, as being essential to bringing about transformation in ourselves.

So, I actually came into Islam through the back door. I was looking for solutions for Afrikan American people. That solution came with Islam, through the teachings of Elijah Muhammad. Today, things are a little different. I think Minister Farrakhan is involved in trying to restore the best of what the Honorable Elijah Muhammad had in mind. We all know the Nation has gone through a tremendous transition. Currently, we certainly do not have a structure anywhere comparable to what Elijah Muhammad had.

Many of us who came into the Nation as I did came into it because of the powerful possibilities of offering something for our people, not only in terms of spiritual answers but also in terms of economic, social, cultural, and other answers, the whole domain. The Nation is nothing like that now. We don't have banks. We don't have farmland. We don't have any of those kinds of structures that were in place. Most of the schools and businesses are closed. All the things that Elijah Muhammad had in 1975 no longer exist.

I think Minister Farrakhan is beginning to put back in place some of those things. We don't really know. It's a reconstruction job that he's engaged in. It's almost like trying to say what Malcolm X would have done, when we never saw what Malcolm's independent program really was. In many ways, what we see

right now with Minister Farrakhan is the effort to try to articulate what the program ought to be like when it's back in force. We have only seen the beginnings of it. We can't judge now whether it will be as good as what Elijah Muhammad had, but what he is proposing is very consistent with what the old Nation of Islam represented.

Personally, my background in the Nation of Islam has augmented my work tremendously. One of the things I've been advocating over the last several years is that the major obstacle to our progress is the problem of identity. We simply have not established an acceptance of reality of who we are. What I argue is that a people's power is rooted in the affirmation of themselves. It doesn't matter who they are. Whatever it is they are able to do as human beings has to grow out of the fact that they see who they are as worthwhile. When they look in the mirror, they should see a person who is worthwhile enough to work the rest of his life to make sure that his life and that of his offspring can become more effective. For example, a man should be able to say, "The woman I'm married to is important enough that I will do anything to make her life protected and worthwhile so that she can develop herself. These children who look like me are so important that I will sacrifice my bad habits, I will make my life different, I will deprive myself of immediate pleasures, I will do whatever I can to make their lives happen." This is the thing that drives people into entrepreneurial and institutional development, that drives people to build new worlds and new societies based upon this fundamental need to affirm who they are.

The fact that we reject ourselves and our basic essence is the ultimate nucleus of the whole self-destructive process that is blocking our progress at this point. This may sound very strange to some people because we are so accustomed to blaming and putting the cause of our stagnation outside of ourselves. That doesn't mean racism does not exist or that we are not the victims of the most diabolical system of oppression in modern history. There is no doubt about that. But, in my thinking, we have now come to the point in our development as a people when the major barrier to our effectiveness is within ourselves. We are not using the strength, the energy, the skills, the capability, nor the destiny that has come to us. We don't acknowledge, affirm, or admire who we are.

The process of making us reject our identity began with slavery. Then, it was necessary, a prerequisite for making us accept the direction of other people's minds. Slaves can't be themselves. That's a contradiction in terms. People who are themselves won't stay slaves. They'll reject it. They'll run away from it. They'll rebel. They'll protest. They'll kill you if you try to make them slaves. In order to make us slaves, it became vitally necessary to disrupt our identity, to make us reject ourselves, and make us reject our fundamental humanity. In the

process of doing so, we then spent generations working against our own progress and our own development.

What we need to begin to do is redefine our reality as human beings. We must have pride and dignity in who we are. I'm trying to say this in such a way that it doesn't sound like the glib, stereotyped things we say all the time like "black pride" and "black is beautiful." It's more than that. That's a part of it—we have to see beauty in who we are. Part of it is the aesthetics of recognizing that black folks are worthwhile, but the deeper part is being able to appreciate the fact we really can think and think well. We really are something to have endured what we've endured in this society and still function as fathers, husbands, doctors, lawyers, teachers, ditch diggers, plumbers, and people who are making it. Despite the fact that overwhelming numbers of us are still in the prison system, it's really quite phenomenal that *all* of us are not there.

Even though crack cocaine is wiping us out left and right, it's still phenomenal that we aren't all crack addicts. We ought to be, you know. Given the realities of what we've had to deal with, it would be justifiable if we were all junkies, lunatics, black-on-black killers, homicidal maniacs, the whole bit. It would make logical sense if we were that way.

Self-acceptance lets us understand the real measure of our accomplishment. We have made it in spite of all those factors that should have made all of us what many of our brothers and sisters have actually become. Pride is beginning to define ourselves, by ourselves; to focus on assets rather than liabilities and to begin to look at our possibilities rather than our defects. Most of all, with pride we begin to develop a vision that takes us some place beyond where we've been or have never been before. We must draw upon the strengths and assets that are there.

Sometimes we have real formidable difficulties, particularly with those who feel they have already arrived. There are ways to reach and deal with the middle class, many of whom are very intelligent people who can be reasoned with. We must try to reach them through a kind of rational dialogue. We must say to them, "Let's talk about who we are. Let's discuss some information we've never had before. If you want to reject the information, that's your choice. We Afrikans do not have to beg for culture. We brought culture to the world."

To begin to show and get that information to our people in whatever way we can, we must work through the media, through music, through the arts. We must show them that kente cloth is more beautiful than anything Gucci can come up with. We must find ways to share the aesthetics of Afrikan people. All of those small and simple things become one avenue. If that fails, leave them alone. They will come home. The racists will send them back. The nature of

Na'im Akbar

racism in this society will send everyone of us back, sooner or later. I have that much faith in the system. It is predictable. Sooner or later they are going to show their true "color," if you will.

What that means, then, is that the brother who is in corporate America, who has worked very hard to get there, who has struggled and demonstrated his skill and capability, and who has paid his dues, is going to end up finding people less competent than himself shooting by him. He's going to discover the ones who shoot by him look one way, while he looks another way. Suddenly, he's going to find out he's black after all. Despite the fact that he's worked very hard, gone to Stanford's business school, never associated with any other black people, and lives in a white neighborhood. Many "buppies" go to the bank with good credit. They've done all the right things the right way, but they discover they can't get a loan to buy their dream home. Then they find out that this Caucasian friend—with fewer resources, fewer assets, less collateral, and a poorer credit record—has gotten a loan only because he looks one way and they look another. Despite their white cars, white apartment houses, white swimming pools, white lacrosse and polo games, they will discover that the social and cultural scene of the Euro-American world still sees them as black. The nature of racism in America brings that reality painfully home.

The realities of this system will drive many of these buppies back to where we are. We thought they were gone, lost to the corporate world, the university world. Then, they start coming around, listening to lectures by Ivan Van Sertima. They want to go to the local black book store to pick up books by Cheikh Anta Diop. They want to read and hear some more of this stuff. These are the same ones who, a few years ago, didn't want to hear any of that "black stuff." They had made it independently, or so they thought. The realities of this system have made them realize they must come to grips with the fact that it is impossible for any individual to achieve independent of his own group.

If the group is stigmatized, if the group has not made it in general acceptability, no matter how successful you may be, you are stigmatized. When I say the group, I don't mean that everybody will attain the same level of achievement. What I mean is that the group itself has to have dignity, otherwise, your individual accomplishments will always be smudged by your undignified group membership.

All of us, no matter how selfish we may want to be, are obligated to help the group attain dignity in order that we can all attain dignity. Otherwise, the only thing we can do is try to leave the group. But one thing about being black in America, you can never leave the group. You will die with it. But there are positive things happening, especially in scholarship.

What people don't understand is that all scholarship emerges out of the experiences of people dealing with their problems or obstacles to their development. Freud was facing a society of people who had a whole set of problems such that Judeo-Christian Europeans were not able to be as effective as they wanted to be as a people. They were concerned about their family problems, personal failures, and societal failures. Their psychology was based upon their efforts to find out what was interfering with the effectiveness of European and European American people. This same goal guided Skinner, Maslow, Rogers, and all of their experts in psychology. Their work doesn't suggest anything to the contrary. In their writings, they tell you that all of the people they studied were white people. Most of their research studies were conducted on white people, in white situations, dealing with white adjustment issues. None of them, none of these great scholars, had any kind of extensive involvement, observation of, or even interest in other than upper-middle-class European, American, Jewish, or Christian people. That was basically their interest. They never looked at Afrikan people, except as cases of deviance.

When they wanted to talk about a deviant group or show deviance at its worst, they would identify us. Deviance was defined as being the way they thought we were. They admitted having deviance, but they thought their deviance could be corrected. Our deviance, they believed, was innate. None of them bothered to address how our minds functioned, how we adjusted, or how we identify the source of our excellence in spite of their mistreatment.

Afrikan American psychologists began to ask the question: How can we black people become more effective as human beings? We found that Freud clearly did not have the answer, nor did Skinner and Maslow. All these people who were supposed to be the major thinkers in European psychology were not equipped to address the issue of improving the effectiveness of non-European or nonwhite people. When we applied the traditional tools of psychology to our people, they didn't work. Not only that, our people wouldn't even stick around long enough to be exposed to that kind of treatment—psychotherapy, psychoanalysis, that sort of stuff. It was alien to us. The techniques and ways of reaching white people were not very meaningful for our people.

Again, this takes us back to what I said earlier about how Elijah Muhammad was successful in solving these problems without putting anybody in counseling. He simply taught self-respect and selfy-discipline and addressed the social, economic, and moral realities of being black in America. He resolved many of our personal and emotional problems by affirming our group identity and group integrity. We began to see our worth as being tied in to that of a worldwide community of dignified people. He was able to infuse his followers with a sense of energy and inspiration that made them transcend whatever that made them alcoholics, prostitutes, homosexuals, or spouse abusers. They were able to transcend those hang-ups and put their energies, devotion, and commitment into building something for everybody. That was a phenomenal curative process. The inevitable question was: Why were we working with the tools of Freud, Jung, Rogers and Skinner that are unable to change our people, when someone with a simple message of strength, power, and dignity of the group was able to change many of our destructive processes?

So, what we began to do as black psychologists was very interesting. Many of us who began to pioneer this whole kind of Afrikan-centered thinking were very much influenced by the work of Elijah Muhammad and Marcus Garvey. We were influenced by those outstanding Afrikan American people who made significant social change, in a massive way, for our people. So we said, "We have assets and tools in our history as a people; we can begin to draw upon those things that help us understand how we can be more effective." That means that when we look at Afrikan people, we find that they have some strong characteristics historically, philosophically, and in many other ways. We also said that typical Afrikan behavior characterized those early immigrants who came, say, to California from Texas, Louisiana, and Missouri and looked after cousins and distant cousins, who often lived in overcrowded apartments with lots of relatives sleeping on the floor until they could get a foothold. They looked out for each other, eating out of one big pot, for a long time. That sense of community is typical Afrikan conduct.

We also said that Afrikan people operate out of a strong sense of spirituality. No matter who they call "God," or even if they don't, they've got a sense that there is a bigger reality that's invisible and more powerful than the visible reality. What's true of Afrikan people all over the world is that belief, that faith, that conviction that there's a bigger reality more effective than the difficulties, contradictions, paradoxes, pain, and evil that's observable. That there's something much bigger and much more potent. That force is what brought us through three hundred years of slavery. That vision told us the circumstances we saw before us were not the whole story. That conviction kept our ancestors going.

Now, Afrikan or black psychology is the effort to try to articulate that process so we can begin to draw upon those resources that have worked for us. If we were sitting around waiting to be reinforced—the way Skinner and Watson say we should be, waiting to get rewards for certain behaviors—if that were the primary force in changing our behavior, we'd still be on the plantation, in worse shape than we're in right now. The mere fact that we have changed, and have been able to move from where we were to where we are, was based upon a dri-

ving vision, inspiration, and spiritual belief that made us stand up against people who had dogs, military forces, and everything else they needed to change society and influence people.

We took on this country. When I say "we" I mean Afrikan people. We came through slavery, the post-Reconstruction era, Jim Crow, and the civil rights era. We actually challenged the most brutal, the most savage, and the most militarily sophisticated nation in the world with nothing but a strong belief in what was right. That was insane on one level, but, on the other hand, it was the clearest manifestation of the strength of Afrikan convictions. And even though we had defeats, we actually won. We beat Strom Thurmond. We beat Bull Connor. We beat the most powerful, most negative, and most barbaric Caucasian people who were in power at that time. We defeated them, based upon our beliefs.

That's what we need to talk about in Afrikan psychology. We don't need to talk about our drug addicts and broken homes, though we've got all those things. The issue is not that we have the same manifestations any people have when you destroy their humanity. Instead, we talk about how we have survived in spite of those destructive influences. That's what Afrikan psychologists try to do. That's why we've tried to reach back to the best of being Afrikan, so we can bring that into the American situation, so we can become the kind of American Afrikans whose foundation is in our true identity as Afrikans, as our spiritual selves.

I advocate that spirituality is the essence of Afrikan psychology. Let me give you an idea of what I mean: It's not accidental that those people who've been most effective in providing meaningful leadership for our people have understood the importance of spirituality. There is not one example of an effective Afrikan American person, leader, or whatever who did not come with a message that was rooted in some spiritual context in order to move our people. Not one. Martin Luther King, Jr., had a spiritual message. Marcus Garvey was strongly spiritual, even though he was also impressively political and economic. Everybody talks about his economic program, but if you read *The Philosophy and Opinions of Marcus Garvey*,[1] it's like reading the spiritual philosophy of Noble Drew Ali, Elijah Muhammad, and Martin Luther King combined.

All of those people represented moving forces, even our most relevant scholars understood spirituality. W. E. B. DuBois, Booker T. Washington, Mary McLeod Bethune—all took spiritual reality for granted in their work. All of those who had a mass movement, those who moved our people and inspired them, were rooted in a spiritual context. That is not accidental. There is no history of a political movement for Afrikans in this country that did not have a spiritual base for a mass movement. We had people who became socialists, communists, and followed various other ideologies, but there has been no mass movement of our people that was not rooted in some type of spiritual message. It got translated in different ways, but it never left out the spiritual aspect. When you look at Afrikan people around the world in Haiti, Jamaica, South America, South Pacific, the continent itself, Europe, and America, the one thing that is consistent in all those settings is a devoutly spiritual people who are constantly referring to that invisible reality I talked about earlier. Clearly, it's important to understand that when I talk about the spiritual self.

When we, as Afrikan psychologists try to talk about this, we are not talking about being "spirited"—that is, emotional. Afrikan people are spirited. Emotions are no more than the most superficial level of the spirit. Spirit is actually a consciousness. It's an awareness of a reality that one is unaware of. It transcends the senses. It's a set of causative forces you ascribe to and accept as legitimate in your life. In Haiti, they understand that when people become sick for no apparent reason, there is always a reason. When people suddenly run into a rash of bad luck for no reason, there *is* a reason. It follows for them that when people do negative things, there are negative consequences. They buy into a set of principles that are as predictable to them as those of the so-called physical science principles. Those principles speak to a spiritual reality.

When we talk about spiritual things, we're talking about laws that determine reality, that work out of sight influencing reality, even though we aren't always able to know how these processes work. Afrikan psychology is one that incorporates those basic assumptions about the nature of life and about spirituality. What gets us into trouble is when we begin to confuse the spiritual with the religious. Religion is simply a set of exercises for cultivating spirituality. For example, Islam brings a set of exercises that cultivate a spiritual consciousness. It teaches us to deal with the larger spiritual reality. It puts it in certain terms, gives you certain descriptions of it, teaches you how to communicate with it, and encourages you to develop certain disciplines to build a bigger consciousness of it. Christianity encourages you to engage in certain kinds of rituals, liturgies, and other symbolic acts that cultivate a certain kind of consciousness. Rastafarians, in order to begin to develop a better sense of Jah, have certain kinds of exercises to cultivate their consciousness. All religions come with more or less effective tools to cultivate a certain kind of consciousness.

Very often, we spend a lot of time arguing about the greater validity of one as opposed to the other, when they all have the same basic objective. They become problematic when we begin to confuse the symbols, for instance, when we begin to believe this white figure who has been represented as Jesus is actually, literally God, that he and all other white people like him are in the privi-

leged position to be the chosen people of God because he *looks* like God. He's white, therefore, he's privileged and better than us. That's an example of religious symbols being used for political purposes that have nothing to do with spirituality. This actually prostitutes our spiritual vulnerability!

We are a people who are always willing to accept the invisible reality and many of the symbols that go along with it. When you begin to convince black people that Islam is legitimate only if it's done in Arabic, when one is dressed like an Arab, or practices only the culture of Arab people, then we're talking about a disorienting religious system. That's an instance where religion has been used for political purposes. It has a motive other than using it for greater spiritual consciousness. It seems to further alienate people from themselves. In other words, you can be as strong a Christian, as strong a Jew, as strong a Muslim, as strong a Buddhist, as strong a worshipper of Amen-Ra, or whatever the case may be, within the confines of your own cultural experience, without having to negate yourself in order to develop spiritual consciousness. We Afrikan Americans are already spiritual, and we have been particularly open to a variety of systems of enhancing that spirituality.

What Afrikan psychology suggests is that we don't need to separate psychology from religion or to separate the healing of our people's minds from the healing of our people's souls. It's all connected. It's all tied together.

How we eat has as much to do with how we think as it does with how we are able to grow spiritually. It has long been established by the ancient priests of the Nile Valley that how one eats, one's nutritional patterns, and the selective use of fasting and discipline are all rudimentary exercises in developing mental and spiritual discipline as well as proper nutrition. The holistic nature of health and healing is something we pioneered. *How to Eat to Live* by Elijah Muhammad refers to physical and spiritual life.[2] He wrote that you can't separate the fact that if you eat like a dog or a hog, you'll literally begin to *think* like one. It begins to contaminate you spiritually; if you become more selective in terms of your eating, you try to eat things with the least amount of contamination. It's interesting that so many things that are indigenous to our thinking, as a people, are now becoming such a part of modern Western thought. The Euro-Americans, the yuppies, are more into proper dieting, proper nutrition, and understanding the relationship of proper diet to proper thought and proper spiritual thinking that Afrikan people pioneered than we are. The very people who once condemned such beliefs as "witchcraft" and "voodoo" are now actively embracing them as the most innovative ideas in Western "discovery."

Afrikan psychology simply represents one of the many kinds of reconstruction of what and who we as Afrikan people are. It provides a direction for us into the twenty-first century. But to be effective in the twenty-first century, our students will still have to go through the Europeanized university training. That's called "paying dues." I tell students, "I empathize with you. I did the same thing. I've suffered through that process of mastering European psychology." But I also tell them that there are several things I find extremely valuable about acquiring that knowledge. Number one, we're living in a society that is still under the leadership of people who think Eurocentrically. Whether we like it or not, you can't get licensed as an Afrikan psychologist at this point in time. I hope we will be able to soon. I hope before the twenty-first century we will have legitimized our own institutions in such a way we can begin to say, "These are the ones who qualify as experts to work with black people, based on what they have been taught and understand." We're not there yet.

Clearly, there is no way to be a practitioner in our communities unless you're licensed by the current power structure. With that in mind, it's a necessary evil to go through the current process. Many athletes don't like the drudgery of doing a hundred push-ups or running up and down a hill in all kinds of weather, but they know that in order to play in Saturday's game, they've got to do it. So I say to students, "Look, you've got to do the push-ups. That's a necessary part of what you have to do to play in the game with its current rules. Once you've gotten into the game following those rules, you can then be equipped to engage in the process of deconstructing and reconstructing the rules." That's what we, as Afrikan psychologists, must do.

I know that I would not be able to get the ear of the Afrikan American students or scholars if I were not "Dr." Na'im Akbar. The fact that the University of Michigan legitimized me as a clinical psychologist helps my cause. By the way, they didn't know they were legitimizing me to do what I'm doing. They thought I was a good Freudian psychologist. They had no idea they'd unleashed a Frankenstein!

I say to students, "Look, go through the process. Endure. Do what they require you to do. It's pretty much a mechanical process. They don't place a lot of emphasis on creative thought, so just memorize, feed it back, and go through the process. It's not that difficult to master most of these programs. Frustration is what causes the greatest difficulty. Take hope in the fact that I and many others survived that process and came out with our consciousness intact. Despite going through that process, you can still commit your entire work life to doing something else."

What students must do is keep themselves connected to progressive Afrikan American thinkers. Become a member of the Association of Black Psychologists. Read the *Journal of Black Psychology*. Read the Association's

newsletter. Talk to those people who are talking about the kinds of things I'm talking about. Work actively, locally and nationally. Listen to and watch the audiotapes and videotapes, and get the books of people like Ivan Van Sertima, Wade Nobles, Asa Hilliard, and psychiatrist Richard King, people who are talking about a new concept of psychology and psychiatry. In those times when you feel most frustrated, pop in one of those tapes, or pick up one of those books. Read those articles again. They'll reinspire you, show you that the picture's bigger than what you get in school. Then go back, and memorize some more behavioral theory, or some more Maslow, understanding that that's simply the strategy for the time being.

I don't mind saying this publicly because so many people, so many of my graduate students—who are primarily European American students in the university where I work—are very disenchanted with the very sterile form of traditional psychology. They want to do more exciting things, but they know that in order to do that they have to get a degree. Even though it's more about them than it is about us, they see it only as a means to an end. Many of them have gone on to do some very exciting things. They've started their own institutes and counseling practices, doing very different things from the traditional things they were taught. I want them to know that they have colleagues and allies.

When I was a graduate student, there were no alternative voices. Kenneth Clark was the only black psychologist I'd ever heard of up until the time I got my Ph.D. But Kenneth Clark believes that integration is the best solution for black people. He's always argued that our ability to interact with white people is our greatest accomplishment. He believes that very firmly. He's never joined the Association of Black Psychologists. He has refused to accept awards from us. He has resigned from the boards of several organizations that wanted to set up Afrikan-centered organizations. He does not see anything that talks about the affirmation of Afrikan people as being worthwhile. He sees such things as very deviant and as "reverse racism."

But he was the only model I had, and he offered the possibility of what I could become in the field. Even though I am nothing like him, nor like those professors that I came into contact with, he showed me that it is possible to maneuver the system in a certain way. From there, I had to seek out other kinds of resources to inspire me. Fortunately, there is now the Association of Black Psychologists. It didn't exist when I was a graduate student. There are also hundreds of Afrikan-oriented black psychologists around the country who are publishing, lecturing, going to conferences where one can be exposed to their thinking. The possibility of finding real inspiration, real direction, and real guidance while going through the credentialing process is much more positive now than

it was then. So if I and others made it when we made it, others can certainly make it now.

I think we're going to have to rely upon people who will take the initiative to begin to build something new. Spike Lee and the kinds of things he's trying to do with film, even though he's young and has some unrefined concepts, bring entertainment but also social commentary. His work pricks people's consciousness and makes them think in a different way about what they're doing. With more of that beginning to happen, we're going to see the creation of a new set of criteria for what arts, telecommunications, and media are all about.

We're going to have to infiltrate, penetrate, and control the media because, increasingly, it's going to become the major source of information for most people in society: Afrikan Americans, European Americans, whatever. If we don't have control over some of those things ourselves, so that we can structure the information they send out, we're going to lose out. Our people will become more confused, more frustrated, more disoriented, and their identities will become even more messed up than they already are.

Clearly, that's not something I can do. The effort Bill Cosby made to establish a liaison with psychologist Alvin Poussaint, who is an expert on the black child, is a very noble and correct gesture, even though neither of them did what I would have done. But that alliance is a very brilliant model. What we need is for those in the limelight like Jesse Jackson, Spike Lee, Arsenio Hall, and Oprah Winfrey to form alliances with those of us who are trying to articulate Afrikan thinking from the perspectives of Afrikan psychology. Those people who have control over the media have an audience of such large numbers of our people that we could make a great impact if we began to talk to them about ways they might use that power to make a difference.

We all know they're being advised. Take Oprah Winfrey. Who's advising her? Who advised her to utilize her brand new production studio, the largest in the country owned by anybody black that I know of? The first thing to come out of it was "The Women of Brewster Place," which is a terribly scathing attack on black men, just a scathing attack, that creates another huge chasm between black men and black women. That program just fed right into that whole mentality that says that black women's worst enemy is black men. Nobody who really understands the minds of our people would have encouraged her to put that out there, unless they were committed to creating images that perpetuated the very thing that was shown in that drama.

The fact that Oprah Winfrey does not even know that the Association of Black Psychologists exists is something that's got to be corrected. Someone

should say to her, "Look, you need to talk to the Association. You need to talk to Wade Nobles. Or Na'im Akbar. Or Richard King. You need to talk to some of these people who are trying to redefine what psychology is really all about for black people." Yeah, I was on her show, but I couldn't even get to talk because I was overwhelmed by the Hispanics, the Jews, and other people who somehow were equating being Jewish, or being Hispanic, or being Asian, with being black. There was no appreciation for the uniqueness of who we are, but Oprah has access to this instrument that can provide an opportunity for our most creative thinkers to share their ideas with the world.

I'm saying the way we reach Mr. and Mrs. Afrikan America, all the hard-working, well-meaning black people, and the buppies who need some other answers, is to make use of the devices that are there, that are available if they could be properly used. The only way we can do that is by establishing liaisons. I wish Bill Cosby did know the Association of Black Psychologists existed, that there was somebody other than Poussaint. Though Poussaint brings one point of view, there's more that can be brought in. Somebody like Cosby or Spike Lee could make use of and expand what the Association is trying to do.

I'm using the example of psychologists, but there are many other groups of people who are doing very progressive things. There are musicians that I think have an intuitive grasp of the importance of music and rhythms as an instrument of change. Everything from music to the theater needs to be rethought. The more we talk with each other and transcend the disciplines that divide us, the more effective we could be in bringing about change.

Probably the most important thing we as individuals can do is to establish, as a part of our regular routine, on a regular basis, a hook-up with one of the many and expanding very fine Afrikan American bookstores we have. There are any number of them around the country, and they have come to serve a very important function in our communities. They serve as a kind of network for information for the conferences and other activities that are going on. They are meeting places for Afrikan people with a desire to learn and grow. The people who run them are almost like reference librarians. They can tell you what you need to read, who you need to listen to—everything from music to tapes of Malcolm X speeches and those of current scholars. They have books of various levels of readers, including children's books. They have really become, in many ways, the archivists for our communities. They serve a very valuable function.

That's one resource. Another is to take the initiative to make yourself familiar with the various study groups that are going on. Make the conferences of the various black associations part of your experience. Many of us in my field have done audiotapes and videotapes of our lectures. In fact, most of my work, sev-

enty to seventy-five of the lectures I have done over the last five or six years, is on videotape.[3] These are things you can continue to go back to, loan out, pass around. All of these are ways of networking to learn about the many things that are going on. If people don't take the initiative to avail themselves of some of this information, the only way they will get it will be accidentally.

Let us not forget the young people. My whole life is for them. On a very personal level, I'm the biological father of three children, twin boys and a young girl. They, for me, symbolize all of the other Afrikan children in the world. My whole life and my life's work and energies are about making a better world for them. Everything that I do, all the teaching I do, all of my efforts to try to reach Afrikan American people, the energy I put into trying to do what I do is because I know there are tens of thousands of them everywhere. Not only do I know they are the hope for us as Afrikan people, I know they are the very hope for the world.

I see Afrikan children generally as the fruits of an experiment that failed. They were supposed to have been killed, but they stand as a triumph of the fact that you can't kill Afrikan people. Everything whites could possibly find to use against us they used against us. I don't believe that dope, gang killings, drive-by shootings, black-on-black crime are accidental. I don't believe that there's an instrument of destruction that we cannot rise above.

My message to young people is this: Don't let anybody convince you this process called life is hopeless. The material you are made of can overcome any obstacle this world has to offer. You've got to believe in who you are. You've got to trust in who you are. Even though it's impossible for you to understand fully what this process is, at least trust that you can do as well or better than anybody else has done. Dream the biggest dreams you can dream. Plan to run the world. In the process of doing so, the power to do it will begin to come to you. What I and others of us in Afrikan psychology are trying to teach our young people is how to develop a vision that will bring Afrikan people back into world leadership.

[1] Jacques–Garvey, Amy (Ed.), *The Philosophy and Opinions of Marcus Garvey* (New York: Atheneum, 1992).

[2] Muhammad, Elijah, *How to Eat to Live* (Chicago: Muhammad's Mosque of Islam No. 2, 1967).

³ Dr. Akbar's books and tapes can be ordered from: Mind Productions, at P.O. Box 11221, Tallahassee Fl 32302.

LOUIS FARRAKHAN
MUSLIM MINISTER, LECTURER, TEACHER, MUSICIAN

Minister Farrakhan continues a deep tradition that goes back to Noble Drew Ali, the Honorable Marcus Garvey, the Honorable Elijah Muhammad, and El-Hajj Malik El-Shabazz (Malcolm X). In his efforts to rebuild the Nation of Islam, he has become the only man of Afrikan descent, neither entertainer nor star athlete, who can fill auditoriums and arenas around the country. Despite the several attacks launched against him by the media and politicians, his broad respect and popularity in the universal Afrikan community is based on his consistent message of self-reliance and resistance to racial oppression. He is also the architect of the historic Million Man March.

I was born in New York City, in a borough that is called the Bronx. I grew up in the city of Boston, Massachusetts. My mother, like many black women who find themselves pregnant, for one reason or another, did not wish to give birth to me due to circumstances surrounding her life at that time. She told me, on three different occasions, that she tried to abort me. She was not successful, so she went on and carried me to full term. Just before she passed away, as I sat with her, she held her stomach and praised God for what her womb had produced. Her child would make a significant difference in the lives of black people in America and throughout the world.

My message to all expectant mothers is this: for your sake, and for the sake of the future of our people, be considerate of what is in your womb. You do not know what you're carrying. If Mary, the mother of Jesus, because of the circumstances surrounding his birth, had committed the act of abortion, we never would have met the Messiah. It is important that we understand that the answer to all our prayers comes through the womb of women. So be careful with your womb. Your womb is the sacred laboratory of God Himself. He brings to this earth every savior, every redeemer, every scientist, every one who advances us in knowledge through the womb. Women, take care of yourselves and your womb.

When I think about my childhood, I would say that I was mischievous, and yet I was quiet and reflective. I was an athlete. I was a musician. I was none of that without my wonderful mother. She put the violin in my hands at five years old, and my brother, she gave him the piano to play. He was six- and-a-half. As a youngster, although I liked to do everything all other young people did and do, there was always a time when I would go off by myself to think and reflect on the beauty of life and the tragedy of black life in America.

As a young boy, my mother gave me *Crisis* magazine to read. I would read the writings of W. E. B. DuBois and others. She would bring in *The Afro-American* and the *Pittsburgh Courier,* which always carried news of the latest lynching or brutality of whites against black people. You could say I was nurtured on the pain and suffering of our people. As a very young child, I desired that God would give us somebody who would deliver us from our oppressor and our oppression.

My mother was from the Caribbean, from a tiny island in the eastern Caribbean called St. Kitts. My father, being from Jamaica, was a follower of Marcus Garvey. My mother always tried to teach us what she knew of our history and heritage, of something that would give us a sense of self and self-worth. My mother grew up in the Anglican Church. In Boston, Massachusetts, we were members of an Anglican Church called St. Cyprians. I used to sing in the choir. I carried the cross. I loved the church. It gave me a wonderful beginning. However, I was always struck, as I matured, with the variance or the hypocrisy in what was preached in Christianity, and what was being practiced by so-called Christians.

I was intrigued by the suffering of black people in the South. I told my mother at a very young age that when I grew up, I wanted to go South. I wanted to experience what my brothers and sisters in the South were experiencing. When I left high school and prep school, I went immediately to college in the South.

In my young years, my religious orientation was Christian, but there was something unfulfilling there. It was the apparent paradox and hypocrisy I found with Christians. There we were, black people, believing in Jesus. When I went South, there were white churches I could not go into. There were other churches I could attend, but I had to sit in the balcony.

Some friends of mine died in the Korean War, but in Washington, D.C., I could not go to a certain movie theater that did not admit black people. I wondered to myself as a youngster: What did our friends and our family fight and die for if we had no justice, no rights that white folk would respect? Yet, they all said they were Christians. I could not understand why the church would see these indignities and inhumanities being perpetrated against Christians, by Christians, and have nothing to say.

I began to look for a religion and a religious message that spoke to the hurt of our people, spoke to the need for justice. So in 1953, I believe it was, I heard about Malcolm X. I was playing in a nightclub in Boston. I came out of the club, and Malcolm was across the street, preaching. I remember this very handsome, tall, imposing man with a brown hat, brown suit, brown coat, brown gloves, and a reddish complexion.

Malcolm had a reputation of teaching hatred against white people.Like most Christians, I didn't want to be involved with anybody who had a message or a doctrine that preached hate. I shook his hand and quickly moved away from him.

In 1955, I was playing in a nightclub in Chicago. One of my friends, who was a Muslim, was in Chicago during the annual Muslim Savior's Day Convention. He asked me if I would come out and hear Elijah Muhammad, whom I had heard about but didn't necessarily believe in. I went, and I heard this man Elijah Muhammad. Although I didn't understand everything he said at that time, I heard enough to know this man was answering something in the depth of my being that cried out to see black people delivered. I became one of his followers that day.

I went back to New York, where I was living at the time. I joined the mosque in New York, under Malcolm. That began my work as a helper of the Honorable Elijah Muhammad in the process we call redemption, or the resurrection of the black man and woman of America and the world, from the mud of civilization to the pinnacle of civilization, which we once held before our fall.

That was at a time when, from my vantage point, Malcolm and I became very close. He was, to me, like the father I never had. He became my tutor, my mentor, my instructor in the principles of Islam, in the teachings of the Honorable Elijah Muhammad, and in the disciplined life of a Muslim. I not only admired Malcolm, I kind of think I adored him as the greater student of the Honorable Elijah Muhammad, who was, I would say, the master teacher. Since I was removed from Elijah Muahammad, Malcolm was my closest link to him. In my judgment, he was the best link to Elijah Muhammad. I stuck to Malcolm like superglue.

I must make a point here about the split between Malcolm and Elijah Muhammad. That split was one of the most tragic instances in the life of the Nation of Islam, the life of Malcolm, his family, those who loved him, my life, my family, and those who loved the Honorable Elijah Muhammad. The blood of Malcolm stains the unity or the potential unity of all of us today. That stain of Malcolm's blood cannot be erased if we walk away from this tragic period in our lives. We have to open it up, as painful as that may be. We have to deal with it—unemotionally, if possible— and come out of it hoping we can heal the wounds. The gaping wounds that are in the hearts of the children of Malcolm, the children of Elijah Muhammad, the children of Louis Farrakhan, the children of Martin Luther King, Jr., the children of Medgar Evers. The children cannot keep bearing the hatreds of the parents. The children have to go on to build a united people.

If we use Malcolm's own words, according to what he said in a press conference announcing his break from the Nation, Malcolm felt he could serve the Honorable Elijah Muhammad better from outside of the Nation, than from within the Nation. He felt there was great envy and enmity among some of the ministers, high-ranking laborers, and officials of the Nation against him.

Those kinds of internal pressures, he felt, made it difficult for him to do for the Honorable Elijah Muhammad and for black people what he wanted to do. So the Honorable Elijah Muhammad, when Malcolm made the statement about "the chickens coming home to roost," did not silence him for making the statement because it was a statement of truth. He silenced Malcolm because he had given all of us strict orders to have nothing to say with respect to the death of John Kennedy. Malcolm broke that order in the ballroom, in the Manhattan Center in New York, around the fifth of December 1963. John Kennedy's body was not yet cold. Malcolm's statement was made at a time when the country was in mourning and grief over the loss of one of the most charismatic presidents in recent history, but also one of the most deceitful in his relationship with black people. Nevertheless, the Honorable Elijah Muhammad silenced Malcolm. You may not believe this, but it is true: he did it as much for Malcolm as he did it for the Nation. If Malcolm had continued to speak during that time, he might have been assassinated then. By silencing Malcolm for ninety days, this gave the country a chance to get its bearing.

During that time, Malcolm began to tell us that the Honorable Elijah Muhammad had wives. He didn't say "concubines." He didn't say "women." He said, the Honorable Elijah Muhammad had *wives*. I was told this by Malcolm personally. When he said this to some of the ministers, many of us were shocked. We had not heard this before. We had not known this before.

Malcolm didn't know what effect his words would have on me. He drove me to the airport that night. He said to me, "Brother, don't tell anyone what I told you tonight." I said, "No, brother, I'm not going to tell anyone but the Honorable Elijah Muhammad."

The next morning, about five a.m., Malcolm called me. He said, "Brother Louis, before you write the Messenger to tell him what I told you, I wish that you would give me a chance to write him and explain." I said to Malcolm, "Well, brother, in the condition that my head is in, it's going to take me some time to write the letter. If you can get your letter to him in the meantime, fine. I do not wish to be put in the middle of two powerful men, both of whom I love." He said, "Well, there's only one powerful man, and that's the Honorable Elijah Muhammad." I said, "I'm well aware of that."

That morning, after the conversation with Malcolm, I took up my holy Qur'an, and I began to study and read. As I read the Qur'an, I opened it direct-

LOUIS FARRAKHAN

ly to the thirty-third sura, or chapter, which deals with the wives of Prophet Muhammad of Arabia. God had permitted the Prophet to have as many as nine wives. Scholars of Christianity, some theologians of the West, and some of the Orientalists have condemned Prophet Muhammad for this and gone so far as to call him a voluptuary, simply because God permitted him to have wives. One of his wives, by the name of Aisha, was, I think, married to him when she was only fourteen years of age. The history writings say that he did not have conjugal relations with her at that time, but he took her as a wife.

Now the hypocrites who claim to love God and his prophets say that Abraham is the father of the righteous. He is known in the Bible and the Qur'an as the "father of the righteous," one who was so close to God that he was admitted into God's bosom, given an insight into the secrets, mind, and spirit of God. So loved was Abraham, God made a covenant with the seed of Abraham that is binding today.

Abraham had a wife. His wife was barren. His wife had a handmaiden whose name was Hagar. Abraham went into Hagar and got his first son. He's buried in the East today with Sarah on one side, Hagar on the other. No scholar of religion will condemn Abraham as being a wicked man. They don't condemn Noah, Lot or David or Solomon. They all had several wives. It is so hypocritical for any man to know anything of the prophetic community, and then turn around and condemn his teacher simply because he learned that his teacher had several wives.

But that is not the reason Malcolm left the Nation, nor did he leave the Nation because someone was interfering with money. The money we gave to the Honorable Elijah Muhammad, you could see where your dollars went. He was a man who built forty-six universities of Islam in America and thousands of acres of farms in Alabama, Georgia, Honduras, and Michigan. He built houses for his followers, supermarkets, canning factories, airplanes, airport facilities. You name it, Elijah Muhammad built it. We, the Muslims, became the largest importers of frozen fish in our first year of operation. The money we gave to Elijah Muhammad was used to put us in business. So that doesn't hold water.

Malcolm was hurt because of the envy and jealousy of many of the ministers and laborers. He was hurt because he worked hard for the cause of Islam, and he would pick up *Muhammad Speaks*, our own newspaper, and see that it did not mention Malcolm's exploits in the path of Islam. Malcolm was hurt because in his own mind, he thought his teacher had become envious of him because he, Malcolm, was getting the press, the popularity.

How do I know what was in Malcolm's mind, what he was suffering? Malcolm would come and sit and tell me of his pain. On many occasions, he would talk about just stopping preaching altogether because the ministers were envious of him. This envy grew to hatred. He did not feel he could continue to work in that environment.

Let me close this question by saying this: The government of the United States, under the counterintelligence program of J. Edgar Hoover, admitted in their documents, which we have in our possession, thanks to the Freedom of Information Act, that they worked night and day to split Malcolm from his teacher. They worked night and day to create the schism and take advantage of it. They inserted their agents among Malcolm's followers and among the Honorable Elijah Muhammad's followers to exacerbate the tensions produced in the split.

Then Malcolm was assassinated. Unfortunately, two innocent Muslims were brought to court and sent to prison for twenty-six years of their lives so that the government could give the lie to the American people that it was, in fact, the Muslims who killed Malcolm X. The daily newspapers in New York and around the country painted the Honorable Elijah Muhammad in the role of ordering Malcolm's assassination. They figured they could take out two birds that they hated with one stone.

I conclude this by saying that I walked in Malcolm's shoes. I was the one who lived in Malcolm's house, or the house that Malcolm lived in, after he left the Nation. I became the minister of the mosque Malcolm headed, Mosque Number 7, after it was burned to the ground. I became the national representative of the Honorable Elijah Muhammad, holding the position Malcolm once held.

Because I was favored by my teacher, the press touted my name. The public began to know of Louis Farrakhan. That engendered hatred and envy among some of the laborers and ministers of the Honorable Elijah Muhammad, even as it did when Malcolm was alive among us. I, too, began to think, Is it possible the teacher could be jealous? I felt much of this envy, as Malcolm felt, was coming from the teacher himself.

One day, I sat with the Honorable Elijah Muhammad and his staff. I was ready to lash out at everybody at the table over the perceived envy that existed among us. I wanted him to answer, because I wanted to know if he was behind it. When I talked about jealousy and envy, the Honorable Elijah Muhammad hit the table. He said, "Brother, seek refuge in Allah from the envier when he envies." He got up and walked out of the room.

A few minutes later, he came back and said these words. They stick with me today. He said, "Brother, if you're going to put a piece of board in the corner of the building to uphold the weight of the building, you've got to put a lot of stress on it. If it breaks under the stress, then you know it's not the board you were looking for. You throw it away. You get yourself another board." It was a long time before I understood the depth of that.

The Honorable Elijah Muhammad knew, like Moses, that he would have to go away, that he would have to leave somebody in his place who could weather the storm of hatred, envy, and jealousy among his own people. That person would have to weather the storm of machinations and of evil plotting and planning by the government of the United States. The Honorable Elijah Muhammad could not put somebody in his seat who was not strong enough to weather that kind of storm. As a master martial arts teacher will put pain on the student, will take the student to the threshold of pain and continue to increase that threshold, because the student is going to have to endure excruciating pain in actual combat.

The Honorable Elijah Muhammad brought Malcolm to the brink of the threshold of his pain. He wasn't trying to hurt Malcolm. He was trying to prepare Malcolm, should Malcolm become the board the Honorable Elijah Muhammad was going to have to use as the cornerstone of the Nation.

But Malcolm became vindictive against his teacher, against his benefactor who took him from prison and taught him what he knew, made him what he was. Even if he thought this were true of his teacher, he could have left his teacher alone and continued on his path.

The Honorable Elijah Muhammad was the best thing that ever happened to black people, and he's the same today. How do I know it? Because as he produced Malcolm for black people, he also produced me.

The government of America, the FBI are following me night and day, listening to my telephone, trying to entrap weak Muslims who may do the bidding of the devil. Yet I, Louis Farrakhan, by God's grace, am no weakling. My father made me strong enough to withstand envy, jealousy, enmity, the hatred of my own people, and the hatred of the American government. I will be the winner who will bear witness that there is no God but Allah, and that the Honorable Elijah Muhammad was and is a righteous teacher who had no envy, no malice for or jealousy of his students. He just wanted to make us able to withstand the heat of the fiery furnace.

There have been allegations that I created the environment for the assassination of Malcolm. That's sick! How could I, a man of limited influence, create the environment in which Malcolm was killed? This was never said until I began becoming popular. White folk had to develop a means, a method of putting that seed out among black people, hoping that those lovers of Malcolm would become haters of Farrakhan and, to this day, seek my death.

It is true, we in the Nation of Islam did not like the fact that Malcolm split from the Honorable Elijah Muhammad. We did not like the fact that he went on radio and television talking about his teacher in a negative manner. No, we didn't like that. I, as a student of Malcolm's and of the Honorable Elijah Muhammad,

was put in the position of a child watching parents divorce. I had to choose between Malcolm or the Honorable Elijah Muhammad. I chose wisely. I chose the teacher.

I stood by my teacher then, I stand by my teacher now. My teacher was right then, my teacher is right now. His message was not a message for yesterday, it is a message for today because I'm speaking that same message. I'm listened to today by black people all over the world. I, in my person, am the vindicator of the Honorable Elijah Muhammad from all the false charges the enemies have laid against him and now wish to lay at my door.

No, I didn't create the atmosphere. I was one of the participants in an atmosphere created by the devil, the white man who throws the stone and hides his dirty hand. The white man, the U. S. government, is behind the assassinations of Malcolm X and Martin Luther King, Jr., the false charges against Marcus Garvey, the murder of Noble Drew Ali, the scourging of Paul Robeson, the exiling of W. E. B. DuBois. This is not black people's doing, this is the enemy's doing. He throws the stone and hides his hand.

Today, we see this devil for what he really is. We will uncover him so that our people will make no mistake. We are not the enemy. The enemy is sitting in Washington, D.C., planning our death, using one of us against the other.

When the Honorable Elijah Muhammad died, everybody thought that was the end, the Nation didn't just lay down and die with him. The Nation of Islam, under Elijah Muhammad, was turned from the direction the Honorable Elijah Muhammad directed us toward. Many of the followers of Elijah Muhammad, who loved him, just went out of the Nation and back into the streets.

Louis Farrakhan tried to stand with Imam Waarith Deem Muhammad.[1] When I saw the Imam was not going in the direction of his father and was attacking his father, I decided I had to leave the World Community of Islam, as the Nation of Islam was called at that time. I would not fight the son of my father, so I just went out and became quiet.

In 1977, I decided I could not allow the name of Elijah Muhammad to be written out of history when I knew he meant so much to me and to hundreds and thousands, even millions, of our people. I knew his message was relevant for black people all over the earth. I decided to stand up and rebuild the work of the Honorable Elijah Muhammad. I must say that God, in His infinite mercy, has granted us success in that effort and in inspiring a new growth, a new movement among the total black community.

This is what has me in trouble with the government today. It is because I today have a growing influence over a larger segment of black people in this

country than even Marcus Garvey held. That makes me a dangerous man to them, because they do not control me.

One thing people do not know, and black men should be aware of: My wife is my rock. She lets me do the talking. I think that's as it should be. My wife is not a public figure, she's a quiet strength behind me. She is the kind of woman who helped to make me into the man I'm becoming under the teaching and guidance of the Honorable Elijah Muhammad.

I met my wife when she was eight years old, I was eleven. I liked her then, but I didn't know how strong this like was going to become. I kept coming back and forth to check on her. When she was fourteen and I was seventeen, that like became real serious. By the time she was seventeen and I was twenty, we were married. We've been married for thirty-plus years. We have known each other since she was eight and I was eleven. That may have been 150 years ago!

I want to clarify a point I made earlier about the Messenger and his wives. There may be some brothers who misinterpret that and think they can go out and have wives too. They can't say that of me. I didn't tell them they could. No, what is for the Messenger is for the Messenger. I don't think it is wise for any black man to just jump up and run out, because the Qur'an gives the male that privilege, to have up to four wives.

Women represent responsibility. If a man does not have a job or even an inclination to create one for himself, what does he need a woman for? Before a man goes out thinking about getting women, that man should think first about becoming a man. He should think about what a responsibility it is to be in a relationship with a woman, about the issues that might come forth from that relationship.

The Qur'an does not just tell us to run out and have wives. Polygamy is a very serious injunction that was given in the Qur'an to correct a social condition. What was that social condition? In the time of the Prophet, through wars, the ranks of males had been decimated to the point where the females were in preponderance over the male. In order to ensure that prostitution, or lesbianism, or adultery would not hold sway in the society, God gave the Prophet and the Muslim followers permission to take from one to four wives. The Qur'an warned those men who took wives to do justice by them. It says, "And since you cannot, one is better for you, if you but understood."

The Honorable Elijah Muhammad, to me, was a marvelous teacher. He set up a class for women, and my wife was a member of that class. He set up a class for men, and I was a member of that class. As a man, he taught us that our duty was the maintenance of our wives. We were to look after them, not only economically, but spiritually and emotionally. It is difficult, but with greater knowl-

edge, you have the tool you need to make your marriage work in a period of time when there is great stress on our marriages.

The stress is produced mainly because we lack the knowledge of ourselves and our natural roles. America does not permit the black male to be the provider for himself and his family. The black female is ofttimes more educated than the black male. She's often more aggressive and displays a greater intelligence, a greater will even, to survive. When she finds her mate in a black man who may not have an education equal to hers or who lacks even the will to make it, then there's a strain on that relationship.

Sex cannot hold marriage together. Marriage is the union of two minds and two spirits that struggle to become one. My wife was well taught in that women's class. As I was coming into my manhood, I didn't always act with wisdom or intelligence. My wife knew how to handle me in the days of my ignorance. She did not strike at me with her tongue, like a two-edged sword, which she could have done to cut up my little growing manhood.

Most of our women study us. They know all of our weaknesses as well as our strengths. When they get angry with us, they cannot fight us with their fists, so they destroy us with their tongues. We run out of the house like a dog with our tail between our legs, go to the pool room, to the barroom, and join the rest of the men in talking down on our women. Our women get together with their girlfriends and talk about how the black man ain't nothing. We all end up the victims of an enemy we don't even see. The stench of the enemy's urine, like that of a skunk, is in our homes, in our hearts, and in our relationships.

I sincerely believe that a careful study must be made of the teachings of the Honorable Elijah Muhammad. Those teachings remove the stain of slavery and the stench of all the inferior feelings we as men have because we are frightened of our wives and their growing assertion of their own intelligence and God-given talents. We've got to work at this. There's not any easy solution.

Because my wife and I have been together for almost forty years, we've had our trials and tribulations. Yet, she loves me with a greater passion today than she loved me when I was a young man. I love her with a kind of love I don't think any other woman could take away. She helped to make me what I am.

I would hope that all of you reading this would go home to your wife, or to your husband, and realize that your husband has the potential to become the man of your dreams and the man you hoped for. Likewise, your wife, brother, has the same potential to become the woman of your dreams and your hopes. It takes knowledge to extract from the woman what God has put within her. It takes skill, sister, to extract from the man what God has put within him for both of us to be happy with each other. But there is an enemy out there who is trying to keep the black man and black woman apart and who is trying to destroy those who work to keep them together.

We need to look at the beloved Martin Luther King, Jr. It's easy to say today that we love Dr. King. There's a holiday for him, but I wonder how many Americans, particularly black people in America, know what the government did to Martin Luther King, Jr., while he and John Kennedy were sitting together? Bobby Kennedy was bugging Martin Luther King's home, his office, everywhere he went. They listened in on his most intimate conversations. They sent letters out to members of the press and planted stories against him. Then sent a letter to the Pope not to meet with him. This is the FBI, now. The FBI did everything they could to stop Dr. King from getting the Nobel Peace Prize. Ultimately, I believe, the FBI pulled the police—the black policemen—from around Martin Luther King in Memphis, Tennessee. There were no policemen around Malcolm X in the Audubon Ballroom the day Malcolm was assassinated.

The same government is doing the same thing to Louis Farrakhan. First, they're tapping all my phones. I believe our home is bugged. Everywhere I go, they follow or precede me. They listen. They are busy sifting all of the Muslim communities for those who have fallen victim to the law of man and the law of God. They're trying to get Muslims who have run afoul of the law to say Farrakhan inspired them to criminal activity. The RICO Act is what they are trying to employ to say we are a criminal organization, so they can justify taking away all of the property that poor Muslims, with their nickels, dimes, dollars, and blood money, have sacrificed to help us build.

They are, right now, looking among the ministers of the Honorable Elijah Muhammad who are with me. People who have desires that may be contrary to the will of God, at this time, are looking to see if they can create a countermovement inside the mosque. They want to kill me, but they can't be seen doing it themselves. They want to inspire one of my own to do it for them. If they cannot do that, their aim is to discredit me with propaganda, to spread it far and wide through the media, as they did in 1984, 1985, and 1986. They are working night and day. The CIA is working on this overseas. When I left this country recently, they had plotted to have me killed while I was on the African continent, but Allah did not permit it. He will not permit them to do that small-time stuff with me.

I am not in America of myself. I am not some little negro, nigger, or colored boy who rolled up yesterday to speak strong words on my own. If I'm not backed by the God of Heaven, then I'm through in America. But if I am backed by the God of Heaven, and I am, then the government of America had better be careful

how they handle me. I could be the trigger that unleashes God's power against America and throughout the world.

If they are wise, as they should be, then they would do well to be instructed, like Pharaoh was instructed, when one of his own senators rose up and told Pharaoh not to slay Moses. If Moses was of God, then a chastisement would surely follow, he said. If he was of himself, he would fall of his own weight. That senator prevailed on Pharaoh to leave Moses alone, but Pharaoh went crazy and said: "They're just a little gang. Let's move in on them."

That's what's going on today. They're looking at the Nation of Islam as just a little gang. It's not a little gang. It is righteous people who want to see justice come to black people. We are backed by a powerful God, who is the controller of the forces of the heavens and the earth. If you doubt it, America, lay your hands on Farrakhan and see what God will do for you.

Let me end this by speaking to the young people. They should know that they are not a "lost generation." They are the best generation we have produced. They seem strange because they were made for this hour. They are unlike any generation before them because they have a work to do that is unlike any work done by any generation before them. They are, in fact, the liberators of our people at last. They are the ones who our great-grandfathers and grandmothers prayed would come and deliver our people. From our own loins and from our own wombs have come the answer to our prayer. We just don't recognize the answer.

I'm saying to the students, to the young: be strong. Get to know who you are and what your purpose is in this world. Do not allow your enemy, my enemy, our enemy, to manipulate your frustration. The Bloods will go against the Crips, the Crips will go against the Bloods—when you both are blood of each other's blood, flesh of each other's flesh, bone of each other's bone. It cannot be that if I wear blue, and you wear red, one of us is wearing the wrong color. We were born black in a world set up to promote white supremacy. We are all born in this world with the wrong color, from their vantage point. So why should we not unite as one brotherhood, as one family, and stand against the oppressor and the oppression who we may go free at last?

It is in the hands of our youth, rightly guided by intelligent elders, that together we will make a difference.

Thank you for allowing me the chance to express myself, forthrightly and with passion, on these critical subjects that affect our unity. May God bless each and every one of you—black, brown, yellow, and white—that we may understand what we are facing and take concrete steps to make a new reality.

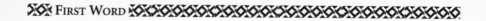

XXXXXX

[1] Imam Waarith Deem Muhammad, the son of the Honorable Elijah Muhammad, sought, after his father's death (in 1975) to move the Nation of Islam in the direction of orthodox Islam. He changed the organization's name to the World Community of Islam.

Barbara A. Sizemore
Educator, Researcher, Administrator, Author

Barbara A. Sizemore is one of the most outstanding educators in the country. She is a strong advocate for the inclusion of universal Afrikan history and culture in the public school curriculum. Her research, identifying schools dominated by American Afrikan students who have succeeded in equaling and/or surpassing schools American European students, has exposed the sharp discrepancies in the educational systems that serve both groups. She has also demonstrated how the development and implementation of sound educational techniques can overcome the harsh social, family, and economic conditions many American Afrikan students face.

I guess you could call my area of specialization educational administration. I'm concerned about the education of Afrikan Americans, and that's the field in which I do my research. The present debate that's going on in education is over the Eurocentric model that is the basis of the curriculum provided in our nation's public and private schools. The assumption is that the foundation of all knowledge was developed by the Greeks and passed down to other Europeans by Europeans, thus forming what is called "the body of knowledge." I call it "the Best-of-the-West Curriculum."

The assumption has been made by people using the work of neoconservative educational theorists like E. D. Hirsch and Allan Bloom that traditional European curriculum is the curriculum we should teach. They say that it represents the very best that we know of human knowledge. This, of course, is contradicted by those who understand that the body of knowledge on which Greek knowledge rested was Egyptian in origin and Afrikan-based. The absence of acknowledgment of this Afrikan-based body of knowledge in the school curriculum leads Afrikan children and children of Afrikan descent to believe that their Afrikan heritage does not exist, that Afrikans contributed nothing to the world, and that Afrikans are inferior.

This is only one of the problems our children face in education. There are several. First, the public schools are the product of a democracy, right? And democracy is based in this society on majority rule, right? So, if the majority of American people are of European origin, this means that the educational product is going to be shaped in their interest and their image of the world. That's one problem. The second problem is that the schools are responsible for teaching children their basic skills—how to read, how to write, how to understand mathematics. That's what we expect the schools to do, but the schools are not doing that. They are not doing that, because the people in them and who run them believe that children of color cannot be taught, that they have a cultural deficit, and that because they are not European they are unintelligent. Like eugenicists William Shockley and Arthur Jensen believe, and like Richard Herrnstein and Charles Murray claim in *The Bell Curve*,[1] black children have an intelligence deficit, so they're not too smart to begin with or their parents and their home conditions militate against their benefiting from education. These authors get this criticism off their backs and dump it on the very children who come to school to be relieved of this condition. It's a circular argument. The problem is that Afrikan American people themselves have come to believe that these arguments are true. In many public meetings, I find myself presenting my research, which contradicts these assumptions, and it is Afrikan American people who will jump up and say, "It's the parents' fault. It's the children's fault. These parents are thus-and-so, and these children are whatever." They themselves are relieving the people in the school of any responsibility or obligation to do what they are being paid to do.

These are the kinds of problems I find. I think these problems exist because most Afrikan Americans do not know that high-achieving predominantly Afrikan American schools exist. They are so overwhelmed with the media reports that simply and frequently say, "Here are these bad schools." Then hear about someone like Joe Clark doing his thing in this bad school, walking around with a bat and a bullhorn, yelling at kids and beating them up, or whatever.[2] They tell you his efforts resulted in all of these positive things, but they do not present you with the evidence of it. People believe these distortions and say, "Well, you really can't do much with these kids because they come from these bad environments, and the parents are not interested."

Afrikan Americans need to believe they can do certain things. Let me give you an example of what I'm talking about. I have a list of schools that are predominantly Afrikan American public schools that service children who live in public housing. These children live under adverse conditions of poverty and single female-headed homes, in high-crime areas, but they are scoring at or above the national norm in mathematics. However, the media suppresses information about these schools. I cannot get *Ebony* magazine to talk about them. I cannot get "Sixty Minutes" to talk about them. I cannot get "The Today Show" to talk about these schools. I find it immensely interesting.

Why are the media hiding this evidence? If someone were killed at one of these schools, they'd be on TV in a minute. If the children were running around selling dope in the school and a principal came in with a bat and a bullhorn, they'd be on TV. But here you have schools where Afrikan American children are living under the most abject conditions of poverty, under conditions that are hostile to normal physical and intellectual development, and they are exceeding the white norm, and no one takes notice. What else can you say but that it's a conspiracy to brainwash Afrikan American people into believing their children are really dumb and really can't learn. Or, if they are not dumb, then they are too oppressed by the conditions of poverty, crime, or whatever indices you to want to use as indicators of the deterioration of the quality of life to say that they just cannot be taught by anybody, no matter how well-meaning they are. That is absolutely incorrect.

Ebony did publish some information about high-achieving Afrikan American schools, but for political reasons. The schools they selected to focus on were run by people who were politically important or friends of people who were politically important. They were not the highest-achieving schools. The schools I have documented in my research were not included. I cannot believe there is an Afrikan American public school that has done better than the Robert L. Vann School in Pittsburgh, Pennsylvania. That school is ninety-eight percent Afrikan American, eighty percent of its students come from single female-headed homes, eighty-one percent of them get free and reduced lunch. It is located in the highest crime area in the city of Pittsburgh. Yet, ninety-one percent of the children at the Vann School scored at or above the national norm in mathematics—fifty-five percent scored in the top quarter! In 1989, it was the highest-achieving elementary school in mathematics in the city of Pittsburgh! Not the highest-achieving Afrikan American school, mind you—the highest-achieving public elementary school in Pittsburgh!

The first thing I noticed about these schools is that the principals are willing to take risks. Most of these principals have just given up on being promoted in the school system, which is kind of like class suicide. They have done this because they realized they had to make some choices about the routines that are established in their schools, which are usually opposed to the regular routines of the system. Let me give you an example of what I mean. One of the routines that was typical of the Pittsburgh public schools was this: when a teacher was evaluated as unsatisfactory, that teacher had what was called the right of transfer. That meant the school system's bureau of personnel had the responsibility to place the teacher in another school. They *had* to find her another place. What they did, however, was dump these teachers on the predominantly Afrikan American schools. Now, the way you got promoted from a principalship to something higher, in the Pittsburgh system or elsewhere, was by going along

with this routine and making life as easy as possible for the personnel people. They, of course, would then say, "Oh, he or she is a good team player." When that principal's name came up for promotion, they would say, "Oh, promote Mr. or Mrs. So-and-So. He or she did this and that" or otherwise went along with the system.

What the principals of these high-achieving Afrikan American schools said was, "No, I'm not taking that person who was transferred. I don't want him or her. Send them back." This created a problem for personnel. They had to find someone else to take these unsatisfactory teachers. But the principals of the white schools would not take them because they certainly didn't want the duds. The principals of the Afrikan American schools then become bad persons because they wouldn't cooperate with this. They reject those kinds of routines.

I sat in the office of one of the principals of one of these high-achieving schools and watched as a person came in to teach at the school. The principal said to the teacher, "Well, are you a reading teacher?" The person responded, "No, I'm a gym teacher." The principal said, "I didn't send for a gym teacher." The person said, "Well, they sent me here." This principal picked up the phone, called personnel and said, "I'm sending this person back. Don't send me any person unless he/she is a reading teacher."

Another example involves choosing materials for children. One of the things going on in schools is the press for whole-language instruction. Whole-language instruction de-emphasizes decoding and phonics. It says you should teach language arts in another way rather than through direct instruction. Children who speak Spanish or another language and children who speak dialects like Black English, often cannot decode the language. Some Standard English sounds are not in their experiential baggage. For instance, Afrikan American children who speak Black English have too many short-vowel sounds in their home language repertoire to speak Standard English correctly. Therefore, what you have to do for these children is to teach them the sounds of Standard English and tell them that these are the sounds they have to use in school. Spanish-speaking children also have a limited or narrow repertoire of sounds. If you want them to make a certain sound, you have to teach it to them if it's not in their experiential repertoire. They can't give it to you. They simply don't have it. Yet, many educators are adopting whole-language instruction just on the basis of the philosophy and the opinion of researchers, who haven't really studied its application to the needs of these students.

In high-achieving Afrikan American schools, the needs of the children determine what is taught, not some philosophy or bias based on a doctoral dissertation. Teachers and administrators in these schools ask: What do these chil-

BARBARA A. SIZEMORE

dren really need to know in order to master certain skills? Probably the most powerful routine I have identified in these schools is their monitoring routines. In other words, they have a strong administrator who monitors the progress of children and the performance of their teachers to see that children are learning what they should learn according to the schedule that has been identified for them to learn it. Each child in these schools is monitored to see that they adhere to certain pacing routine, placement routine, and instructional routine.

A pacing routine is necessary for those children who come into the school and fall behind. It says, look, this kid is going into second grade reading at a first-grade level. When he comes out of second grade, I want him to go into third grade reading at the third-grade level. That means the kid has to do double-time. He has to learn twice as much in this year as he would if he were progressing normally. He has to have a routine that says he must finish this by a certain time. The teacher must identity activities to accelerate the instruction of the child until he catches up.

Forty-seven percent of the children at the Vann School turn over every year. That means forty-seven percent of the kids are new every September. In spite of that, this school is producing this kind of scholarship among these children. The point I am trying to make is that we know how to do this, how to produce Afrikan American students who can excel, but we're not doing it because we don't *want* to do it.

Afrikan American people are not making the people in the public schools responsible because they don't believe the kids can do it. Any kind of information that contradicts this belief is suppressed. Why is that? There are many reasons. People object to a strong administrative leader, especially teachers' unions. Teachers' unions, some administrators, and other people in academe say that the schools need to create a collegial atmosphere in which teachers make all of the decisions. That may be true and it may be the ideal experience, but the fact is that right now many teachers do not believe Afrikan American kids can learn. If you put teachers like that in charge of accelerating the growth of children whom they do not believe can learn, you are going to be in deep trouble. You need to find teachers who believe the students can learn. You have to put someone who believes this in charge of teachers to make sure that they behave in ways that remove this negative belief. In other words, someone who says that if these children are going to learn so-and-so by such-and-such a date, then this is what you have to do. Then the kids learn it.

This changes the behaviors of teachers, but it may not change their attitudes. Some people argue that you have to change attitudes before you change behaviors. What these principals are saying is that they can't wait for that. The kids are in school now. They want to change teachers' behaviors right now, so they can accomplish their objective for these children. Changing attitudes can follow, if it follows at all.

How do they do that? They evaluate teachers' performances every year. In some cities and states, teachers are only evaluated every five years. That is absolutely ridiculous! Do you know how much a kid's life could be ruined in five years? How many kids? If there are on average thirty kids in a classroom, five times thirty years equals 150 kids who could be messed over before a teacher gets evaluated. That is insane!

In high-achieving Afrikan American schools, teachers are evaluated every single year. The prime criteria is the teacher's performance in achieving the objective, which is high student achievement. That's the basis of it. At these high-achieving schools, if you can't cut the mustard, you simply cannot stay. As Ron Edmonds once said, "We know everything we need to know to teach our children. The fact that we are not doing it means we don't want to do it."[3] It's a political problem.

Besides that, some teachers and principals simply do not care. Someone has to evaluate teachers and administrators. They have to be responsible for what they do in schools. The outcome of an organization or an institution is the result of what people do in it. Who is in the school?: principals, teachers, and children. Parents aren't in the school, but teachers, principals, and children are, along with teachers' aides and janitors and secretaries. The unit we have to examine is the school.

Within the school, the instructional unit—that is, what goes on in the classrooms—is the most powerful element. Anyone who teaches a group of children—anyone, a music teacher, a singing teacher, any kind of teacher who teaches a group—understands one thing: when you teach a group of people anything, they string out in a line. Somebody learns it first, somebody else learns it second, third, fourth—until the last person learns it. People don't learn things at the same time. They learn differently and at different times.

What do you do about those who take a long time to learn? You have to divide them into groups so you can teach them and they can catch up. Everybody understands this. Look, if you never teach the child who is taking a long time to learn, he or she never catches up. They're lost. If he or she catches up with the class, everything's cool. It's not the grouping or the track that's the problem, it's what we do with the groups or tracks that is important.

If I had my way in developing a school, I would first look for the schools that are performing well for Afrikan American children. They are in every city. You don't know where they are because nobody wants you to know. I would then take that school and use that school as a model. I would attach other schools to it, and take the principal of that school and those teachers who know how to do this right, and let them teach other schools. I would keep multiplying that model until I got all the schools up to the place where I wanted them to be in terms of competence and skills. That's one thing I would do.

The second thing I would do would be to integrate the curriculum and make it multicultural so all children understood that the United States of America is a culturally diverse nation, that there are many people in it, and that these people come from every place. I would let my curriculum of music, art, drama, literature, mathematics, and science reflect all these groups of people and let these subjects reflect the struggle all of these people as equal partners in this country.

What is basic to all of this? Teaching children how to read. Many don't know how. Children *have* to learn how to read, write, and do mathematics. I don't care if the teacher is Afrocentric or Eurocentric, there's one thing they must do and that is to teach children how to read, write, and understand mathematics. There are no excuses for not doing that. Absolutely no excuses. A child should be reading by the time he or she leaves first grade. It shouldn't take 180 days to teach anybody anything, to be truthful. I mean, you could teach a dog quicker than that.

The school system has to teach those who do not know how to teach reading. Then, once those teachers know how to teach reading, someone has to monitor their routines. Are too many children sitting in the back of the room? Are too many children being ignored? You must look at all the different instructional routines that go on in a classroom in order to be sure things are functioning well for all children.

Knowing how to read and write and do math helps build self-esteem in children. The thing that generates self-esteem more than anything else, of course, is competence. What can you say to a child who is in first grade but who can do third-grade math? Hey, that child *knows* he's great. There is no substitute for competence in building self-esteem, absolutely none. Most of our children come to school with high self-esteem. They are competent in coping with their lives before they get to school. It's only when they come to school, with its often-hostile environment, immense limitations, and restrictions imposed on their ability to cope, that they acquire low self-esteem. I think it's only in school. Once they get out of school, they don't seem to have a self-esteem problem. But once a child is competent in school, the self-esteem problem vanishes. A problem arises when a teacher focuses on self-esteem and not on learning.

Repetition is very important if a child has low self-esteem. If you keep doing something over and over, what does the child think? He or she thinks,

"This teacher really thinks I can read." If you give up on the child and say, "Well, he or she has low self-esteem. I can't do anything with him." If you ignore him or her, what's going to happen? If I find a child who believes that he can't learn how to read, I intensify my belief and keep telling him, "Look, you're not getting away with this. I *know* you can learn how to read, so we'll just sit here and we'll keep going through this until you do. I *know* you can read. I don't know why you're not doing it, but I know you can. I know *you!*" I just keep persisting with a variety of approaches and materials until I find the successful strategy. In the face of this persistence, the child either comes to believe he can do what you tell him to do, or he starts thinking you're crazy!

One thing parents can do in this whole equation is not pass on their beliefs about the inferiority of black people to their children. That's one thing. Too many mothers think they're incompetent in mathematics. They either didn't like it in school or were brainwashed into believing they couldn't do it, or they made bad grades in it. Or they stopped taking math because they were uncomfortable with it. For whatever reason, many mothers pass on their insecurities about mathematics to their children and let their children drop off or out of mathematics. They'll say, "Yeah, well, I wasn't good in mathematics, either. I understand." I would encourage Afrikan American parents not to do this. Our children *can* learn mathematics.

I have so many examples of schools where Afrikan American children are reaching white norms and where the gap between their performance is being eliminated. I think if parents had more security around their ability to do certain things, they would be more secure in counseling their children. That's first. Second, parents must encourage children to read. Try to encourage them to spend more time in academic pursuits like doing homework and studying, rather than looking at TV. All of these are things parents can do. Parents can turn off TVs, video games, and radios, just to show their children that they think academic pursuits are important.

It isn't always possible to have a little desk and quiet study place for your child if you have a family of five children and only three bedrooms. It's important, but not possible in the environment in which you find yourself. But some things are possible in any environment. One of them is to constantly encourage your child to do well in school, to constantly encourage your child to do his or her homework. To ask them all the time, "Have you done your homework? It's important to me." Or to say, "Turn off the TV. You haven't done any homework yet." Things like that. Those kinds of positive, pushy things you can do all the time, just to let your children know where you stand on the matter. If necessary, provide some penalties for not performing: don't buy them those "Air Jordan"

gym shoes they want, buy them "Jeeps" or "Keds." There should be certain penalties for not doing what parents consider important.

The third thing black parents can do is to make sure that their children have chores to do at home. This is exceedingly important. Children must learn their responsibilities. If they don't have any responsibilities to execute at home, they are not going to be responsible for the things they have to do at school or when they are away from you. They should be taught how to wash dishes, take out the garbage, clean the house, get their own food, and cook their own meals. Instead of sitting on the couch looking at the soaps all afternoon, waiting for Momma to come home and cook, a teenager ought to be able to cook a meal for his or her mother when that mother has been out working fourteen hours a day and comes back home tired. These are the kinds of obligations and responsibilities members of a family should share in order to keep the family secure and the quality of their living high. There is no reason why a child should live in a dirty home because Momma is the only one who cleans it up, and she's tired and she doesn't feel like doing it while everybody else is lounging around listening to Michael Jackson. Parents should teach their children early that they have these chores and responsibilities as a member of the family. These are things you are supposed to do, and children should be held responsible for them.

Another important element in the educational process is bringing up positive Afrikan American examples in the lessons. This is not just a European problem, there are many Afrikan American teachers who don't do this. All of us are victims of a Eurocentric education. One of the things we have to learn to do is to integrate the curriculum so that teachers have to teach Afrikan or Afrikan American content or information on other people of color because it's in the textbook. That's our responsibility: to write more textbooks that integrate the Afrikan experience into the mainstream curriculum. That's our responsibility. A lot of work is being done on this issue, but not enough. Asa Hilliard and others have gone in to consult with the Portland, Oregon schools to design a multicultural educational experience. A lot of work is being done in this area by Geneva Gay and James Banks at the University of Washington, and by Charsee Charlotte McIntyre at the State University of New York at Old Westbury.

If I had to identify the three must crucial problems in education, first would be the need for multicultural education—that is, the need to change the curriculum so it reflects the diversity of the people in this country. Second, we need to strengthen the skills of the teachers and administrators who teach the basics to children of color. Third, we need a change in the structure of school systems so that they operate from a different kind of model that is more inclusive of parents, students, teachers, and principals working together as equals.

If I could line up all the young people, I would tell them that they must understand the world in which they will live as workers. I'd tell them, "Listen, you will work for about forty years of your life. For forty years, you will work for a living in a world that is exceedingly different from that in which your parents lived and worked. It will be a technological world that will demand an understanding of the language of mathematics and computers." My suggestion to them would be to study as much as they can, to read as much as they can, to take as much mathematics as they can, and to learn how to use computers. Doing those things would equip them for the future.

1 Herrnstein, R. C. & Murray, C. J., *The Bell Curve: Intelligence and Class Structure in American Life* (New York: The Free Press, 1994).

2 Joe Clark is an Afrikan American educator whose strong-willed principalship of an inner-city high school in New Jersey was chronicled in the popular film, "Lean on Me," starring Morgan Freeman in the lead role.

3 Ronald Edmonds (1935–1983) was an Afrikan American teacher and Harvard-trained educational researcher whose concept of "Effective Schools" has been heralded by educators as a culturally effective and relevant means of reforming education for Afrikan American and other children of color placed at risk of failure.

Kwame Ture (Stokley Carmichael)
Political Activist, Organizer, Author

During the civil rights era, Kwame Ture (then Stokely Carmichael) was a towering, youthful figure who ushered into the movement a new ideology and philosophy: "Black Power." Influenced partly by Martin Luther King, Jr., and partly by Malcolm X, Ture's relentless energy and keen insights forced the older activists to embrace him as a full participant. He was a key figure in organizing both the Black Panther Party and the All Afrikan People's Revolutionary Party.

I was born on an island of the Caribbean, Trinidad, in the capitol city of Port-of-Spain. I was born in 1941, June 29th. At that time, Trinidad was colonized by the British. I was born a British subject, contrary to all the laws of nature. My early life was spent in the Caribbean. I stayed there until I was about ten. The education I got there was rooted in the struggles of the masses of the people to gain independence from British colonialism. The formal education I received, under the British system, was certainly far more disciplined than that of the American system of education.

The changing of my name was just something that had to be done. In the sixties, many people were changing their names. Muhammad Ali, for example. Some changed theirs in the sixties and then changed back to their slave names in the eighties and nineties. I have always thought I wanted to wait before I changed my name. I didn't want to let people think it was a fad. I knew it was something that was going to continue, and I wanted to *earn* my name.

My active participation in political struggles began in high school in New York at the Bronx High School of Science. Many political groups sought to recruit us for their different causes. One of the first political buttons I ever wore was a "Sane Nuclear Policy, Ban the Bomb" button. I also wore a "Fair Play for Cuba" button. In 1957 or 1958, while I was a high school student, the civil rights activist Bayard Rustin was organizing some youth marches in Washington, D.C., in a move to speed up the desegregation of schools in the South. The Supreme Court decision in *Brown v. Board of Education* had already been handed down, but it was not an active decision. So Bayard Rustin started going around, organizing youth activities. I played a role in these activities. We carried picket signs around Woolworth's and other stores in the North that had segregated facilities in the South. We also supported hospital workers strikes.

I went to Howard University in Washington, D.C. I'm very proud of that. I entered Howard in 1960. One of the reasons I decided to go to Howard was because of a political activity I attended in my senior year of high school. A group of us from the Communist Party Youth Group, which at that time was called Advance in the Head, traveled to D.C. to picket the House Un-American Activities Committee (the HUAC). I was eighteen years old. I was the only Afrikan in the group, everybody else was white. I didn't imagine I would find many Afrikans—by that I mean Afrikans born in America—on the picket line in Washington, but a whole contingent of folks from Howard and an organization called NAG, or the Nonviolent Action Group, showed up. NAG was part of the Student Nonviolent Coordinating Committee or SNCC. The Howard students picketed under the socialist banner, but they were not members of the Socialist Party. When I saw them, I asked, "Where are you all coming from?" They said, "Howard University. We work for SNCC. We've got a strong chapter at Howard. We do a lot of work." I said, "Right on! I'm coming to Howard for sure now!"

My college years helped shape my political direction. Before that, the period from 1941 until I left Trinidad in 1952, was the fermenting stage of the movement for independence. The pull of Garveyism was very strong within the Caribbean. Strong strands of Garveyism were present in the United States too. In New York City, I was attracted to 125th Street and what we called soap-box speakers. A lot of them were Garveyites. I owe them a lot. Though I was unconscious of it, they had a strong impact upon me and upon my speaking techniques. To be a speaker up on a soap box in Harlem, talking about Afrika in the fifties, you had to be sharp. You had to have your wits about you, and you had to be extremely alert on all points to answer the sorts of questions condemning Afrika and all the people who seemed to be running away from Afrika.

In high school, I participated in a lot of the study groups organized by the YSA or Young Socialist Alliance, which was the youth group of the Socialist Worker's Party. My activity was directed toward the area of the Afrikan struggle or what was then incorrectly called the civil rights movement. I did Friends of SNCC work and stuff, but I was involved in the North.

I remember my actual movement to the South began during my freshman year at Howard. The campus is no more than twenty minutes by car from the Maryland line or the Virginia line. Both Maryland and Virginia were segregated. That meant that if I went more than twenty minutes away, I couldn't go into restaurants and I'd have to sit in the back of the bus. As a student, driving from Washington to New York, I had to pass through these segregated states without stopping to eat or use a restroom until I got into New York. I remember the first time I was faced with this was on the trip to Washington to picket the HUAC. I

was traveling with many white people. They were communists and very consci-
entious. People who were hungry kept saying, "Stop here, let's get something to
eat." And the organizers of the trip would say, "No, we can't stop here. They
won't serve everybody. They only serve some people. They are not to be dealt
with."

When I worked for SNCC, I never held an elected position. I had always
been a field secretary. I had never been a member of the central committee. I
never sought any of these positions. The work I did in the field was sufficient
and rewarding; I even thought it was far more important. I just had too many
things to deal with to be concerned about being a member of the central committee, or being in any elected position.

There was a strong struggle occurring inside SNCC between the nationalist forces and the non-nationalist forces. The nationalist forces saw Afrikan
nationalism as a necessity in the struggle. Consequently, they not only high-
lighted it, but used it as a pivotal and cohesive force to bring people together.
There were others who didn't see nationalism as having any key role to play in
the struggle. The issue was extremely complicated. Unfortunately, nothing serious has come out about it in the press. Some books have made some attempts,
but even those do not properly comprehend all of the aspects of the problem.

SNCC had always been a majority Afrikan organization. There were, from
its very beginning, a few whites here and there, but they had played no dominating role. Some people in the organization suggested the idea of bringing
thousands of white northern students down South during the 1964 Freedom
Summer Project. Their understanding was that if we brought a lot of young
whites down to the South who had never seen the types of oppression our people were living under, they would consequently develop some hatred for those
conditions, become incensed by them, and move the nation to activity. The subsequent presence of these young whites created a lot of confrontation in the state
of Mississippi, but this confrontation had already been created by those of us in
SNCC, who were all Afrikans. Many people were being killed in Mississippi
before these white students came in '64, but they were all Afrikans. Nobody mentions their names. Even today, when people talk about the three civil rights
workers who were killed—Michael Schwerner, Andrew Goodman, and James
Chaney—they usually talk about the two white ones and not the Afrikan one.

So the thinking was that bringing these white students down there would
bring about an explosive situation in the South. Since they were white, and students, and many of them had contacts in the North, their arrests or torture or
even death could not go unnoticed, and that would have an impact on the political scene in America. This was correct. There was no question about it.

They also felt that these white students had certain skills and contacts that could be used to speed up the process of organizing the movement in the deep South. This was true, but the consequences of this truth were not worth the price. What happened was that whites came to completely dominate the organization with their administrative skills, and consequently they came to want to dominate the political line of the organization. Certainly, there was a conflict there. That was very clear.

Those of us who were nationalists didn't feel we needed them. We felt we should continue on with the struggle without whites. What would that mean? It would be a longer struggle. Once we had people properly organized, we figured, the confrontation would not depend upon the press, which would play a crucial role in blowing up the confrontation with white youth, nor on the liberals. It would depend upon the forces of the determination of the Afrikan masses. Ours was a longer, longer road; a more protracted struggle. Theirs was one that would bring quicker results, but those results would be of a reformatory rather than a revolutionary nature. Those of us who were seeking a protracted struggle understood that we were talking about revolutionary struggle. If we were victorious, the Afrikan masses themselves would come to be able to wield the power, and play power politics when necessary, if they went into electoral politics.

Well, those of us in the nationalist wing didn't win. The 1964 Freedom Summer project was approved, and all of the things we warned about actually happened. Several white students were certainly brutalized and tortured. That brought a lot of press attention to the state of Mississippi and a lot of political pressure against the southern wing of the Democratic Party for their racist policies. It created a situation that helped speed up the process for the signing of the Voting Rights Act.

The nonviolent tactic was effective because we wanted to advance the cause and were willing to do anything to achieve that goal, including giving our lives. Being nonviolent was a tactic. The confusion arose when it was seen as a principle and not a tactic. That was the error Dr. King made. He made nonviolence a principle. Those of us in SNCC, we knew it was a tactic. If it could be shown effective one day, we said "Use it." If it wasn't effective the next day, we said, "Use a hand grenade." King's position was that it must be used at all times, under all conditions, even when it was no longer effective. That was not our position.

It took no great strength or courage to be nonviolent in that respect. If you were, you were just advancing the cause. If you said you were willing to give your life for the cause, then that was the forum in which you gave your life. Once one had this type of political awareness, it took no extra courage to apply it. It was

Photo credit: Dedon (Ken Carr) Kamathi

KWAME TURE (STOKLEY CARMICHAEL)

only to people who didn't have this political awareness that nonviolence seemed to take so much courage.

Matter of fact, I think it took more courage to go to Viet Nam with a gun than it took to take a nonviolent demonstration to Mississippi. Because in Viet Nam, it was a no-win situation. So it took more courage to go fight in a place where you knew you would lose than it did to give your life for a fight that was eternal, whose purpose was to bring about eternal glory.

We worked with King. We saw him, not on a daily basis, but certainly on a weekly or monthly basis in different campaigns, in different meetings, under the same circumstances. When Malcolm X emerged as a new voice, those of us who were in the deep South working for SNCC used to have all of his tapes sent to us. We were playing his tapes for everybody. Everybody in SNCC knew who Malcolm X was, what he was talking about, what he was doing. We knew what King was doing, and we knew what Malcolm was doing. We were listening to both. Discussion was rampant. Malcolm, we said, was going straight to revolution. King was arriving at revolution through the path of reform.

By taking certain stands and by calling for "Black Power" in a militant fashion, we began to undo the movement's Uncle Tom policies and also to push King a little bit further to the left. For example, SNCC was the first civil rights organization, the first Afrikan organization, in the country to take a position against the war on Viet Nam. It was not King. King was pushed by SNCC, not in a hostile manner but in a nonviolent manner, if you will, to take a position against the war in Viet Nam. SNCC was the second national organization in this country to denounce Zionism. That was in 1967. The first was the Nation of Islam, immediately after the Israeli aggression against Egypt in its war against Syria and other Arab states. Consequently, as a spokesperson for SNCC, the role I played was the role history had imposed on the organization. I had the task of advocating these ideas in a very militant fashion. The position was one I really didn't like, but in revolution, you don't do what you like, you do what has to be done.

The press thought we were irresponsible and didn't know what we were talking about. They thought we didn't represent the aspirations of the masses of our people. On all three counts, the press was wrong. We were quite responsible, we certainly knew precisely what we were speaking of, and we represented the aspirations of the masses of our people, without question. Once the slogan "Black Power" came flying out, even though the press, the presidents, the political structure, and all the Uncle Toms did everything possible to stop it, they could not. We were advocating properly and were in perfect harmony with the aspirations of the masses of our people.

SNCC soon posted me out of the South, back to the North, to Washington, D.C. Their reasons for expelling me were quite childish, actually, and totally untrue. The real reasons for my expulsion was my political ideology. I was expelled from SNCC for ideological reasons. Everything is ideological. I refused to compromise with Zionism in any way whatsoever. Much of SNCC's support came from Zionists. I also refused in any way to compromise on the solid stand I had taken with regard to Afrikan nationalism, that is, the need for Afrikans to have their own organization, to run them, to control them, and to finance them. Apparently, these were points SNCC felt threatened its organization, so they expelled me.

One of the reasons they listed for expelling me was I had bought a $70,000 house. I have never done such a thing, up to this time in my life, and I'm 44 years old. I don't *own* a house. I have never bought a house in my life. The FBI lied, as they usually do, pigs that they are, and put out a story in the newspaper saying I bought a house for $70,000. SNCC never even called me to ask whether or not I had done this—they knew better than anybody else the newspapers were always lying about our organization—but without even checking, they fired me. This was one of the reasons listed. They listed about four other reasons that were just as untrue as the first one. So I was expelled.

Before I was expelled, however, under SNCC's auspices, I helped to organize the first Black Panther Party in the country in Lowndes County, Alabama. The Party caught the imagination of young brothers and sisters throughout the country, especially Huey Newton and some others out on the West Coast. They asked SNCC's permission to start a Black Panther Party. It was granted.

The Black Panther Party on the West Coast asked me to come and work with them. I realized I would have to leave SNCC. I was hoping I could find, in the Black Panther Party, the type of base that would help our people rapidly develop the type of organization necessary. I accepted the invitation to work with them, yet even in doing so, I realized that there would be contradictions. I worked with the Panthers quietly, through Eldridge Cleaver and Bobby Seale, while Huey Newton was in jail.

I have always recognized the need for organization. As an organizer, I will never find myself outside of an organization. I may be a pretty bad brother, but I know that I can't bring this beast down by myself. There must be organization to do this. I don't want to be bad, I just want to bring the beast down, so I need organization.

I've said I had great contradictions with the Black Panther Party. They wanted to make me their prime minister. I saw the contradictions they were experiencing and knew that unless we resolved them, it was clear I couldn't be their prime minister. I got out of that by letting them call me their "honorary

prime minister." I was made honorary prime minister of the Black Panther Party within two months after being expelled from SNCC.

The contradictions had a lot to do with the Party leadership. Huey Newton was in jail. I had a lot of respect for him. While he was in jail, Eldridge Cleaver and Bobby Seale headed up the organization, but they had no understanding at all of how a political movement operates. As a matter of fact, their stupidity was sometimes astounding. I remember once coming to them and saying we have to do political education classes inside the Black Panther Party. I said, "Our people are not really educated. They are just running on instinct. We can't fight the enemy on instinct. We have to have reasoning." We had a meeting for three hours in which they tried to inform me that the masses of our people didn't need political education. They were saying this while they were calling themselves Marxist–Leninists. I thought they, Bobby Seale and Eldridge Cleaver, were stupid.

You know, you can't be a Christian and not read the Bible. I have met a lot of stupid Christians who can read and write, but they don't read the Bible. And they call themselves Christians! They say they can *feel* Jesus. That's their problem. You cannot be a Marxist–Leninist and not study Marxism and Leninism. It's a science—it's not a religion. You have to study it. Those in the Black Panther Party were calling themselves Marxist–Leninists and many of them had never read one book by Marx or Lenin! When I tried to bring the issue up for discussion, they told me I was "bourgeois."

I'm just showing you the stupidity that was rampant inside the Black Panther Party. It was clear to me that neither Eldridge Cleaver nor Bobby Seale had even *thought* of revolution. *I* was a revolutionary. My credentials were made while Eldridge Cleaver was sitting in jail for raping women. I was sitting in jail for fighting for my people. While Bobby Seale was playing jokes and going to jail for gang-fighting, I was going to jail for fighting for my people. I had been to jail more than they had ever been, and I had never been to jail for anything except for fighting for my people. Consequently, I was a revolutionary; they were *talking* revolution. They had no understanding of it at all. The stupidity I had to put up with in that party, it was just not worth it. That's why I had to resign from the Black Panther Party. They didn't want revolution. They wanted *reform.*

Before you know it, Eldridge Cleaver was running for president with the white Peace and Freedom Party. The Panthers formed an alliance with the Peace and Freedom Party. It was a step backward; just like what we had experienced with whites in SNCC. The Black Panther Party was dying in the streets with the police. The Peace and Freedom Party wasn't dying.

It's just like people come telling me today that the Afrikan people in Azania, South Afrika, must have their white allies. White allies? The only people dying in the street are us. If I have an ally, and I'm the one dying in the street, and the ally ain't dying in the street, what do I need him for? I don't see any white people getting shot by the South Afrikan police. I don't see any white people throwing bricks or bottles at them. The only ones actually doing that are the Afrikans. Consequently, they have no allies. When you are fighting, if your allies are not fighting, you have no allies.

So here was the Peace and Freedom Party, an electoral political party, and Eldridge Cleaver, telling me this is what we are going to make alliance with. When he got finished with the Black Panther Party, they were giving breakfast to children. Now, I'm not against giving breakfast to children—nobody can be. But I'm not for the Black Panther Party becoming the Salvation Army. I'm not for having a charity organization. I'm a revolutionary. By the time they were finished, they were trying to outdo the Salvation Army. That's where they are to this very day.

Looking beyond petty internal differences, political education has to be kept at the forefront. Between '66 and '67, before the contradiction with SNCC, a lot of people in SNCC were attacking me. Many of us in SNCC wrote books, but every penny of my book was given to SNCC. I hope all those who attacked me gave the money they made from the books they wrote to some organization. Every penny from my book went to SNCC. I financed the organization, to the tune of thousands of dollars, while it attacked me. That's how much that book made in the first year. SNCC paid me that year—seven dollars a week—out of my own book earnings!

The book was called *Black Power*. The term has been around. As a matter of fact, Richard Wright, wrote a book called *Black Power*, which he dedicated to Kwame Nkrumah.[1] Adam Clayton Powell was also using the term quite a bit within the American Afrikan community. It was not a new term at all. It just came at the right time. The powerlessness of the oppressed masses of Afrikans in the deep South was just too clear and blatant for it not to catch on like wildfire.

Black Power caught on like wildfire because, prior to that slogan, the idea was that Afrikans could gain their liberation in the deep South through moral struggle. Dr. King was talking about "quickening the moral consciousness" of the country. You don't get liberated through morality. You get liberated through *power*. Of course, those using power must be moral, but if morality could make us free, we would be free, because our oppressors are certainly immoral.

One of the strongest and most moralistic persons I've ever worked with was Mrs. Fannie Lou Hamer. I worked with her for many, many, many years in the Second Congressional District of the Mississippi Delta. That was when I worked for SNCC as a congressional director. Mrs. Hamer was one of the people who worked on the projects in my congressional district. I knew her. I slept on her floors many times.

As a matter of fact, it was Mrs. Hamer who came to resolve the problem for SNCC on the question of violence or nonviolence. I remember it very well. We were having a discussion and Charlie Cobb, who was field secretary for SNCC at that time, raised the issue. He said, "I know I'm nonviolent or at least I'm *supposed* to be nonviolent, but let's say, for example, I go to Mrs. Hamer's house"—Mrs. Hamer always kept guns in her house—"and let's say that white terrorists like the Ku Klux Klan know that I'm in the house, and they come by to shoot into the house because I'm there. Let's say Mrs. Hamer and them are not nonviolent. She and the family pick up guns and start shooting back, and there is a gun right there next to me. What should I do?" Nobody answered the question. Nobody. We knew what the answer was. It was clear because I myself had slept in Mrs. Hamer's house when shots were fired into the house and guns were brought out. We returned the fire. Definitely.

Mrs. Hamer was the salt of the earth. She was a strong woman. She demonstrated to me that you cannot limit human beings in their political development. There is just no limiting them. Just think, here was a share-cropper, a woman who could hardly read or write, who had undergone so much suffering, and her grasp and understanding of political concepts, her ability, not only to articulate them but to mobilize the people around them, was outstanding. No man, if he had read or written thousands of books, could do it any better.

Looking back, SNCC and the Black Panther Party aided me in developing my ability to analyze our situation better. I moved on to the All African People's Revolutionary Party in 1967. I traveled. I met Fidel Castro when I went to Cuba. I met Ho Chi Minh and had lunch with him in Hanoi. I met Sekou Toure of Guinea. I met Ghana's Kwame Nkrumah. I met Julius Nyerere of Tanzania. I met many, many heads of state.

When I was in China, I met Mrs. Shirley Graham DuBois, wife of Dr. W. E. B. DuBois. I didn't know she was in China. I was on my way to North Viet Nam and passing through China when she heard I was there and sent me a message to come and have lunch with her. I saw the name, "Mrs. W. E. B. DuBois," on the card, and I said, "What? She's in China? She wants to have lunch with *me*?" I said, "Of course, I will have lunch with her! Is she kidding?"

Lunch was, I think, at one o'clock. I was there at noon. We talked, talked, talked. She talked, talked, talked. I listened, listened, listened.

While we were having lunch, she looked up and said, "Have you ever met Kwame Nkrumah?" I said, "No ma'am, I have never met him." She said,

"Would you like to meet him?" I said, "I would give my right arm to meet Kwame Nkrumah." She said, "Okay, you'll meet him," and that's all. She continued talking some more. After lunch, I thanked her. She asked me what my plans were. I said, "Well, I'm going to go fight with the liberation movement in Afrika." She said, "What are you going to do about America?" I said, "Later for America, I'm going to tear up my passport. I don't need them." She said, "Well, okay. You may not need them, but don't tear up your passport. Put it in your back pocket. That's what my husband and I did. When we really needed to go to the U.S. to help do some activating work for the Afrikans there, we couldn't because we didn't have our passports. So just put it in your back pocket." I said, "Alright, okay," and I thanked her. You see how you can learn? People pass on news of the errors they have made to others so they can avoid repeating those mistakes.

I went from China to Hanoi, North Vietnam, while the Americans were bombing. From North Vietnam I proceeded into Algeria. I was a guest of the Algerian government. This was before Eldridge Cleaver and them had ever thought of going there. After doing a lot of work with the Algerians, the Algerian government came to me and brought me an invitation to attend the eighth congress of the PDG, the Democratic Party of Guinea. The invitation came from Guinean co-presidents Sekou Toure and Kwame Nkrumah.[2]

Guinea. I couldn't believe it. I couldn't understand it. But I certainly was going, that was for sure! I thanked my brothers and sisters in Algeria so much for what they had done for the movement, through me, and proceeded on to Guinea.

When I arrived at the airport, I was taken to my hotel. I went to my room and put down my bags. My face was greasy. I bent over a bowl to wash my face. I had just put water on it, when I heard a tap at the door. With water still on my face, I grabbed a towel, put it around my neck, and opened the door. There before me was Mrs. DuBois. She said, "Come, Dr. Nkrumah is waiting for you." I told her, "But I just got here." She took the towel off my neck, threw it on the bed, pulled me out the door, closed it, and led me to a car. The next thing I knew, the door of the car opened and she was taking me into a building.

"Wait here," she said. "He's here, he's here, he's here," she said, "Here he is." And there I was, and there was Dr. Kwame Nkrumah, standing right in front of me! We spent much time together there while I was attending the congress.

After the congress, I went to see President Nkrumah again. He had given me the manuscript of a book he was writing, the *Handbook of Revolutionary Warfare*, which forms the basis of the All African People's Revolutionary Party.[3] As I was reading it, I realized immediately that all the problems had been put into their proper place. We discussed it quite a bit.

Before I left Guinea, I went to say goodbye to him. He asked me, "Well, what are you going to do?" I told him I had decided to go to Tanzania to fight with the liberation forces there. We talked about it a little bit. He said, "Well, it will be good for you to go there, but you know there are a lot of contributions you can make in different fields." I agreed with him, but even I couldn't see clearly what form that contribution would take. As I was walking out the door, he said, "You know what you ought to do? You're going back to America first, right?" I said, "Yes, I do have to go back there to put some final things in order before I go to Tanzania." He said, "Well, even if you are going to go and fight with the liberation movements, you ought to come and be my secretary for a while."

I said, "What?" He said, "Yes, come." Maybe he was joking, but I wasn't. I walked out the door, and that's all that was ringing in my head, "Wow! I'll be Kwame Nkrumah's secretary. I'll be dynamite, no matter how stupid I am."

When I went to say goodbye to President Sekou Toure, he told me, "Well, you know Afrika is your home." I said, "I know that, sir. Of course, I know it's my home." He said, "We in Guinea want you to know that anytime, anywhere, if there is anything you need, just let us know. You can come here anytime you want and live here, and we would be very honored if you did that." So I thanked him too.

With both their words ringing in my ears, I went to Tanzania. I spent some time there with the liberation movements. Unfortunately, the CIA activity there was extremely strong. The people there did not have a proper understanding, at that point, of the CIA's maneuverings. Thus, the CIA was able to create some slight problems—not significant ones, but enough to cause hesitations in my plans to work with the liberation forces.

I returned to the United States. I had every intention of putting all my business in order within two months and of returning to Guinea. But when I arrived in the United States, the State Department illegally seized my passport and held it for about nine months. That meant I couldn't leave for nine months. I decided to use that time to my best advantage, by beginning to lay the groundwork for organizing the All Afrikan People's Revolutionary Party until I returned to Guinea.

The *Handbook of Revolutionary Warfare* stayed in my head. At that time, Nkrumah was hesitant speaking about Afrikans in America. I said, "We are Afrikans." He said, "There is no question you are Afrikans." I said, "Well, are you saying this party is for *all* Afrikans, or are you saying it's for *some* Afrikans?" Of course, that was not the point. The point was that as far as Nkrumah's thinking was concerned, regarding the All African People's Revolutionary Party, the

Afrikans in America were so far away, he himself could not conceive of the organizing efforts it would take to mobilize them for the liberation struggle. Once I mentioned my interest in doing so, he could not say no. That was clear. He said, "Well, you can try." I said, "No, we *will* organize it." He said, "Yes, well, you know Afrikans know that Afrika is theirs." But still, he was not too sure anything could be done in the U.S.

So this All Afrikan Peoples' Revolutionary Party comes out of his book, the *Handbook of Revolutionary Warfare.* Coming out of the '60s, we had a high quality of cadre in the Party. He would get the opportunity to meet some of that cadre from the United States who were doing work for him, going into Ghana, setting up plans to blow up things in Ghana. Our level of organization really shocked and surprised him. He began to see the possibility of this organizing and combat activity. He sometimes became overjoyed at little things, things I thought were not important, that we were able to do.

Many people are perplexed by the discussion of ideology and economic systems. This confusion has been imposed upon us by capitalism. It seeks to create confusion in this area, so that there is no clear thinking about it. As a matter of fact, it makes people respond to these important issues on instinct. I mean, if you say "communism" in America, the people are ready to pick up the gun and come after you. They don't know what a communist is, and they aren't even concerned with finding out. This only helps America when it wants to confuse the people.

Look at that stupid man, Ronald Reagan. He wants to confuse the people. All Reagan did was scream "Communists in Nicaragua!" and the people go crazy. They have no understanding of what being a communist means and don't seek to learn what it means. This confusion is imposed on everybody in America. It's even more imposed upon us Afrikans here.

We can begin to separate the confusion from the truth by learning the difference between an ideology and an economic system. When we speak of socialism and communism, we are speaking of scientifically objective economic systems that are the same in Afrika, Europe, America, and Asia.

Ideologies are something different, however. When we speak of ideologies, we are speaking of principles. Economic systems have ideologies that direct the people in building and controlling their economic systems. Ideologies are principles that hold a society together and direct the people's energies toward predetermined goals. Ideology comes from the culture of the people. Thus, the ideology coming from the culture of Afrika is different from the ideology coming from the culture of China—it's as different as their cultures. This doesn't mean they are hostile to each other or antagonistic to each other. It simply means they are *different* from each other. I think the confusion arises when somebody confuses economic systems with ideology, thinking they are one and the same, or when someone thinks the ideology comes from the economic system, or when they think all ideology is the same.

Afrikans can and must be socialist. Afrikans are fighting to construct socialism in Afrika. The route they take will be different from the route taken in Europe, America, or Asia. This difference will be reflected in the ideology, not in the system of socialism. Socialism, as I said, is an economic system.

There are only two economic systems in the world, just two: capitalism or socialism, the latter of which leads to communism. There can only be two because each economic system must answer one fundamental question: Who will own and control the means of production, the wealth, of the country? The question can only be answered in two ways: Either some will own or all will own. It's as simple as that.

Under the capitalist system, only a few have the right to own. A socialist system says that everybody must own and control the means of production and the wealth of a country. You can see the clear division. Socialism is the only just economic system. This is clear, crystal clear. Those of us who are revolutionary *must* be socialist! Our ideology may be different—for example, I'm an Nkrumaist. That is my ideology. It comes out of the struggle and culture of Afrika vis-à-vis imperialism and the kind of society it wishes to construct. This Nkrumaism, this ideology, is no different from Marxist–Leninism. Just as Islam and Christianity, as religions, both serve the same God yet have different rituals. Both have different ideologies, but both are doing the same thing. Thus, socialism in Afrika and socialism in Europe are no different. If Nkrumaism is directing that socialism, it is just like any other philosophy, with different branches and different means of arriving at the same conclusions.

Socialism is truth, and truth is universal. Two plus two is four in China. Two plus two is four in Afrika. In Afrika, we represent this equation with cowrie beads. In China, they use the abacus board. But it's the same two plus two. It's just represented in different ways in different cultures.

To understand and establish socialism, you first have to abolish private ownership of the means of production. When there is no longer any private ownership of the means of production, everything belongs to the people. Then the struggle to make the distribution equal begins. For example, the Soviet Union had limited private ownership of the means of production.

There was nobody in the Soviet Union who owned the means of production. It was owned by the people. There may have been corruption among those politically responsible who abused the confidence the people put in them, who stole money, or were corrupt. But once the people are limited from owning the means of production, the fight toward social progress is nothing but constant progress.

Confusion can set in again when we bring the spiritual element into this discussion of ideologies and economic systems. Karl Marx and Friedrich Engels in *The Communist Manifesto* wrote that "Religion is the opium of the people."[4] If you looked at religion in Afrika and then look at religion in Europe, you would see two different roles being played by the same agent. In Afrika, religion has always been tolerant; in Europe, religion has always been intolerant. There are more fights over religion in Europe than probably anywhere else in the world. As a matter of fact, those Europeans who you find in America today, those Europeans you find in Australia, in New Zealand, in Azania—many of them are there as a result of religious intolerance and religious conflict in Europe.

Europe started from many nations and went from nations to states. That is to say, they already had their nationhood, they sought next to build up state structures. These nations always used religion as a means to help confuse the people. So when Marx and Engels said religion was the opium of the people, they said it in reference to Europe. If one looks at Europe, one cannot but say that Marx and Engels are correct. This statement, however, is not correct outside of Europe.

If one would look properly, if one were religious, one would have to be a socialist. One really couldn't take any other aspect toward life. If one would read the Bible, one would see that in the early days of the Christian religion, when the rich wanted to join the church, the first advice they were given was to sell off all their worldly goods. The very symbolism of the Bible is nothing other than communism! It's as communist as you can get! Jesus Christ taking a few loaves of bread and a few fish to feed the masses of the people—that's nothing but symbolism for sharing the wealth with the masses of the people, seeing that they are properly fed. Anyone who is religious *must* be socialist. The enemy takes Marx and Engels's statement, which is a correct statement in Europe, and blows it out of proportion, making it an incorrect statement. They make it appear as if Marx and Engels are saying that anyone who is religious cannot be a socialist. To the contrary, anyone who is religious *must* be a socialist.

Here again, some elements will manipulate this for their own gain or deception, based on the ignorance of the people. As I said, most Christians don't even read the Bible, so they don't even know what Israel is, except what they think they know about it in the Bible. They don't read the Bible, so they really don't know. That ignorance is manipulated by Zionism. It is also manipulated in connection with the problems surrounding the holocaust the Jewish people suffered at the hands of Hitler. So playing on these two aspects—one, the worldwide ignorance of the people about Israel and what it really means; and two, the sympathy they can get for those Jews who were slaughtered by Hitler—the Zionists try to combine, in collusion with imperialism, the stealing and occupying of the land of Palestine and the terrorizing and genocide of the Palestinian people. That's how it works.

We have the same thing in South Afrika. Properly organized, we could begin to effectuate the policies of this country toward Afrika. The Zionists in this country are quantitatively far less than we Afrikans—they are not even ten percent of our numbers—yet they effectively control the foreign policies of the United States with regard to the state of Israel: illegal, racist, immoral, and unjust as it is. We Afrikans are not organized. That is our major problem.

A principal solution for many of the problems we face lies in a united Afrika. The objective of the All African People's Revolutionary Party is Pan-Afrikanism. Pan-Afrikanism is the total liberation and unification of Afrika under scientific socialism. Our objective is a unified, socialist Afrika. We understand that until Afrika is free, no Afrikan anywhere in the world will ever be free. Our task is not stopped, not even slackened until we achieve this. We are intensifying our efforts. We know Afrika is going to be unified, socialist, and free.

Thinking about the young, I would tell them that life is not what they acquire. It is not about the material goods they acquire. Life is only the service they render to humanity. Consequently, at the young age they are now, they need to study and work very hard for their people. They must do everything they can to help their people. The more they grow, the stronger they are, the more they must do for their people. I promise them that they will have no reward higher in life than serving the people.

Ready for the revolution!

※※※※※

[1] Wright, Richard, *Black Power* (London: Dennis Dobson, 1954).

[2] Ghanaian President Kwame Nkrumah had by that time been overthrown by the CIA and, in exile, was serving as co-president of Guinea.

[3] Nkrumah, Kwame, *Handbook of Revolutionary Warfare: A Guide to the Armed Phase of the African Revolution* (New York: International Publishers, 1969).

[4] Marx, Karl and Friedrich Engels, *The Communist Manifesto* (New York: Washington Square Press, 1964).

LEONARD JEFFRIES, JR.

POLITICAL SCIENTIST, EDUCATOR, ADMINISTRATOR, AUTHOR, LECTURER

Leonard Jeffries's Afrikan-centered scholarship has made him a prime tar-
get of maligning attacks by those who want the Eurocentric view of the
world to retain its hegemony both inside and outside the academy. His
right of free speech was recently threatened by Western traditionalist forces
who condemned his efforts to put into place a curriculum of inclusion in
the schools of the state of New York and to present a truer picture of the
realities of Afrikan enslavement and various groups' role in that process.
Despite the efforts of his critics, Dr. Jeffries is a warrior who has accom-
plished many positive achievements throughout the country and around
the world.

My roots are in Newark, New Jersey. I was born there in 1937 and raised there. My father's side of the family comes from Kelly, Georgia, which is south of Atlanta. My mother's side comes from Virginia. My parents came together and produced two sons. I am the oldest, and my brother Marland was born two years after me.

I've been fortunate in that I've travelled to and lived in many parts of the world. I lived on the West Coast from 1969 to 1972, when I was asked to set up the Black Studies department at San Jose State in California. That was one of my greatest experiences, to be able to build, from nothing, a department of Black Studies. It was one of the largest on the West Coast and one of the largest in America, with eleven faculty lines, forty courses, a summer institute, and a teacher training program. The impact of that program is still being felt. I meet people all the time, all over the world, who went through that program.

I tell everybody that I've been blessed to have had one of the best educational experiences in the world. That's why, when I look at knowledge and experience, I think in terms of a polarity–duality concept. I use a pyramidal framework to try to explain a lot of things. I call it "pyramid analysis." If you look at the true pyramid, it has two polarities at the base, then it has the summit. At one polarity of my own life is the European experience. That began formally with my education in the Newark, New Jersey schools. I was an honor student, a top student all the way through: president of my grammar school class, president of my junior high school class, president of my high school class. I integrated many of those schools. My classmates were predominantly white.

I attended Lafayette College in eastern Pennsylvania. There were only two blacks there when I arrived with a fellow from Atlanta. We doubled the black population by one hundred percent, from two to four. There were 1,400 white boys and four of us, but I became one of the top students there. I was an honor student and head of the Knights of the Round Table, the honor society there. I was also the president of a fraternity. Ironically, it was a Jewish fraternity: Phi Lambda Phi.

I graduated from Lafayette with honors, majoring in political science, government, and law. I received a Rotary International grant to study overseas. Where? In Switzerland, in Europe. In what context? French. I studied political science, international affairs, diplomacy, and political economy in France. After two years, I received my certificate and came back to the United States, where I did my master's in government, law, international affairs, and Afrikan Studies at Columbia. Then I went on to get my Ph.D.

From the point of view of the European, I have had the best that he gives his own. But that is not what I am all about. My strength and the thing I am most proud of is that other polarity: the Afrikan polarity. It's the Afrikan multibillion-dollar education that I am really proud of. The European million-dollar education puts me in good stead. It gives me their qualifications. But the billion-dollar Afrikan education began in the beginning, in the mind of my mother.

Somehow or other, my mother conceived greatness for her young people. She said her youngsters were going to have a foundation from which they could grow and develop. She married an Afrikan brother, my father—a big, tall man, who had strength and character. Together they built the family unit that is my foundation, and they did this with other family units.

I grew up on 14th Street in Newark. Of the twenty kids I grew up with, eighteen of us made it big—that is, they're doctors, lawyers, Indian chiefs, and concerned people. They go back and forth to Afrika all the time. It was an Afrikan community and an Afrikan communal process that I grew up in. That's the foundation I had.

Wherever I went, some strong black person put their hands on me. The Sunday school teacher who lived at the end of our block, Mrs. Smith of the Mt. Sinai Baptist Church, said she was going to transform all the young people who came into her midst. So in that little Sunday school class she devised an educational process to build character in us. She would have us come to her house on Mondays and Wednesdays, ostensibly to get some more lessons in the Bible. In reality, she was trying to teach us to read and write, to analyze, to know our history, and to develop character and respect for each other. This black woman, in that little church, set aside a goal for herself, and for fifty years she did this. A few

years ago we had to go back. Fifty years of us had to go back to pay homage to Mrs. Smith.

That is what I am talking about. That's my education. That's my coming up with my mother, my father, and all these old people putting their hands on me. Then, when I went to school, everybody singled me out because they saw that I had this special desire to learn. Even white folks would slip me special books and what-not.

Miss Grace Baxter Fenderson came into my life when I was a teenager. My mother told me to go down to the NAACP office and join the NAACP Youth Council. This was in 1951. So, there I was, a little boy, thirteen years old, going down to tell the people at the NAACP that I wanted to be in on the deal. When Miss Fenderson saw me coming through the door, she wasn't going to turn me away. So I became involved in a leadership process through the NAACP.

At that time, the NAACP was considered a radical organization. We were sitting-in and doing all kinds of things, like filing lawsuits and such. It was that youth experience that helped me grow. By the time I got through high school, I had traveled around the country, struggling for civil rights. Then in 1955, I went off to Lafayette College and became one of the leaders there.

In 1959, I went to Europe. While I was in Europe, the world opened up to me. My Afrikan contacts became very real. I had heard about Afrika, studied it in school, but then another black person came into my life: the Reverend Dr. James Robinson of Knoxville, Tennessee. He was a little, short man. My mother is a short one too. All these short black people have left their mark on me. Reverend Robinson set up a program to link black people with Afrika. It was called Operation Crossroads Africa. I learned about his program while I was in college, and I helped raise money to help his efforts.

When I was in Europe, Afrika became my reality. Everybody thought I was Afrikan. See, while I was running around Europe studying, I mastered French. Whenever someone over there heard me speak, they'd say, "Well, you must be from Afrika because Americans don't speak French that well." When I told them, "No, I'm a poor boy from Newark, New Jersey," they'd say, "No, no, no. If you're studying in Switzerland, with the elite of the world, you must be an Afrikan bigwig's son. You must be an Afrikan *prince.*" I had to go through Europe to be an Afrikan prince! It never dawned on me that a year or two later Afrika would be a very real part of my life.

It was when I came back from Europe in 1961 with this Afrikan consciousness, having been exposed to it and what with everybody thinking I was an Afrikan and all, that I met Reverend Robinson. He said, "You're the man for my program." I started going back and forth to Afrika after that. I've been eighty times. I lived there for two years while I was doing my master's and my Ph.D. My wife had gone to Afrika before I knew her. I met her through the Crossroads program. She went to Nigeria in 1960. We met when I came back from the Ivory Coast and Senegal in 1961. From that point on, we started going together. By 1964, we were ready for marriage. Who married us? Reverend Robinson. Where did we go on our honeymoon? To Afrika, of course. I took the money I had gotten from a Rockefeller grant for my doctoral research, and we went away for two years, honeymooning and studying in Afrika. It's been the most fantastic experience of my life to have had that Afrikan education.

After two years of studying political and economic development of the Ivory Coast and traveling around Afrika, we came back to the States. This was during the crisis of the sixties. Our cities were boiling over. There were explosions in Watts in '65, New York in '64, Newark in '66, Detroit in '67, and in hundreds of other cities. I couldn't just be a esoteric scholar and simply work on my dissertation. I put it on the shelf and got involved in manpower training and community organization work in Newark. I was right there when things blew up. We were busy organizing the Black Power conferences and establishing the Committee for a Unified Newark.

By 1968, I was combining both my Afrikan scholarly interests and my interests in community development. I participated in international conferences. In fact, in 1968, I went to Los Angeles to an international conference of Afrikanists, a meeting of the African Studies Association. It's white folks, mainly; white scholars involved in Afrika. At any rate, I went to L.A. to present a paper at this conference. When I saw the level of these scholars' presentation, these so-called outstanding white scholars, I was shocked! I decided right then and there that those people weren't going to fall asleep when I made *my* presentation! When I laid down my theories and ideas, everybody, and I mean everybody, woke up!

In Los Angeles, I met another little black man—a little man, just like James Robinson, just like that little black Sunday school teacher, just like my little mother—a leader in the world of Afrikan scholars, a special dynamite scholar named Dr. John Henrik Clarke. He was out there in Los Angeles organizing black scholars. He organized a black caucus to demand equity and some justice for us in the Afrikan Studies Association.

The white folks didn't respond effectively. We decided we would meet with them at their next conference in Montreal the following year. We said that if they didn't meet our demands, we would establish our own association. Well, we went to Montreal and challenged them. Again, they did not give us the proper response, so we left there, after disrupting the conference, and established the

LEONARD JEFFRIES, JR.

Afrikan Heritage Studies Association. That was in 1969. I was one of the founding officers. Dr. Clarke was the founding president.

Ironically, in 1968, when I was in Los Angeles presenting my scholarly work on the Ivory Coast, someone told me about some trouble brewing in Mexico. At that time, the Olympics was taking place, and some of our brothers were raising hell around the principle of Afrikan struggle. Three brothers from California, led by John Carlos, had raised the Black Power fist from the victory stand in Mexico. A storm was brewing, so this scholar said, "We need to go down and help the brothers out." I said, "We don't have the money to do that." He said, "For another twenty-five dollars on your ticket from New York to Los Angeles to New York, you can go to Mexico City. I said, "Count me in." We jumped on a plane and went down to Mexico City, to the Olympics, and met with John Carlos and the brothers. We tried to help them out with the international struggle they were involved in.

Later that year, I was teaching political science at the college level at City College in New York, and someone asked me to teach a course on Black Studies, the first Black Studies course at City College. I did. From January through May, the black students there had been demanding Black Studies programs, more black faculty, more black support programs, and greater access to the college. There was a special consciousness spreading among our people at that time. It was spreading across the country. You not only had the scholars demanding equity, you had the black students demanding it too. You had black psychologists, black lawyers, and black caucuses in all the organizations. This was a lot of ferment, and there I was, right in the middle of it, at the Olympics, at the African Studies Association, and at City College.

The black students at City College made four demands: one, new admissions standards that gave our people a better shot at getting into college; two, support for those youngsters once in college; three, more black faculty; and four, the creation of Black Studies programs. These demands were made in February. They were rejected. By April, the students, not getting an effective response, took over the college. They formed a leadership group called the Committee of Ten. There were only 250 black and Latin students at City College during that time. Sixty of those students were in my Black Studies class. Most of the Committee of Ten were in my class.

When they made and stood up for their demands, by taking over the college in April, I was in the middle of that. They stopped the college for two weeks and organized community support. By May, the school's political leadership realized they had to give some concessions to these youngsters.

By May, some people from California, led by Mel Whitfield—I don't know how they heard about me—sent a group to City College to ask me to come out to a conference in San Jose. They wanted to look over some people for the possibility of heading their Black Studies program there. I went out there, along with another great scholar and partner of mine in the struggle, Dr. James Turner; and with a scholar from Detroit, Dr. Carlene Young. We were there at this conference, and they were looking us over to see who would head the Black Studies department at San Jose. James had a commitment to go to Cornell. He went, and he set up one of the greatest programs in the world: the Africana Studies and Research Center at Cornell University. I was asked to head the program at San Jose State.

At San Jose, we began to put into place one of the strongest programs on the West Coast. The beauty of it was that, when I got there, the students, these black youngsters, gave me a copy of a proposal for a Black Studies degree program that had been approved by the state's board of regents. Someone had written across the front of it, "THE WHITE PROPOSAL." They threw it on the ground and said, "Now you develop us a *real* Black Studies program!"

So from scratch, with no models, we had to develop these programs on these white college campuses. Do you know what an enormous task that was for someone like myself, who had only taught on a university campus for six months prior to that? In that six months—half the time we couldn't teach because the students had taken over the college—but I accepted the challenge. I didn't blink or say, "Well, we don't have the ability to do this on a major university campus." San Jose had 26,000, almost 30,000 students. It was a major school. But I didn't hesitate. I knew I had the capability to set up a degree program. So that's what I did.

It was that experience that opened up another dimension for me. Somehow or another, this young man had heard that I was an expert on Afrika, and he wanted to attach himself to me. We met at a dinner. He had this fantastic research he was working on. He said he wanted to come to my house; he had a proposal for me to look at. That young man was Alex Haley.

Alex Haley came to my house and told me he needed support for the work he was doing on his family, which eventually became the book, *Roots*.[1] We came up with a proposal for a library on black family history that we submitted to the Carnegie Corporation. We submitted the proposal for a quarter-million dollars. They turned it down. They said the proposal "wasn't tight enough."

Well, I didn't have time to work on a really tight proposal; I was putting together one of the first Black Studies programs in the country, traveling to Afrika, doing my thing. So they gave us a planning grant of thirty-thousand dollars, which is what they should have done in the first place. With that planning grant, that summer I brought on board other scholars like Dr. Lawrence

Reddick, who used to head the Schomburg Center for Research on Black Culture in New York; and Dr. Herman Blake, who was head of Oaks College at the University of California–Santa Cruz. We divided up our responsibilities. I took care of the overseas portion: Afrika, the Caribbean, Brazil; Larry Reddick looked at the archival portion; and Herman Blake looked at the issue of oral traditions and the American struggle.

We came together in the fall with our data and saw the enormity of the field of study of the Afrikan family that *Roots* epitomized. So then we came up with a million-dollar proposal, but we said, "White folks ain't going to give us a million dollars!" So we pared it down to eight hundred thousand and submitted it to the Carnegie Corporation. They gave us about a half-million, $460,000, to go along with the earlier grant of thirty thousand. That's $490,000. That's a half-million dollars given to private scholars, not an institution! It was the largest grant of its kind ever given to black scholars. It was that grant that I coordinated with Herman Blake and Larry Reddick that put the foundation under the research around *Roots*.

Some of our scholars like to point out that they, and we, are children of the sixties. In the sixties, there was a growing Afrikan consciousness, but we referred to it as "black consciousness" or the "Black Power movement." Afrika, for us, was not as clear then as it is now. There was a black consciousness— with our marching and sitting in during the fifties and Autherine Lucy and James Meredith trying to get into "Ole Miss"—but the worldwide Afrikan consciousness, the full understanding of this Afrikan phenomena, was not quite there. We had Adam Clayton Powell, Jr., one of our leading legislators, going international, going to the Bandung Conference to represent black people from the U.S. In 1956, we had the independence of the Sudan. In 1957, we had the independence of Ghana, led by Kwame Nkrumah, who had been educated in America at Lincoln University. By 1958, Sekou Toure of Guinea said "No" to France's President De Gaulle. By the mid-sixties, dozens of Afrikan nations had their independence, or rather, their pseudo-independence—we now call it "neocolonialism." This independence explosion was taking place in Afrika while we were exploding on the streets of America. We had this growing context of understanding Afrika, but the full depth and meaning of it was too new to us.

Then in the middle of the sixties, a new organizational phenomenon takes place, with black caucuses becoming institutional structures and organizations. The Organization of the Black Lawyers, the National Council for Black Lawyers, the National Black Social Work Organization, and the Afrikan Heritage Studies Association were created. We began to structure our consciousness and to add in an Afrikan component. But the real meaning and understanding of this Afrikanness was not quite there the way it should have been. We knew it was *supposed* to be there, but the content was missing. I was aware of the content because, while I was in the struggle in America, I was going back and forth to Afrika two and three times a year, living there for months at a time. I had seen both worlds. I had this polarity of struggle in America and struggle in Afrika. I was seeing both dimensions.

It is clear to me that the sixties was the "seeding period" for this present Afrikan consciousness. In order for this growth to be effective, we needed to involve some "agricultural scientists" in the process. Most of us were out there struggling. Our target was white supremacy, but we didn't divide ourselves up effectively enough to neutralize it. But we worked that garden! Some seeds did not take root effectively, some were choked out by weeds. Fortunately, nature works in such ways that even the remnants of something can remain in the ground and start to bear fruit decades later.

The eighties was the beginning. In the nineties, a new Afrikan consciousness is beginning to bear fruit with some true understanding we did not have in the sixties. We've had thirty years to see our mistakes. We've had thirty years to see the weeds destroying the seedlings. Now we are weeding the garden. Now we know that our independence was not a real independence. We know now that the system of white supremacy is not going to allow a full and true Afrikan independence as long as it exists. Now we know that the thrust in America for integration and the Black Power movement did not have the substance they needed to have.

We did not have a systems analysis; we had a *paralysis* of analysis. We thought in a race dimension. We thought in a class dimension. We thought in a cultural dimension. We did not see that all those things were working together against us, that we were up against a worldwide system of global white supremacy that has an economic, a political, and a cultural dimension. And if we are going to deal effectively with that and develop something of our own, we need to think in terms of an Afrikan world system that has an economic dimension, a political dimension, and a cultural dimension. We can't look at the cultural nationalists and say, "Well, they are incorrect because they don't have a political analysis." Or look at the political dimension as the only dimension and leave the economic dimension to someone else. We have to see economics, politics, and culture as interrelated in order to have the capacity to do what we need to do at every level.

Our people now are more conscious of this. Dr. Clarke has produced a new book called *Africans at the Crossroads: Notes for an African World Revolution.*[2] In it, he calls for an Afrikan world union so that we can come to see each other as brothers and sisters: Even though we might be citizens of America, we are

Afrikans; even though we may be citizens of Jamaica, we are Afrikans; even though we may be citizens of Brazil, we are Afrikans. We need to think in terms of our linkages to Afrika. That does not mean we do not effectively function as citizens of America, but we share our wealth and our expertise with the motherland, the fatherland. We have an obligation to do this. That's the center of what our new system has to be built upon. A new reality is at stake.

We know integration is the deal, but not integrating with white folks. The integration we have to have, first and foremost, is the integration of Afrikan peoples with themselves! First, we need the integration of the Afrikan personality, mind, body, and spirit of individual Afrikans. Then we need an integration of the extended Afrikan context—meaning, we have to see each other as brothers and sisters. That's the true Afrikan value system and true Afrikan understanding: that we are spiritually connected. It says that if we're blood, we're connected, but even if we're not blood, we're connected. That is the kinship model we must now understand to its fullness.

We have to integrate ourselves, even though we have this "twoness," these "two souls in one dark body" that W.E.B. DuBois referred to. Looking at the polarity, the thesis–antithesis condition at the base of this pyramidal duality, we see that we have to integrate thesis and antithesis into synthesis. An Afrikan soul, that's our reality, that's what we are born with. That's what Mother Nature, that creative force of the universe, gave us. It's our God-given blessing. But our experience is in a European context. That's what slavery, colonialism, and neo-colonialism has wrought upon us.

Our Afrikan legacy is our being and essence, but our reality is European and American. Our reality is white global supremacy. We've got to find out how to interrelate these two and come up with a synthesis that helps the Afrikan side of the equation and neutralizes the European side. That's the only way we can be true to ourselves. You can't integrate the European side into the Afrikan side. You'll become schizophrenic. You've got to integrate the *old* Afrikan side, which is our heritage, and the new Afrikan side, which is our reality, to produce a new Afrikan consciousness.

We're much more aware of this now than we were twenty or thirty years ago. That's why there's a qualitative difference in what we are doing now. We've weeded out some of the weeds. We know that when somebody is "wearing blackface" and becomes a mayor of a town or city, it doesn't necessarily mean he is going to be acting in the Afrikan interest, because he's a part of the European system. We know when some black man becomes the head of a police force, we don't necessarily know whether or not he is going to do anything for us. That might not necessarily be the case. The skin game is not the real game, it's what is in our hearts and minds that matters. What has been these people's socialization process? What is their commitment to our people?

In fact, I have a formula. Again, using this pyramidal analysis, think in terms of three elements; that each has to be analyzed in order to understand whether or not a person will be true to his calling to Afrikan peoples. You have to put that person through what I call the "Afrikan VIP Test." At one polarity, you have the "V," for Values. At the other polarity, you have the "I," for Interests. At the summit, you have the "P," for Principles. We have to put into positions of leadership persons who are Afrikan VIPs, whereby they have Afrikan values and understand them, whereby they can discern Afrikan interests and are willing to defend and fight for them, and whereby they are able to espouse real Afrikan principles and operate around them.

Unfortunately, most of our people have been processed into Europeanness. We have what I call the "European VIP Syndrome," or "Very Important Person Complex." We get caught up in being very important persons, like when we become the mayor or the head of the police or the head of the school system. We forget that our real essence is the Afrikan VIP.

Whether we appreciate Afrikan values, whether we understand true Afrikan interests, whether we operate around Afrikan principles, or not, that's the test we have to apply. Don't go for the skin game when you get your mayor, your police chief, your superintendent of schools, or even your teachers. Afrikan parents need to have this in their mind when they go into the school system. Don't just take your youngster in there and just send them off to school. Don't just put your youngster in a classroom with Mrs. Muriel Greenberg or Mrs. Beulah Green without first going in there to see what that teacher is like. You have to give them the Afrikan VIP test. You've got to put the Afrikan VIP test on both Mrs. Greenberg and Mrs. Green. You have to give them the European VIP test to find out whether they think they are very important persons, or whether they understand that they've got to have Afrikan VIPs in order to reach and teach our youngsters.

You have to teach out of love and respect. You cannot teach out of contempt. If a teacher, whether it is Mrs. Greenberg or Mrs. Green, is teaching out of disrespect or is unable to love Afrikan youngsters, no matter how black, or wayward, or smelly they may be, you have to give them their walking papers. You *have* to teach out of love and respect—that's operating out of the Afrikan VIP system. That's Afrikan humanism. That's seeing the spiritual worth in everybody and everything.

But there's this European concept we operate out of. If a student is not a potentially rich person, or someone who's going to "be somebody," we can't seem to reach out for them or love them and have responsibility for them. That's why our teaching is such a negative process. That's why we're not achieving pos-

itive socialization in the teaching arena. We're into negative socialization. We've got to turn that around.

It's not a "color game," it's a value system game we need to play. It's a game of understanding spiritual development. Education has to be seen within the context of this pyramidal framework I'm talking about, within the context of this duality and polarity.

Again, at one polarity, at the base of the pyramid, education is the Afrikan context. From the beginning, in ancient times, Afrikans understood that education is socialization. Socialization is how you get your beliefs, your role models, your patterns of behavior. It's how you become what you are going to be. Around that socialization, culture is key. You can't have cultural confusion— that is, be caught up in the white world—and expect to have a positive socialization. Is it any wonder we've got confusion in our community?

If you are socialized in the Afrikan sense, you appreciate who and what you are. You believe you are one of "the chosen," that you are a descendant of the first of the human family—the first to bring forth an understanding of the God concept of the universe; the first to develop science, mathematics, and philosophy; the first to develop architecture and urban planning; the first to develop morality, ethics, and an ethos about how people should live within the larger context of the great value systems of the world and the laws of the universe.

We Afrikans were the first to do that. When Europeans were in caves and had no idea what the world was all about, Afrikan people—the people of the sun, the melanized folk around the globe—were raising up civilization and cultures and had been sustaining them for thousands of years. At the essence and core of their cultures was the concept of spiritual development, of humans as spiritual entities, linked with all the spiritual forces of the universe—an awareness that one had to develop first a formula for raising oneself into a God consciousness of spiritual character development.

Education begins with what I call "character development" or CD. CD is the socializing function of education. It has to be in place before anything else can happen around learning. If you do not have character, there's no need to give you knowledge and understanding. Without character, you would misuse that knowledge and understanding.

The other polarity is "skills development" or SD. SD is the tooling function that provides the technical skills you need to begin to understand the universe.

SD and CD have to be integrated; they grow parallel with each other. That way you will have somebody who has knowledge and wisdom *and* the ability to use what he or she learns in a wise way. Otherwise, you could give students technical knowledge—say, for example, teach them how to use science and technology—and they will become like mad scientists. You will produce someone who has learned how to create and/or use weaponry in order to destroy the enemy but who doesn't know who the enemy is. They will turn their knowledge on themselves, fire at themselves, like some of our young people are doing today, because we gave them knowledge without wisdom.

In the Afrikan socialization process, these things went together. Socialization was a process that started in the womb, in the minds of the women that were going to bear the children, and continued until one was in the tomb. Then, as an ancestor, if you lived a decent life, your life was maintained in the living realm of the dead. You would be a revered ancestor. Your name would be called upon, and your memory would be kept alive.

Then comes the third factor, which is serious or meaningful "educational development" or ED. ED is built around the truth. The ED that we have today is a negative process because it's built around lies. It's built around the lie of white supremacy. It's built around the lie that white folks were the firstest with the mostest on the planet. *That is not true!* Any scientific examination of the global experience of the human family will tell you of the Afrikan origins of humankind. That's what Afrikans stand on. We don't stand on no "anti-other peoples." We stand on an understanding of truth. That's what an education has to be all about. But again, that polarity comes into play.

You have to have an understanding of education from the point of view of intent. What is the educational endeavor designed for? If it's just designed to train you to be a better cog in the wheel of white supremacy, in the accumulation of wealth for rich white boys, then that education is bankrupt. Education with an intent to liberate you and develop your mind is a spirit force that can change the universe. That's the true educational process. That's what the Afrikans devised. That's what the Greeks were interested in when they went to Afrika; to learn at the feet of the ancient Afrikans of the Nile Valley. Education as a liberating process that liberates the mind, body, and spirit.

With that intent, we have to look also at content. Content is what is taught. The content must be truth, and it must be searched out. We've got to look at both the intent and the content.

So, you see, as Afrikans, we're blessed because we have this duality–polarity. We have this Afrikan dimension, which has come from our family and from our world experience. Then we have the European experience, which has come from the Ph.D.s, the Ed.D.s, from the Europeans and their schools. When you integrate the two dimensions, you have a "monster" mind, a monster experience capable of taking on the world.

But that's what people are afraid of, that we Afrikans will now analyze the historical development of the human experience while looking for our truth. Once our truth is raised up, it shines. It wipes out white supremacy. All those folks have got to go hide. This is what the reaction we are seeing is all about. Once you raise up Afrikan truth and put Afrika at the center of the global experience, everything else is amplified.

If you put Afrika at the center of your experience, you come to understand the beginning of humankind. You understand, number one, the Afrikan origins of humanity. All the scientific historical data points to that—millions of years ago humankind emerged out of Afrika. Dr. Cheikh Anta Diop, in his great book, *The Afrikan Origin of Civilization: Myth or Reality*, deals with this.[3] He also deals with it in his great later book, *Civilization or Barbarism*, which I have to take the credit for, because I was familiar with his work in the late fifties and sixties, and I was directly responsible for getting an eight thousand dollar grant, seven thousand of which came from the Black United Fund, to get his work translated from French to English.[4]

In the seventies, I was involved with *Roots*, with getting a half-million dollar grant to coordinate thirty scholars from around the world to put together one of the most dynamic bodies of information on the enslavement of Afrikan peoples and their Afrikan retentions and survival in the New World. So when I raise the questions and issues I'm raising, or make the analysis I'm making, I'm basing it upon twenty years of researching and coordinating the work of black scholars.

People frequently ask me, "Well, when are you going to publish this research?" I say, "If white folks have trouble with what I *say*, can you imagine what's going to happen when I bring a book out? My research involves scholars like Dr. Diop, like Dr. Iangoran Bouah, the leading scholar of the Ivory Coast; Dr. I. Ade Akinjogbin, a Yoruba scholar from the University of Ife; Dr. Bakari Sidibi, head of the archives of the Gambia, who was the one who introduced Alex Haley to the village of Juffure and who introduced him to Kebba Kanji Fofana, the griot who revealed his history. It also involves Camara Laye, who wrote the book *The African Child*, which gets into heavy research on the oral traditions of Afrikan peoples.[5] This is the type of scholarship I am privy to, that I coordinated and have at my fingertips. That's what I'm now developing for publication—the real book on what happened to the *Roots* scholarship can only be done by me. And that's what I'm working on now.

I'm very proud to say that our part of the *Roots* phenomena, the publications, will continue. Now that Alex has passed, we don't have to deal with the constraints he put on this research. We agreed in North Carolina not to go forth with the research around *Roots* because it became too controversial. Now, Herman Blake and I have said, "Let's go forth with it." Alex Haley and a fellow named Jim Dyer from the Carnegie Corporation always said we weren't ready. That research has been in our basements and in our libraries for the last fifteen years. I've been amplifying it this summer, and in the past six months I've added quite a bit to it. Dr. Clarke asked me to do a couple of chapters on slavery, so I'm working on that. I deal with slavery in Brazil, Guyana, and the Caribbean as well as the enslavement process in Afrika.

The key to all this is Europe. I am mastering the knowledge of the enslavement process that began in the Iberian Peninsula of Spain and Portugal. I know that this knowledge was transferred when the economic center of Europe moved from the Iberian Peninsula to Protestant northern Europe—to Amsterdam, Rotterdam, the Hague, London, Liverpool, Bristol, Hamburg. It then became a part of the process of the New World, in Brazil, the Caribbean, and the Americas. I am putting this data together. People are waiting for what I have. I've really got something for them.

I wrote the document that became the *Curriculum of Inclusion*, which upset, it seems, the whole world. Again, I ask, if they were upset by that analysis, what's going to happen when I bring out these other things? As a result of my curriculum work, I was the target of unscrupulous, amoral, and unethical attacks. I began to understand that when Afrikan truth is raised and the devastation wrought by white supremacy is revealed, all that people hold dear comes into question. I know that there will be a reaction from the white community, whether Jew or Gentile—even some of our "Negro" brothers and sisters will have a problem with this whole Afrikan understanding thing.

The blistering public eruption against me came about after I made a speech in Albany, New York, in 1991. The historical context of that speech needs to be understood. The attacks that came after it happened because people of color had won an enormous victory in the struggle for curriculum change in the state of New York. Because New York is so key and crucial to the world, the powers that be arrayed against us. They knew that they had to prevent these blacks from having a victory in New York. But we had our victory, and most people don't understand that. That's why, in the fall, when I go into court to struggle against the unscrupulous way they have tried to take the chairmanship of the Black Studies Department at City College away from me, I am bringing the lawsuit for twenty-five million dollars against them for violating my First Amendment rights and my academic freedom.[6] I want to be able to deal with the content of what was involved as well as the intent. Those forces attempted to destroy my constitutional rights, but they could not. The reason they did this was that they were in fear of my *content*, of the truths I am in possession of and synthesizing.

My Albany speech, in July of 1991, was the culmination of a three-year struggle over the state curriculum that goes back to 1988. In 1988, I was asked, along with three other scholars, to become involved in the process of educational change in New York by evaluating the state's curricula. We evaluated over one hundred documents from the New York State Education Department, documents covering every area of education from science, mathematics, philosophy, languages, art, and culture to drug and health education. These documents were the curricula and guidelines used by the state's public school teachers and administrators. Each of us was asked to look at these documents critically, line by line. We had teams of scholars and researchers working with us.

One scholar was Dr. Shirley Hune, a scholar of Asian American background, who looked at things from the Asian perspective. Another scholar was Dr. Carlos Rodriguez–Fraticelli, who looked at it from the point of view of Latinos and Puerto Ricans. Another scholar was Professor Lincoln White, who looked at it from a Native American perspective. And then there was me. I was asked to look at it from the Afrikan and Afrikan-American perspective. All of us looked at these documents separately and concluded that not a single curriculum document in the state of New York adequately reflected the global experience of peoples of color, first-world peoples, the foundation peoples of the world, the people who represent nine-tenths of the global family. We called for a curriculum of inclusion. We said that what we had was a curriculum of *exclusion*, of white supremacy, white nationalism, and pseudo-American nationalism. We called for change. Each of us submitted our proposals for change separately to a committee that was supposed to develop implementation procedures for those changes. Thus, in November 1988, we became a threat to the educational establishment of New York and, by implication, to the country and the world.

I was asked to do a summary of the four proposals. I did that in January 1989. The proposal I submitted used an Afrikan-centered model to look at the multicultural dimensions of the Asian perspective, the Latino perspective, the Native American perspective, and even the white perspective. The model was too heavy for the committee. It said my report was "too black." I told them that the Afrocentric perspective was just a paradigm to use for the global experience. The committee started to fight over that issue. Finally, it voted, eight to three, to proceed with my model, which became the heart of *The Curriculum of Inclusion* document. In April 1989, I was asked to revise that document, which I did. After that, I was out of the picture, in terms of New York State curriculum development and reform. The committee took our proposals, my summary, and their recommendations, and published them as one document in July 1989.

The document, *The Curriculum of Inclusion,* was given to five or six scholars around the country to review. One of them was our great scholar, Dr. Asa Hilliard, who reviewed it favorably. The others, in the main, also reviewed it favorably. Diane Ravitch of Teachers College–Columbia University reviewed it negatively. Apparently, she saw it as a great threat to the educational establishment. She went to her partners, people like Albert Shanker of the American Federation of Teachers, and others, and they devised a strategy to attack me personally and designate me the whipping boy and scapegoat for the curriculum reform movement. Instead of critiquing the proposal in an analytical way, they launched an attack on the person who had the major responsibility for the proposal: me. So from fall 1989, I was under constant attack for my involvement with this document.

By the beginning of 1990, my detractors knew *The Curriculum of Inclusion* was being discussed around the country. They also knew the Board of Regents of New York was going to vote on its acceptance soon, so they went into high gear with their attacks. The *New York Post* ran a two-column editorial on February 12, titled "Commissioner Sobel's Obsession." Commissioner Sobel was the chief educational officer for the state. His so-called "obsession": trying to put into place a multicultural education. The subtitle of the editorial was "Conspiracy Theorist." And who was the conspiracy theorist, the *eminence gris,* the boogeyman behind all this?: Dr. Leonard Jeffries of City College, with his theories about worldwide white supremacy rule. Dr. Len Jeffries, who once stated on the "Geraldo" show that AIDS may have been part of a conspiracy to devastate Afrikans and people of color. (What I actually said is that we need to look at all the possibilities for the origins of the disease, given our knowledge of the Tuskegee Institute experiment on syphilis initiated in the 1930s. In that experiment, conducted at a black institution among a black population and organized by the U.S. government and leading health officials, the subjects' illnesses were purposely untreated for forty years, even after penicillin was developed. I merely stated that we need to look at all the possible causes for devastating epidemics like AIDS. Certainly, I based my analysis on that—Tuskegee.)

The key point I am trying to make is that, by February 1990, these supremacist forces had singled me out as the big hand behind curriculum reform in New York, and they had stamped me as a conspiracy theorist. Now, within the context of the Jewish community, when you label somebody a conspiracy theorist, you immediately turn him into the worst person in the world. For many centuries, the conspiracy idea was used by white Christians to devastate and persecute Jews. So when someone who is Jewish, or when elements of the Jewish community stamp you as a conspiracy theorist, they are calling you the arch-enemy of the Jewish people.

Why was this happening? The third week in every month is when the Board of Regents meets. The third week of February was when the vote on *The Curriculum of Inclusion* was to take place. My detractors thought it was going to take place in February, so that's why they wrote their editorial. But the vote didn't take place in February; they put it off until March. So, the week before the vote was supposed to take place in March, a series of editorials came out across the country attacking the *Curriculum* and attacking me. For what purpose? Again, to try to influence the Board of Regents' vote, which didn't take place in March either. Finally, by April, they are sure the vote is going to take place, because the Board of Regents doesn't have many more months to meet that year.

So, April becomes the crucial month, and those arrayed against me, the Diane Ravitches, the Albert Shankers, the Arthur Schlesingers, they decide they can't take a chance on the *New York Post's* treatment of the issue, so they go to *The New York Times*. The *Times* sends one of their educational editorial staff, a young man named Joseph Berger, who happens to be a graduate of City College and who also happens to be Jewish. Berger called me up and asked me for an interview. I said, "I have nothing to hide. I have been interviewed by people from around the world on these and any other questions people are interested in. I want people to get at the truth."

So Berger comes to my office to get the interview. Actually, he came to one of my classes. Fortunately, we taped everything. We not only have the audiotape, but we have the videotape too. The tape shows Mr. Berger in the class, before I got there, trying to stir up trouble by asking loaded questions of the students. Other people interested in the struggle for curriculum reform were there, other news reporters and TV people were there. The famous black writer, Clayton Riley, who writes for *Newsday*, was there. The tape also shows my arrival in the classroom and me presenting my lecture, as I normally do, dealing with global white supremacy, with the Afrikan foundations of human development, and the question of enslavement.

At no point in that lecture did I ever single out the Jewish community on the question of their involvement in Afrikan enslavement. I raised that issue in the context of a systems analysis. I stated that the slavery system began with the trans-Atlantic slave trade, which had the approval, acknowledgment, and support of the Catholic Church. It began in the 1400s, with the Catholic Church giving the Portuguese throne the right to "enslave the infidels." By the 1500s, Spain, which was being led by King Ferdinand and Queen Isabella, wanted in on the slavery business.

The Italian, Christopher Columbus, convinces Ferdinand and Isabella to finance an expedition sailing West. When new lands are discovered, they want to exploit them. They need labor. They try white labor, but the whites can't handle the New World ecology. They try Native American labor, but they are dropping like flies due to European diseases, So, they bring in Afrikan labor. The Spanish throne then fights with the Portuguese throne to gain the acknowledgment and approval of the Catholic Church as leaders of the slavery system. In the 1500s, the "Protestant Reformation" takes place, and as soon as the Protestant nations—the Dutch, the English, the Germans, and the Swedes—become national entities, they fight against the Catholic nations to take control of the system.

That's the context I put the Afrikan enslavement system in. I also noted that merchants from around the world were asked to become involved in it. When the Sephardic Jewish merchants from the Iberian Peninsula were pushed out of Spain after the Spanish Inquisition, they went looking for a home. The Dutch Protestants invited them to Amsterdam, Rotterdam, the Hague, and Zealand to become part of their merchant class and help them in their slaving activities. Now, I never singled out any group, but I put each group's involvement into an historical context. I stated that when the Dutch moved their slaving activities across the Atlantic Ocean to try to rip off the business from the Portuguese in Brazil, their Jewish merchant partners, planters, and sugar developer friends were right there with them. The Portuguese fleet came down and chased them out of Brazil in 1654, and the Dutch moved, with their Jewish partners, to Surinam, Curacao, Barbados, Jamaica, Martinique, Guadeloupe, and Haiti in the Caribbean, and to Charleston, New York (then called New Amsterdam), and Newport, Rhode Island, in North America. This is history. There is no need for any particular group to be upset. People who understand are now beginning to appreciate this.

The message has gotten to Rome. This February, the Pope apologized again to Afrikan peoples for the Catholic Church's initiation and involvement in their enslavement. He did it in the early eighties; he has done it again in the nineties. As of yet, however, we have not had a similar statement from any particular group who happens to be part of the Jewish community for the involvement of the Jewish merchant class, bankers, and planters in the enslavement process. There's complete denial and hysteria. But I understand that, too. It's what I call "cognitive dissonance," the inability to process new information due to the discomfort and disharmony the new information produces.

Many people really don't know their history. Afrikan people are obligated to raise that history because we were in the middle of it. The enslavement process is an important part of the centrality of Afrikanness in the modern world. It is our obligation to raise these questions. When we do, some people are going to be uncomfortable, even some of our own people. The question of Afrikans' own involvement in slavery is an important question we have to raise. I do it all the time. We've got to raise these questions, but that's to be done within the family. When we deal with things outside the family, we've got to raise serious questions. We can't have a paralysis of analysis and let people bring up the civil rights movement or the idea of some kind of coalition that might have developed between blacks and Jews during that movement and have that blind us from the real deal.

Other people operate from the European VIP perspective. The rich bankers and merchants have a fraternity of interests they operate out of. It doesn't make any difference to them whether one is Jewish, or Christian, or Muslim; it does not make any difference whether one is Christian Catholic or Christian Protestant. They have a fraternity of interest. It is this economic analysis we need. We do not need to be blinded by a civil rights coalition. There are economic interests across these groups that were working against us then and that are continuing to work against us now by establishing imperialism, neocolonialism, and the impoverishment of black people and people of color around the world. These forces continue to work in South Afrika, against the interests of black folk, because they want the gold and diamonds. Continuing to work in this economic realm, which is so important to them. They are willing to compromise the historical integrity of Israel, which rose up out of the ashes of the European Jewry that was devastated by the Nazi holocaust. The state of Israel's integrity is compromised by leaders who have an economic interest to wed themselves to the fascists of South Afrika and thereby help white supremacy maintain power in South Afrika. There is no justification for that relationship at all, except that it is in the economic interests of those who are at the heart of white supremacy, and who believe in the European system of control and exploitation.

We have to make these kinds of analyses. We're obligated to do so! This is what we were trained to do, in the European dimension and the Afrikan dimension. But when we do it, everybody is devastated.

Getting back to April 1990 now, we're still on the curriculum issue: *The New York Times* took the lead with Mr. Berger's article, but I got them caught with their drawers down, because I got it on videotape. I got raw footage. I didn't doctor anything. The tape shows me lecturing in the context that I always lecture, dealing with the global enslavement system, not singling out any one group, but making sure I include as many people as possible.

Let me say this, first and foremost, it is not in our interests to finger the Jewish community for their involvement in our degradation, enslavement, or exploitation. It is not in our best interest to put the Jews at the center of this controversy. That might blind us from seeing the Protestants, the Catholics, the Swedes, the Germans, the Dutch, the French, the Italians, the Spanish, the English, and the white Americans who were all involved. I never raised this issue in the context of singling out the Jews. Unfortunately, the Jewish community, or certain elements of it, raised it in that context, hoping to create a red herring or a red flag to scare people.

The person who took the lead in doing this was Joseph Berger in his April 20th article in *The New York Times*, the product of his visit to my class. The article was titled, "Two Professors at City College Stir Up a Storm," referring to myself and a Professor Michael Levin at City College, whose beliefs in the inferiority of black and Latin people and the superiority of Jewish people were well known. The subtitles were "Uproar at City College" and "A Turmoil at City College." There was no turmoil at City College. There was a little bit of controversy, but no turmoil. Professor Levin had been teaching his thing about black and Latin people for some years. He was tolerated. He had the right to have his opinion. But they wanted to compare me to Levin in order to discredit my work with *The Curriculum of Inclusion*.

Bergman also put in his article the capstone of charges aimed to destroy me and the curriculum movement: that I was anti-Semitic. He wrote that Professor Jeffries, "in his classes makes reference to rich Jews' involvement in slavery." He also said that, "Professor Jeffries also mentions that the swastika may have been an ancient Afrikan symbol, or some people's symbol, that's older than the Germans and the Jewish people themselves." In other words, these things were put in as a red herring. But I have a copy of the tape. I know what I presented. I am having a transcript made of it. These are the things that are going to be published in the Fall, once the court situation has been cleared up. Unfortunately, the people are trapped. This attack is something being engineered by Jewish media people to beat back the struggle over curriculum reform.

People began to call me from around the world. The one thing they wanted to know was, "Do you have a theory about black people being superior

because of the amount of melanin in their skin?" Of course, Berger mentioned that in his article. When the article came out I was at a scientific conference on melanin. But if you read the article, you'll see that he did not say in it that *Jeffries* has a theory that black people are superior because of their melanin, rather he states that I passed out to my class "an article that implies that black people have an advantage, intellectually and physically, because of melanin." Now look at the wording of that very carefully. He doesn't say that *I* say anything about melanin; he says that I pass out some information on it to my class. He does not say whether I am for that document or against it. He does not say what my analysis of it is. He simply leaves it there for the world to pick up. He words it in such a way to say that the document implies black people have physical and *intellectual* advantage over whites because of melanin.

Well, I have read that document over and over again to find out whether it implied this. It does not. It does state clearly that we have a physical advantage. That much seems to be quite clear and is documented by scientific evidence. The inclusion of the intellectual advantage aspect was planted by Berger to parallel a statement by Levin that black people are intellectually inferior because of their IQ scores. This was a masterful stroke. He beat me back by tying me down to theories on melanin, black superiority, and anti-Semitism.

But it didn't work. In spite of all the print and TV coverage the story got, it has not worked. Within a week after the Board of Regents voted and the *Times* article went out over the wire services, some people from London's BBC called me and asked, "Dr. Jeffries, do you have a theory that black people are superior because of their high melanin content?" I answered, "No." "Well, what kind of theory do you have?" I said, "I don't have a theory. I have a paradigm, a framework of looking at the world that involves understanding the Afrikan centrality of the human experience." Other people called: Australia's "Nightline," the Canadian Broadcasting System, *Ebony*, and *Jet*. They all wanted to know if I had a theory on black folks and melanin. I told them no too, but I also told them I had something more important to say, as I tell all reporters.

I told them that I knew the most important story in the history of humanity, a story that could make their careers if they took it and ran with it. They said, "What is it?" I told them, first of all, that what I and other scholars like me were saying was that there is an Afrikan origin to humanity; two, there is an Afrikan evolution of society; three, there is an Afrikan cradle of civilization, particularly in the Nile Valley; four, a diffusion of this Afrikan culture to other people has taken place over centuries; five, the legacy of Afrikan peoples was stolen by the Greeks; and six, there is an Afrikan foundation to Judeo-Christianity and Islam.

But I usually lost them before I could finish these points, or I got no response from them. Nobody wanted to deal with the truth. They just wanted to deal with the hysterical points that had been raised by Berger about theories I did not have and attacks on people I did not make. Because the *Times* is such an important communications vehicle, these lies have remained out there, and I've had to deal with them. But I haven't shrunk from the task, because I know I am operating out of truth.

Here's the sequence of events thereafter: Within a week, on April 26, the Board of Regents voted seventeen to nothing to accept *The Curriculum of Inclusion* and begin the process of curriculum reform it outlined. Most people do not know about this enormous victory. Within a few months, the state commissioner of education puts in place a committee of twenty-four persons, dominated by white people, many of them Jews, including the great scholar from Harvard, Nathan Glazer, and other people such as Arthur Schlesinger, Jr. This committee was supposed to look at the social studies area and come up with recommendations for curricular change. It met for a year. After that year, in June 1991, it issued a report entitled "One Nation, Many Peoples: A Declaration of Cultural Interdependence." Even a conservative like Nathan Glazer went along with the committee, saying its ideas for reform were ideas whose time had come.

But Arthur Schlesinger, who was fighting for the old establishment and white supremacy, couldn't accept them. Along with a Professor Ken Jackson, Schlesinger was one of two members who voted against the report. But listen to this: After two meetings of the committee, Schlesinger, seeing that this Afrikan truth, and the truth of native peoples and Latin peoples and Asian peoples, was going to be put on the table and seriously discussed—not by me, because I wasn't a part of the committee—but by others like Asa Hilliard and a third-grade schoolteacher named Diane Glover and a beautiful Ethiopian sister, Dr. Elleni Tedla, of Colgate University—when he sees that these Afrikans were strong enough to raise the issues I had raised, he asks to be removed from the committee as a full member. He wanted to hang around so he could claim connection and be listed as a consultant, but he did not want to be a part of the process of enlightenment the committee went through in looking at this larger truth. He wanted to hide behind a cloak of white supremacy. So he and other conservative scholars begin a campaign to discredit the report.

Schlesinger produced a volume called *The Disuniting of America*,[7] funded by right-wing monies, which is a purely political tract that tries to block the idea of multicultural curricula. In that book, he attacks all the Afrocentric scholars— DuBois, John Hope Franklin, John Henrik Clarke, Asa Hilliard—all of us had our pictures in there, in the margins, teeny-tiny little pictures. The one scholar who had a half-page photo was Dr. Len Jeffries. Okay, now this is important to understand: When Schlesinger tries to block the success that the committee has had, when he puts my picture in his book, it becomes clear to me, and to my people, that I was being targeted for destruction and death. I had to make sure I put out a statement about what this thing was all about.

When I went up to Albany in July 1991, a couple weeks after the Schlesinger book came out and a couple weeks after the "One Nation, Many Peoples" report was issued, I outlined the things I talked about earlier. At no point did I single out the Jewish community. When the Jewish community was mentioned, it was in reference to a conversation I had had with that outstanding Jewish leader, New York City Mayor Edward I. Koch, on May 16th, 1989, after *The Curriculum of Inclusion* had been accepted.

After the publication of *The New York Times* article, within a couple of weeks of it and shortly after the Board of Regents voted to accept *The Curriculum of Inclusion* document, Mayor Koch had asked me to come visit him and bring the materials I used to document all these controversial things I was saying. Before we met, he had stated on his TV program, to a million-plus people, that Leonard Jeffries was wrong, that I was teaching racism in my class; but that Levin's theories of black people being inferior were right, and he was not teaching racism in his class. Now, Koch had never been to my class. I had several outstanding nationalist and Zionist Jewish students in my class, and not one of them testified against me as being anti-Semitic. They were in my class for four-and-a-half months, three times a week, listening to my presentations on every conceivable thing in the universe, but none of them had anything to say against me. In fact, I received letters to the contrary from some of my Jewish students. See, but because of the hysteria created by the media, people saw or thought there was another reality out there.

Well, Mayor Koch thought he could destroy whatever integrity I might have had. I went down to his office with all my books: the Diop books, the ben-Jochannan books, the Chancellor Williams books, the George M. James books, the books by white scholars such as Martin Bernal and Gerald Massey, the books by outstanding Jewish scholars like Melville Herskovits and Herbert Aptheker, who support the thesis of the Afrikan origins of humankind. There is a whole tradition of Jewish scholarship supporting this Afrikan understanding. Well, when Ed Koch saw this material, he was taken aback. We met for an hour-and-a-half. Fortunately, it was his recommendation that we tape that meeting, also, so I also have that conversation on tape. I call it "The Afrikan Education of Edward I. Koch." I give it out to people so they can see what the real deal is. I like to let them know that in May 1990, Len Jeffries was willing to go to one of the leading members of the Jewish world community and lay out before him what it was that we Afrikan scholars have been saying and why we have been saying it.

He wanted to see what I had, thinking he would be able to devastate and ridicule me. Well, he saw it, and for a year and a half, Ed Koch had nothing to say about Len Jeffries. I had hoped, when I went into his office, me with my brother and him with the senior partner of his law firm, that he would take this information and give it to Jewish scholars so a more meaningful dialogue and discussion could take place between us. But of course, that did not happen. There was only silence on Ed Koch's part, for a year and a half. He did not resurface against me until after the Albany speech on June 20, 1991, in which I mentioned Mayor Koch, Diane Ravitch, and others, as the leading emissaries of the neo-conservative forces who rallied against me.

As I said, I made that speech in the context of trying to put the whole framework of what the struggle was all about before the world. It was clear my life was threatened. Most people told me, "Don't be bothered." The Afrikan Holy Ghost told me, "When you are with your truth, you can go anywhere and deal with anybody. Since Koch is the biggest and baddest they've got, you've taken on their best, so you don't have to worry about the rest."

When Koch wrote me to ask me to come see him, the letter said, "Dr. Jeffries, I would like for you to come down to my office so we can discuss your documentation." I thought he wasn't serious. So I called him up and said, "I'm interested in your proposition, but I have a condition. I want you to come to my office." Koch said, "Oh no, I couldn't come up to your office." I said, "Well, I have all the books and everything up here." "Oh no, no, no, I couldn't do that. That would cause, you know, too much publicity." I said, "Well, I'll come down to your office, but first you've got to give up my pyramids."

He didn't know what I was talking about. I told him, "I have a picture of you from several years ago, riding on a camel around the pyramids and talking about how your ancestors built the pyramids thousands of years ago. I have another picture of Israeli Prime Minister Menachem Begin dancing in front of the pyramids, claiming that *his* ancestors built them thousands of years ago. I want our pyramids back, and there is no need to even dialogue unless you are prepared to give them up."

I explained that, in the current mythology of the world, the pyramids have been claimed as a part of the legacy of the ancient Hebrews. In point of fact, there is no historical evidence linking the ancient Hebrews with the pyramids. The Great Pyramids of Giza were built from the fourth to the seventh dynasty, in a period between 2600 and 2100 B.C. By their own tradition, the Jews do not indicate their spiritual ancestor Abraham emerging until 1700 or 1800 B.C. In

fact, there wasn't a Jewish community in Egypt that had anything to do with the ancient pyramids. It is clear to me that this was a part of the stolen legacy we had to reclaim. He was taken aback by my request, but he agreed to give us our pyramids back.

The point I am trying to make is that you have to operate from a position of strength. If you operate from weakness and doubt, you won't know what you are doing, and there's no need for you to even get into the ballgame.

The first thing I raised with Ed Koch was the question of the Statue of Liberty. On the tape, I say, "Ed, we have to deal with that Statue of Liberty, because clearly the historical evidence shows that it had nothing to do with your immigrant forebears. The Statue of Liberty has a great deal to do with my forebears who fought for liberty in America." Most people do not know this. The statue was standing in the harbor in 1886, long before the waves and waves of immigrants from eastern, central, and southern Europe began to stream into New York. It was a gift to commemorate the struggle of black folk during the Civil War. It was conceived by a Frenchman named Edouard-René Lefebvre de Laboulaye, a political scientist who wrote a three-volume history of the United States and who was the head of the French Anti-Slave Society.

Frédéric Auguste Bartholdi, the statue's sculptor, was a friend of his. When the first models of the statue were built, they were of an Afrikan woman holding the broken chains of enslavement in her hand and at her feet, but this model could not be accepted by a racist America. Eventually, the Statue of Liberty was modeled in a white context, but the basis for the idea came out of the Afrikan experience. Standing in the harbor, with its beacon of light, the Statue of Liberty was co-opted by the immigrants coming to New York, who took it and made it a spiritual symbol for themselves. The real spirit of it, however, comes from our ancestors, who fought like no other people against the slave system and produced this enormous victory against enslavement. The Statue of Liberty has an Afrikan center, but this is not in the history books. I didn't learn about this when I went through school. That history has to be known. It has to be told. I intend to tell it with the last breath in my body.

I told this to Ed Koch, and he accepted it. He didn't have any information to the contrary. But, for some reason, if you're black and you raise these issues, you become "anti"— anti-immigrants, anti-Italian, anti-Poles, anti-Hungarians, and anti-Jews. I'm not "anti," I'm trying to deal with the truth.

I'm presenting my information, and after about a half-hour, Koch starts getting what I call cognitive dissonance. I would prefer to call it something much deeper, like "racial pathology," but cognitive dissonance is good enough for those who cannot digest that term. Cognitive dissonance started to set in, and after a while, he got so uncomfortable he asked me, "Well, what is it that you said, something about rich Jews' involvement in the enslavement of Afrikans?" Now, this is Ed Koch asking me a question about the Jews. So I ask him back, "Where do you want us to start? What period of history? Do you want us to start at the beginnings of Afrikan enslavement in the 1400s? Do you want me to start in Amsterdam and Hamburg, where the new Jewish community in those areas continued the slave trade for the Dutch, the Germans, and the English? Or do you want me to start in Brazil, the Caribbean, or Curacao? Or in New York or Newport, Rhode Island? Newport, at the time the American Revolution, was the leading slave center in America. It was the home of one of the largest, most active, and wealthy Jewish communities in America. Do you want me to start there?"

Koch responded, "Well, uh, uh, uh, what books do you have?" I told him, "Well, I have a book about a man named Aaron Lopez of Newport, who, in the 1750s and 1760s, was one of the biggest slavers out of Newport, which was a community that had a large number of wealthy Jews who controlled a hundred or so of the slave ships. Aaron Lopez, himself, controlled a dozen. These ship-owners also controlled most, if not all of the thirty distilleries that processed molasses from the Caribbean into rum, which was sold to the Native Americans and Afrikans as 'firewater.'"

I kept on. "Do you want to go back into the Spanish and Portuguese Sephardic Jewish community? Then get Stephen Birmingham's book *The Grandees.*[8] That book claims that the rich Jewish Sephardic community supported the Spanish throne and helped lay the foundations for Afrikan enslavement in the 1400s and 1500s. It further claims that even after the Jews were persecuted during the Spanish Inquisition in 1492, plenty of them converted to Christianity and stayed in Spain to help Queen Isabella, who was notoriously anti-Semitic, maintain the Spanish slavery system."

"Do you want to go to Amsterdam? Then get a book by Jonathan Israel entitled *European Jewry in the Age of Mercantilism, 1550–1750.*[9] It shows a picture of the Amsterdam Synagogue, which was the center of slave trading for the Dutch and notes that Amsterdam was the leading port in this period of time for slaving. Before that time, the Dutch and the English had seen slaving as some type of pirate operation. Well, the Jewish merchants said, 'Wait a minute, let's make this thing into a business. There's no need to send out a fleet and have it waiting in the Atlantic Ocean for months to see whether it can catch up with the Spanish galleons. Let's make this thing into a serious business operation. Let's send ships loaded with cheap manufactured goods out of the ports of Europe, down to the West Coast of Afrika, to trade with Afrikan wayward chiefs and

insane Afrikans, then let's fill these same ships up with Afrikans. Then, let's take them across the ocean and make a profit, not only on the trade goods for Afrikans, but by trading the Afrikans in the New World. Then, we'll take the products of the New World, put them in the same ships, and bring them back to Europe. We'll establish a system.' This system became huge, and it was the merchant bankers of Amsterdam, Protestant and Jewish, who took the lead in this activity.

"That is the history. People have got to deal with that. I am not singling out the Jewish people. They were persecuted throughout Europe, even to this day, but I am talking about the wealthy who had a fraternity of interests in maintaining the system of enslavement, which is the genocide and the Holocaust of Afrikan peoples. It is my sacred mission to raise these issues. I do not single out any particular people, but since the Jews singled themselves out on this matter, we need clarity."

I was trying to bring that clarity to Ed Koch. I told him, "Now, I'm not talking about *most* Jews. *Most* Jews were being beat up and down Europe, persecuted for being Jewish. I'm talking about the *rich* Jews, specifically making that distinction. Just like I'm not talking about white folks in general when I talk about oppression, I'm talking about wealthy white folks, the powerful white folks who make the decisions.

Now, Diane Ravitch can say, "Black people sold black people into slavery." She does not hesitate to say that. She doesn't specify that *certain* Afrikan chiefs may have sold Afrikans into slavery; she says black people, indicting *all* black people, sold black people. Schlesinger says the same thing. We're the only people asked to specify. You can't say "Jews sold black people," you have to say "certain Jews." Well, I say "certain Jews," but apparently that's not enough, even saying "rich Jews" is not enough—I have to specify the specific Jews. We're the only people called upon for that type of specificity.

So I did that. I said, "Okay, let's talk about who financed, planned, operated, maintained the slave trade. Let's talk about every slave ship being blessed by a Protestant minister and a Catholic priest. Let's talk about the Catholic Church. Let's talk about the Danes, the Dutch, the Portuguese, the French, the Scots, the Swedes, the Brandenburg Germans, the Jews, Gentiles, Arabs, and Christians, who were involved in slavery for hundreds of years. Let's deal with the whole ball of wax. Let's not just say 'Afrikans sold Afrikans into slavery.'"

So I told Ed Koch, "Let's get some clarity on these things. Let's talk about them. The documentation is there."

I am currently preparing a ten-volume work dealing with the Jewish relationship to the black community, with reference to slavery. If we put it in the school system, there will be no question about Diane Ravitch, Arthur Schlesinger, *or* Miss Daisy!

An anti-Semitic person does not stay at City College for twenty years as chairman of a department and have friends. Many of the people at City College are Jewish. In fact, the "head Jew" at City College, Dr. Bernard Sohmer, came up to me after the *Times* article appeared and said, "Len, everybody knows rich Jews helped finance the slave trade." I said, "If everybody knows it, then let's put it in the classroom."

Now, Bernard Sohmer is an individual who's been at City College a long time. He was a student there in the forties and a young professor there in the fifties. He became a dean in the sixties and seventies, and has been a leader at the college for over thirty years. He's either head of the faculty senate or the faculty council. He is the person who filters Jewish interests and speaks on behalf of Jews at City College. Even when we had a Jewish president at the college, an outstanding physicist, Dr. Robert Marshak, persons who wanted to deal with Jewish alumni, faculty, or students interests went to Bernard Sohmer. He was the "head Jew in charge," just like we have this tradition in our community of the HNIC, or "head Negro in charge." Well, at City College, even though we have a black president, I'm the head Negro in charge. When people want to deal with something around black folks, they come to me. I protect Afrikan interests.

To say my partner, Bernie Sohmer, is the head Jew in charge is not a reference that beats him down; it is a reference that acknowledges him and raises him up. It's not an anti-Semitic reference. It is a reference based upon our mutual understanding of our interests. Bernie and I have a working relationship. I respect the man. Unfortunately, the way this controversy has been raised has produced a poisoning in our relationship. We still talk, but we don't have the same let's-sit-down-and-work-out-the-problems relationship that we once had. If there is a major crisis at City College, we'll get together, which we did when the students took over the college. I worked with Bernie Sohmer to settle that issue so people weren't killed.

In one of the greatest attacks on a single individual in the history of the world for being "anti-Jewish," or anti-Semitic, I was depicted as a "crazy professor." My credentials were questioned. My enemies even went so far as to say I didn't have a Ph.D., even though they knew I got my master's and my doctorate from Columbia

University. They even went to the extent of saying I got my position as chair of the Black Studies department in 1972 based upon no experience or credentials.

An important thing that needs to be added is that the scholarship and the research I began thirty or forty years ago is continuing. I want people to know that I didn't get into this ballgame of trying to search for the truth yesterday. In the fifties, as a young scholar at Lafayette College, I was involved in studying the urban crisis. I was still a teenager, nineteen years old, and I concluded, in a 148-page document I wrote for my honors work in 1958, that the nation's cities were about to explode because of racial segregation, discrimination in employment, overcrowding, and the lack of understanding about these things. I wrote about metropolitan segregation, about the ring of white cities around the suburban areas. I was before my time. Within a few years, the cities exploded.

By 1961, I was in Afrika, getting this Afrikan consciousness, playing a part in the awakening of Afrika. In the sixties, I did my master's thesis on the economic development plan of Senegal. I did my dissertation on the politics of economics in the Ivory Coast. I was in the vanguard of research on Afrikan development.

In the eighties, we began to institutionalize Black Studies, worldwide. We formed the Association for the Study of Classical Afrikan Civilizations, so that hundreds of scholars could come together and commune about this research and share it, and not through the traditional thing of hiding our research until it could be published. Our thing is to *share* the research, to go to the site of the research and see the documents for ourselves. Dr. Jacob Carruthers of Chicago was the first president of the Association. I was the regional vice president and also the national secretary. We started taking hundreds of our people to the Nile Valley. They came back with firsthand knowledge of the monumental buildings of the Afrikans, of Afrikan science and mathematics, of the great temples of learning that became the models for the universities of later times.

As we build this Afrikan pyramid of knowledge for the world, a new keystone is being fashioned to hold up all this truth, and it is the truth about the Nile Valley. Without this truth, Afrikan history hangs in an imbalanced situation. With it, it's grounded on a firm foundation. The culture and civilization that emerged out of Afrikan people's communion, for ten thousand years, in that Nile Valley, produced the foundations for civilization and culture for the world. It produced the foundation for science, philosophy, and medicine; the foundations for social development, understanding of the spiritual worth of individuals and the universe—all that comes out of our people's experience in the Nile Valley.

I have a formula that says, "Afrikans create. Europeans imitate." There's nothing wrong with imitation, it's flattery. But if you imitate and, because of

your power dynamics, you colonize information, lands, or people and then say those you've colonized had no history, no culture, and contributed nothing to culture and civilization, that's a dastardly act. And that's what the European world has imposed upon us. That's why we have a sacred mission to change all that.

1 Haley, Alex, *Roots* (Garden City, NY: Doubleday, 1976).

2 Clarke, John Henrik, *Africans at the Crossroads: Notes for an African World Revolution* (Trenton, NJ: Africa World Press, 1991).

3 Diop, Cheikh Anta, *The Afrikan Origin of Civilization: Myth or Reality* (New York: Lawrence Hill, 1974);

4 Diop, Cheikh Anta, *Civilization or Barbarism: An Authentic Anthropology* (Brooklyn, NY: Lawrence Hill, 1990).

5 Laye, Camara, *The African Child* (London: Collins, 1954).

6 In 1993, Dr. Jeffries won his case and retained his chairmanship. In 1995, the New York Supreme Court ruled against Jeffries maintaining his chairmanship. However, the Black Studies faculty at CCNY re-elected him as Chairman, but Jeffries declined for the good of the department.

7 Schlesinger, Arthur M., Jr., *The Disuniting of America* (Knoxville, TN: Whittle Books, 1991).

8 Birmingham, Stephen, *The Grandees: America's Sephardic Elite* (New York: Harper & Row, 1971).

9 Israel, Jonathan I., *European Jewry in the Age of Mercantilism, 1550–1750* (Oxford: Clarendon, 1985).

ENDNOTE

The insistance that Afrikans have accomplished nothing of significance in the world is an effort to promote and embrace the idea that Europeans have created everything of significance in the world. This denial persists despite the availability and dissemination of information documenting the contributions of Afrikan people, past and present. The scholars presented in this volume are under constant attack. Indeed, they are involved in continuous warfare regarding the exclusion or inclusion of their work in the canon of the arts, sciences, humanities, history, literature, and other disciplines.

An example of this is the statement published in the Spring 1994 issue of *American Educator*, a publication of the American Federation of Teachers, referring to many of the scholars included in this work: "Although they claim to advance long-ignored facts and to correct Eurocentric distortions of history, many of their claims and theories turn out to be little more than 'Africanized' versions of discredited and discarded European ideas." The foundation for this line of thinking is grounded in Western civilization's greatest collective mental illness: white suprmacy.

Nevertheless, good things continue to occur. I continue to receive volumes of letters related to my radio broadcasts that refer to the kinds of discussions included in this book. An excerpt from one letter reflects the practical results of such programming.

> When I came in contact with your program, I was at a point in my life where I was involved in destructive behavior in the Los Angeles area. I had embraced a criminal lifestyle that involved affiliation with gangs and selling drugs in the community. After one night listening to your program, my life was changed. It was "Afrikan Mental Liberation Weekend" that really pushed me over. I never lacked the intelligence. I attended the University of California-Berkeley, California State-Dominguez Hills, and California State-Los Angeles, but it was only until I listened to you and your programming that I took up a lifestyle that I know saved my life.

The facts have been presented. It is now up to you to judge the veracity of the information. Nothing on this earth should have the power to influence your thinking besides your own scrupulous investigation of the sum total of this work.

Truth, the most potent of principles, embedded in spiritual reality inspired the Afrikans of the Nile Valley to call their literature *Medew Neter* or "Divine Speech." The positive elements of this literature—Afrikan history, art, culture, and science—must permeate the consciousness of the present. Only after they are included in all educational curricula and information systerms will positive change occur and the Afrikan world united.

Those with the greatest control and influence over scholarship, publishing, literature, entertainment, and the flow of information have encouraged their intellectuals to appropiate the best of the past—and the present—making it evolve from their culture and reside in their history.

Afrikan people will not be denied the contributions they have made to the development and welfare of the human family. The Afrikan people will not be detered from telling this story so that others will change their thinking. Until the words and ideas of Afrikan people are fully realized, we cannot evolve beyond the petty issues of color and race, nor can we grow with one of the Creator's most essential elements: Enlightenment.

First Word

To A

New Word

For A

Clear Word

Or A

Last Word

-K. P.-L.

BIOGRAPHIES

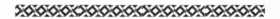

NA'IM AKBAR

Dr. Na'im Akbar is a celebrated clinical psychologist, author, and lecturer, whose work has been lauded throughout the United States, the Caribbean, Afrika, and Europe for its Afrikan-centered, humanistic, and holistic approach to human development. He has been interviewed on several episodes of "Tony Brown's Journal," "The Phil Donahue Show" and "The Oprah Winfrey Show," and travels thousands of miles each year to meet the spiraling demands for his combined talents as a lecturer on college campuses and community and professional forums. He is the author of over twenty significant scholarly papers and several widely acclaimed books, including *From Miseducation to Education, Chains and Images of Psychological Slavery, Visions for Black Men,* and *Light from Ancient Africa.* An early work, *Natural Psychology and Human Transformation,* which addresses the limitations and failure of Western psychology to deal with the Afrikan experience, was recently expanded and reissued.

A graduate of the University of Michigan, whose undergraduate and doctoral degrees are both in psychology, Dr. Akbar has taught at Norfolk State University and Morehouse College, where he was chairman of the Psychology Department. He also served as director of the Office of Human Development of the American Muslim Mission in Chicago, and has served on the boards of directors of several important organizations, including several terms on the board of the National Association of Black Psychologists, to which he was elected president in 1987-88. He was the associate editor of the *Journal of Black Psychology* for eight years and is currently a member of the editorial board of the *Journal of Black Studies.*

Dr. Akbar has received numerous honors for his progressive and landmark contributions to his specialized studies of the psychology of the Afrikan American. Among those awards is the Annual Member Award from the National Association of Black Psychologists for his outstanding scholarship and research. He is listed in *Who's Who in Black America* and has received the prestigious Community Service Award from the National Association of Black Social Workers. The mayors of Atlantic City, New Jersey (in 1986) and Cleveland, Ohio (in 1988) both declared a "Na'im Akbar Day" in their cities in recognition of his contributions to the field of black psychology. He was the second recipient of the Dr. Martin Luther King, Jr. Distinguished Scholar Award from the National Human Relations Task Force at Florida State University in 1987. During that same year, he was also a recipient of a McKnight Foundation Faculty

Development Grant, which afforded him a year's funded sabbatical for research and writing.

Dr. Akbar currently holds a joint appointment in the Department of Psychology and in the Black Studies Program at Florida State University. He lives with his wife, Renee, their daughter, and their twin sons in Tallahassee.

Yosef A. A. ben-Jochannan

Yosef A. A. ben-Jochannan was born in Ethiopia and received his early education in Brazil, St. Croix, and Puerto Rico. He subsequently obtained a bachelor's degree in civil engineering, a law degree, and dual doctorates in cultural anthropology and Moorish history. He practiced law as an assistant prosecutor in Puerto Rico and has worked as a civil engineer in both Puerto Rico and the United States. From 1945 to 1970, he was the chief of the Afrikan Desk of UNESCO (the United Nations Education Scientific Cultural Organization) and served as the civilian advisor to the permanent African missions to the United Nations from 1957 to 1964.

Throughout his career, "Dr. Ben," as he is affectionately called by his many loyal students, has taught at numerous universities in Afrika, the Caribbean, and North and South America. Though he retired from full-time teaching at Cornell University in Ithaca, New York, he is presently professor of religion and history at Al Azar University in Cairo, Egypt. He also conducts educational tours to Kemet (Egypt) and the Nile Valley, and is the chairman of the Alkebu-Lan Foundation and Alkebu-Lan Books and Educational Materials.

The author of twenty-nine books, including *We, the Black Jews; Black Man of the Nile; Africa: Mother of "Western Civilization";* and *The African Mysteries System of Wa'set, Egypt and its European Stepchild, "Greek Philosophy,"* Dr. Ben is currently working on a seven-volume *Encyclopedia of Africa.* He is married and the father of twelve biological and six adopted children.

JOHN HENRIK CLARKE

John Henrik Clarke was born in Union Springs, Alabama. He grew to young manhood in Columbus, Georgia, then traveled to New York City with the ambition of pursuing a career as a writer. After four years in the U.S. Air Force, earning the rank of sergeant major, he attended New York University and majored in history and world literature. From his early years, Dr. Clarke studied the history of the world and the history of Afrikan people in particular. He traveled extensively in Afrika, visiting every country except South Afrika. His travels took him to Latin America, western Asia, the Caribbean, and Europe, mainly to attend conferences on world history, culture, and politics.

As a writer of fiction, Dr. Clarke has published over fifty short stories, which have been distributed in this country and abroad. His best-known short story, "The Boy Who Painted Christ Black," has been translated into more than a dozen languages. His articles and conference papers on Afrikan and Afrikan American history, politics, and culture have been published in leading journals throughout the world. Dr. Clarke has also written or edited twenty-one works of history or social criticism. The best known are: *American Negro Short Stories*; *William Styron's Nat Turner: Ten Black Writers Respond*; *Malcolm X: The Man and his Times*; *Harlem, U.S.A.*; *Marcus Garvey and the Vision of Africa*; *New Dimensions of African World History*; and *Africans at the Crossroads: Notes for an African World Revolution.* He has served as a staff member on five different publications, including the *Pittsburgh Courier* (1957–1958), and was, for twenty years, the associate editor of *Freedomways* magazine (1962–1982). Among the other positions he has held are: feature writer for the First African Heritage Exposition; special consultant and coordinator of the CBS TV series, "Black Heritage: The History of Afro-Americans"; and consultant to Anheuser–Busch's "Great Kings and Queens of Africa" series, the Carver Federal Savings Bank historical series, and Harcourt Brace Jovanovich's *African American Experience Resource Guide.*

Among several other organizational affiliations, Dr. Clarke is the founding president of the African Heritage Studies Association, and one of the founding members and chairman of the Council of Elders for the Association for the Study of Classical African Civilizations. He is also a founding member of the Black Academy of Arts and Letters, and served for several years on the Consultative Council of the International Organization for the Elimination of All Forms of Racial Discrimination as one of their nongovernmental organization representatives at the United Nations. During his long career, Dr. Clarke has

been instrumental in the establishment of several libraries. The new library at Cornell University was dedicated in his name in 1986. The John Henrik Clarke Africana Collection at Atlanta University was dedicated in 1993. The John Henrik Clarke Children's Library at P.S. 123 in Harlem has been functioning for several years.

Dr. Clarke has received over a dozen citations for excellence in teaching. He is also the recipient of several honorary doctor of letters degrees from the University of Denver, the University of the District of Columbia, and Clarke Atlanta University. He was accepted into the Alpha Beta Upsilon Chapter of the honor society of historians, Phi Alpha Theta, when he received his Ph.D. in history from Pacific Western University in 1993.

Dr. Clarke taught Afrikan history as the distinguished visiting professor of African History at the Africana Studies and Research Center at Cornell University. He is presently professor emeritus of African world history in the Department of Africana and Puerto Rican Studies at Hunter College in New York City.

WILLIAM LaRUE DILLARD

A native of Suffolk, Virginia, Dr. William LaRue Dillard is pastor of the historic Second Baptist Church of Monrovia, California. A dynamic and gifted preacher and teacher who effectively communicates profound biblical truths with a powerful and compelling appeal, Dr. Dillard earned his bachelor of divinity and doctor of divinity degrees from the American Bible Institute, and earned the doctor of philosophy degree in clinical psychology from Hamilton University. He received his Christian education teaching credentials from the Evangelical Teacher's Training Association of America and L.I.F.E. Bible College. He was baptized, licensed, and ordained to the gospel ministry at Mount Zion Baptist Church in Los Angeles, California.

Dr. Dillard is internationally known throughout the Christian community, having preached the gospel in West Africa, England, Israel, the Philippines, Mexico, and throughout the United States of America for more than three decades. As the author of eight books, including *A Burning and a Yearning in My Soul* and *Biblical Ancestry Voyage: Revealing Facts of Significant Black Characters*, he continues to share his findings of faith through the written word. In *Biblical Ancestry Voyage*, he traces the Afrikan ancestry of significant biblical characters based on historical, social, political, and cultural facts neglected by the white scholars who have dominated biblical research.

LOUIS FARRAKHAN

For almost two decades, Minister Louis Farrakhan has been the leader of the Nation of Islam, a Muslim community based in America that was founded in 1930 by Master Fard Muhammad and guided from 1934 to 1975 by the Honorable Elijah Muhammad. Born Louis Eugene Walcott on May 11, 1933, Minister Farrakhan and his younger brother Alvin were raised by their mother, a native of St. Kitts, in the Roxbury section of Boston. He attended Winston–Salem Teacher's College in North Carolina on a track scholarship. During his junior year, he married his childhood sweetheart and left college to begin a family, earning a living through his talents as a musician and performing artist in Boston. Popularly known as "The Charmer," he achieved fame as a vocalist, calypso singer, dancer, and violinist.

In 1955, while headlining a show called "Calypso Follies," on Chicago's Rush Street, the young entertainer was invited by one of his friends to attend the Nation of Islam's National Saviours' Day Convention. He immediately accepted the teachings of the Honorable Elijah Muhammad (and later the name Louis X) and began processing into the Nation's Temple No. 7 in New York, under Minister Malcolm X. In May 1965, three months after Malcolm X's death, Louis X was appointed to the post of Minister of Temple No. 7 and given the name "Farrakhan." From that post, he was able to restore respect for the Nation of Islam in the Harlem community and throughout the country, establishing numerous businesses and other employment opportunities for black people, disseminating news and religious information through Nation of Islam newspapers and tapes, and establishing and redirecting the Nation's independent Muslim schools.

After the death of the Honorable Elijah Muhammad in 1975, the Nation of Islam suffered drastic changes under the leadership of his son, Wallace D. Muhammad (now known as Imam Warithuddin Mohammed). The changes disoriented many of the followers and led to the Nation's financial ruin. After an agonizing reappraisal of the condition of black people and the efficacy of the teachings and programs of its founder, Minister Farrakhan decided, in 1977, to restore those teachings and rebuild the Nation of Islam in over 80 cities. His efforts and the widespread acceptance of his message by the black masses propelled him into media attention, most of which was generally critical. In 1984, Minister Farrakhan accompanied, provided security for, and otherwise supported the Reverend Jesse Jackson in his bid for the presidency. He extended the outreach of the Nation of Islam to the African continent with the creation of the

newspaper *The Final Call* and establishment of the Nation of Islam's Ghana mission in 1991. In October 1995, Minister Farrakhan organized, with the Reverend Benjamin Chavis and other black leaders from a diverse cross-section of interests, the monumentally successful "Million Man March" and Day of Atonement gathering of black men in Washington, D.C.

Minister Farrakhan resides in Chicago's Hyde Park community with his wife of forty years, Khadijah. He has five daughters, four sons, and twenty-three grandchildren.

ROBERT HILL

Robert Hill was born in Jamaica and educated at the University of Toronto and the University of the West Indies. As the editor of the now-classic collection, *The Marcus Garvey and Universal Negro Improvement Association Papers,* he is known worldwide as one of the foremost scholars on the life and movement of Marcus Garvey. His lifelong quest to provide an accurate account of Garvey's leadership and philosophies began when he was a young student in Jamaica and won an essay contest on Garvey. His scholarly efforts have also focused on presenting the true nature and character of Jamaican, particularly Rastafarian, culture to the world. His historical accounts and cultural analysis of the Rastafari way of life are equaled only by the learned elders of Rastafari. He also serves as literary executor to the papers of the noted Jamaican scholar and author C. L. R. James. His research guides, bibliographies, and manuscript collections, compounded with his many and various publications, have catapulted him to the elite of Jamaican Afrikan scholars.

Dr. Hill has received numerous awards and professional appointments and maintains a busy schedule of lectures and international research. He is currently an associate professor of history, with a special emphasis on Afrikan American and Caribbean history, at the University of California, Los Angeles. He is currently working on a book, *The Rastafari Bible: JAH Version.*

ASA G. HILLIARD, III

Dr. Asa Hilliard is the Fuller E. Callaway Professor of Urban Education at Georgia State University, with joint appointments in the Department of Educational Policy Studies and the Department of Educational Psychology and Special Education. A teacher, psychologist, and historian, he earned a B.A. in psychology, and M.A. in counseling, and a Ph.D. in educational psychology from the University of Denver. He began his teaching career in the Denver (Colorado) Public Schools and at the University of Denver. He served on the faculty at San Francisco State University for eighteen years, during which time he was a department chair for two years and dean of education for eight years. He was also a consultant to the Peace Corps and Superintendent of Schools in Monrovia, Liberia, for two years.

Dr. Hilliard has written numerous technical papers, articles, and books on testing, teaching strategies, public policy, cultural learning styles, and child growth and development. As a result of his expertise and background, he has participated in the development of several national assessment systems for children and adults. He has also been active in forensic psychology, serving as an expert witness on the winning side in several landmark federal cases on test validity and bias, including the *Larry P. v. Wilson Riles* IQ test case in California and two Supreme Court cases on test bias.

As a consultant to numerous school districts, universities, government agencies, and private corporations, Dr. Hilliard has shared his knowledge of valid assessment approaches, curriculum equity, and teacher training. Several of his programs in pluralistic curriculum, assessment, and valid teaching have become national models. He has worked on projects with the National Academy of Sciences, NASA, the Smithsonian Institution, and the National Geographic Society. Recently, he served (with Dr. Barbara Sizemore) as chief consultant on the "Every Child Can Succeed" television series produced by the Agency for Instructional Technology.

Dr. Hilliard is a founding member of the Association for the Study of Classical African Civilizations and currently serves as its first vice president. Over the past decade, he has conducted several ancient Afrikan history study tours to Kemet (Egypt). He has produced videotapes and educational materials on Afrikan history through his production company, Waset Education Productions. He is the co-developer of a popular educational television series, "Free Your Mind, Return to the Source: African Origins," which has been shown throughout the United States and in several foreign countries. He is the co-

founder of an annual National Conference on the Infusion of African and African-American Content in School Curriculum.

For his efforts in the promotion of American Afrikan and Afrikan education, history, and culture, Dr. Hilliard has been the recipient of numerous awards, including the Morehouse College "Candle in the Dark Award in Education," the National Alliance of Black School Educators' "Distinguished Educator Award," the American Evaluation Association's "President's Award," the Republic of Liberia's "Knight Commander of the Humane Order of African Redemption," and the National Association of Black Psychologists' "Outstanding Scholarship Award."

LEONARD JEFFRIES, JR.

Leonard Jeffries was born and raised in Newark, New Jersey. He received his bachelor's degree from Lafayette College, and his master's and doctorate from Columbia University. His area of specializations are political science and Afrikan and Afrikan American Studies. He has traveled extensively throughout Afrika, the Caribbean, and Latin America, and has conducted more than forty international educational study tours.

Dr. Jeffries has conducted enormous research in the West Afrikan countries of Senegal, Sierra Leone, Liberia, Ghana, Dahomey, and Nigeria—and in Jamaica, Haiti and Brazil—concentrating in such areas as family lineage, slavery, slave fort castles, and oral tradition. He also served as a Peace Corps evaluator in Central Afrika and as director of its Zimbabwe Field Study Project. With his expertise on Afrika he has garnered numerous professional achievements. Among the most noted are his efforts spearheading the establishment of the first Black Studies program at San Jose State University and the research assistance he provided author Alex Haley in the establishment of the Kinte Library Project of Black Family History, which led to the enormously successful book and television series "Roots."

Dr. Jeffries is one of the founding members of the National Council for Black Studies, the African Heritage Association, the Association for the Study of Classical African Civilizations, and the National Melanin Consortium. He has also served on numerous editorial boards, including those of the *Journal of Black Studies, New Perspective on the Caribbean,* and the *Journal of African Civilizations,* and he was a columnist for *African Commentary.*

As professor and former chair of the Department of Black Studies at the City College of New York, Dr. Jeffries was one of the co-authors of the New York State educational policy report, *The Curriculum of Inclusion.* As one of the most visible proponents of this document, he bore the brunt of the considerable strategic opposition mounted by conservative scholars opposed to multiculturalism and Afrocentrism in education in their efforts to discredit the work and its authors. Despite this opposition, the *Curriculum* document was adopted by the New York Education Department in 1989. For these efforts and for his presentation, in his classroom lectures, of historical evidence of incriminating Jewish involvement in the American slave trade, Dr. Jeffries was the focus of severe media attention and criticism, culminating in his removal from his position at City College. He waged a successful legal counter to the College's moves to dismiss him, and currently retains his professorship there.

DEBORAH MAÁT MOORE

A native of Detroit, a graduate of the University of Detroit College of Engineering (with bachelor's degrees in mathematics and computer science), and a graduate of the Andover–Dartmouth College Math Teacher's Institute, Professor Deborah Maát Moore has had much success with American Afrikan students by including a focus on the contributions of Afrikans in her daily math lessons. In the 1980s, Professor Moore began tracing the origins of mathematics back to the Afrikan people who lived along the Nile Valley. She also investigated the mathematical details involved in the construction of the ancient pyramids. Her research resulted in the book *The African Roots of Mathematics* and in the pamphlet *The Pineal Gland and Melatonin: Their Relationship to Blacks.*

As a former instructor at Wayne State University and teacher in the Detroit Public Schools, Professor Moore recruited students for the Detroit Pre-College Engineering Program (DAPCEP) and founded the Kemet Math Club, a group made up of accelerated American Afrikan math students from various middle and high schools in Detroit. Kemet Math Club students are taught the ancient Egyptian techniques for solving math problems. They are also shown how math can be applied to their everyday life and are given instruction in their current math subjects.

Professor Moore is presently working as a mathematics consultant with Professional Educational Services. She is also currently the director of the Ahmose Math Clinic in Detroit, where American Afrikan students from ages five to forty-five come to learn the secrets of math achievement.

BARBARA A. SIZEMORE

Barbara Sizemore was born in Chicago, Illinois. She received her bachelor's and master's degrees from Northwestern University and her doctorate in education from the University of Chicago. Throughout her career, Dr. Sizemore has spearheaded research in the area of high achievement among American Afrikan children. She worked for several years in the Chicago Public Schools teaching English to Spanish-speaking students, providing Special Education to primary and secondary students, and serving as a principal and project director at both the elementary and high school levels. She then accepted an associate professorship at the University of Pittsburgh, later becoming a professor and interim chair in the Department of Black Community, Education, Research and Development, where she pioneered innovative research on American Afrikan elementary school children.

The author of numerous book chapters and journal articles, Dr. Sizemore has been exceptionally effective in identifying high-achieving predominantly American Afrikan schools and in studying the techniques and methods used in obtaining high achievement in those schools. She is also a strong advocate of a multicultural curriculum as an effective means of teaching and enhancing self-esteem among children of color.

Dr. Sizemore has received three honorary doctorate degrees, the Northwestern University Merit Award, the United Nations Association Human Rights Award, and the Presidential Award from the National Council of Black Studies for community service, promotion of Black Studies, and scholarship. She is presently the dean of the School of Education at Depaul University in Chicago. She is the mother of six and the grandmother of two.

KWAME TURE (STOKELY CARMICHAEL)

Kwame Ture (Stokely Carmichael) has been an active participant in the struggles of Afrikan people from the civil rights movement to the Black Power movement to the Pan-Afrikanist movement. His biography is virtually a synopsis of the history of all three campaigns. Born in Port-of-Spain, Trinidad, on June 29, 1941, at the age of 10, Ture's parents brought him to the United States. He graduated with honors from Howard University in 1969 with a major in philosophy. During the 1960s, his early political activities included participating in community and college sit-ins, chairmanship of the Student Non-Violent Coordinating Committee (SNCC), organizing (with Martin Luther King, Jr.) the "Selma to Montgomery March" in 1965, working with the antidraft movement, and establishing the first Black Panther Party in Lowndes County, Alabama. He was also intimately involved with the activities of the Mississippi Freedom Democratic Party, and worked with the United Farm Workers in support of migrant laborer's boycotts of grapes and lettuce. Ture was also at the vanguard of the struggle to free the civil rights and Black Power movements from Zionist domination and control. Under his leadership, SNCC was the first national organization to publicly denounce Israel's aggression in occupied Palestine.

In the course of his revolutionary activities, Dr. Ture (he is the recipient of an honorary doctorate of philosophy from historically black Shaw University) has traveled extensively in Afrika, the Middle East, North Viet Nam, Cuba, Puerto Rico, Europe, and North America. His work in nations and communities struggling to resist oppression has expanded his knowledge of the issues that effect people and revolutionary movements throughout the world. During the late 1960s, Ture traveled to Puerto Rico to re-affirm SNCC's support of the independence of Puerto Rico from American colonialism. He also went to North Vietnam, where he met with President Ho Chi Minh. It was in the People's Revolutionary Republic of Guinea, at the invitation of President Ahmed Sekou Toure, that Kwame studied with "Osageyfo" Dr. Kwame Nkrumah, the deposed president of Ghana and co-president of Guinea, founder of the Organization of African Unity, and cornerstone of the African revolution. In Guinea, Ture's Pan-Afrikanist ideology became more precise. Upon his return to the U.S., he immediately began to build the base for the emergence of the All Afrikan People's Revolutionary Party, conceptualized by Dr. Nkrumah.

Always studying and evolving, Ture has been hailed as a genius of social science, a gifted orator, and a true revolutionary. His goal: the total liberation and unification of Afrika under scientific socialism.

IVAN VAN SERTIMA

Ivan Van Sertima was born in Guyana, South America, and educated at the School of Oriental and African Studies at London University and the Rutgers Graduate School, where he received degrees in Afrikan studies, linguistics, and anthropology. He has made a name for himself in all three fields.

As a literary critic in the field of Afrikan studies, Dr. Van Sertima is the author of *Caribbean Writers*, a collection of critical essays on the Caribbean novel. He is also the author of several major literary reviews published in Denmark, India, Britain, and the United States. He was honored for his work in this field by being asked to nominate candidates for the Nobel Prize in literature for the period from 1976 to 1980. He has also been honored, as an historian of world repute, by an invitation from UNESCO to join the International Commission for Rewriting the Scientific and Cultural History of Mankind. As a linguist, Dr. Van Sertima has published essays on the dialect of the Sea Islands off the Georgia Coast. He is also the compiler of the *Swahili Dictionary of Legal Terms*, based on his field work in Tanzania in 1967.

Dr. Van Sertima is perhaps most widely known as the author of *They Came Before Columbus: The African Presence in Ancient America*, which is currently in its twenty-first printing. This work received the Clarence L. Holte Prize in 1981, "for a work of excellence in literature and the humanities relating to the cultural heritage of Africa and the African Diaspora." He is also the editor of the *Journal of African Civilizations*, which he founded in 1979.

Dr. Van Sertima has taught at Princeton University and at Rutgers University, where he is currently an associate professor of African Studies. He has lectured in the United States, Canada, the Caribbean, South America, and Europe.

FRANCES CRESS WELSING

Frances Cress Welsing, M.D., was born in Chicago, Illinois, the daughter and granddaughter of physicians, Drs. Henry Noah Cress and Henry Clay Cress, respectively. By training a psychiatrist, she earned her bachelor's degree at Antioch College and her medical degree from Howard University College of Medicine. She completed her internship at Cook County Hospital in Chicago and did a residency in general psychiatry at St. Elizabeth's Hospital in Washington, D.C. For seven years, she was an assistant professor in the Department of Pediatrics at Howard University. She also served as clinical director of the Psychoeducation Institute at Hillcrest Children's Center in Washington, D.C.

Dr. Welsing first received nationwide attention when she debated the issue of black genetic inferiority with William Shockley on the national television program, "Black Journal." In that encounter and others, she dared to argue that black people's subordinated status in the world was not due to any inherent intellectual inferiority. Rather, she claimed, it was the result of a highly sophisticated system of racism and white supremacy. Since then, Dr. Welsing has written and lectured extensively on the topic. Her work, *The Cress Theory of Color Confrontation and Racism*, is a remarkable publication that serves as the basis for her remarks when she speaks on the lecture circuit, as does her later compilation, *The Isis Papers: Keys to the Colors*, a collection of several of her articles from scholarly and popular periodicals.

Dr. Welsing presently resides in the District of Columbia, where she is in private practice as a child psychiatrist. She is in frequent demand for television appearances and speaking engagements.

ANNOTATED
BIBLIOGRAPHIES

NA'IM AKBAR

Books

The Effects of Race and Paranoia on Power Involvements. Unpublished Ph.D. Dissertation, University of Michigan, 1970.
  An analysis of how race and systematic paranoia function in greater society.

The Community of Self. Chicago: Nation of Islam Office of Human Development, 1976.
  A collection of essays intended to assist the layperson to better understand mental development and self-improvement for the effective development of the American Afrikan community.

Natural Psychology and Human Transformation. Chicago: World Community of Islam in the West, 1977.
  This is a discussion of the limitations and failure of Western psychology in dealing with the Afrikan experience.

From Miseducation to Education. Jersey City, NJ: New Mind Productions, 1982.
  This brief monograph discusses the limitations of traditional European-American education for American Afrikans, adding a prescription for a more valid form of education.

Chains and Images of Psychological Slavery. Jersey City, NJ: New Mind Productions, 1984.
  An analyses of the effects of slavery on the Afrikan mind, and how images effect behavior. Included is the solution.

Visions for Black Men. Nashville, TN: Winston–Derek Publishers, 1991.
  An excellent work on the American Afrikan male evolving into manhood.

Light from Ancient Africa. Tallahassee, FL: Mind Productions, 1994.
  An essential work focusing on the lessons of ancient Afrika as the origin of human psychology.

Natural Psychology and Human Transformation. Tallahassee, FL: Mind Productions, 1995.
  An expanded re-issue of the original publication by popular demand.

Articles and Essays

(and Walker, E. L.), "Speed and Basal Resistance Level (BRL) in a Segmented Straight Alley as a Function of Alteration of the Stimulus, Gentling and Isolation," *Psychology,* 1964.

(and Wolowitz, H. M.), "The Relevance of Power Themes Among Male, Negro and White Paranoid and Non-Paranoid Schizophrenics," *International Journal of Social Psychiatry*, 1964.

"Awareness: The Key to Black Mental Health," *Journal of Black Psychology*, No. 1, 1974.

"The Black Community Research Needs: Methods, Models and Modalities," in L. Gary (Ed.), *Social Research and the Black Community*, Washington DC: Institute of Urban Affairs, Howard University, 1974.

"The Rhythms of Black Personality," *Southern Exposure*, Atlanta: Institute of Southern Studies, Vol. 2, 1975.

Khatib, S. McGee, Nobles, W., & Akbar, Na'im. "Voodoo Or IQ: An Introduction to African Psychology," *Journal of Black Psychology*, Vol. 1, February 1976.

"Rhythmic Patterns in African Personality," in L. M. King, V. J. Dixon, & W. Nobles (Eds.), *African Philosophy: Assumptions and Paradigms for Research on Black Persons*, Los Angeles: Fanon Research and Development Center, 1976.

"Community Psychology and Systems Intervention," in L. Ramey (Ed.) *Manual for Study of Community Psychology*, Atlanta: Southern Regional Education Board, 1978.

"African Metapsychology of Human Personality," *National Association of Black Psychologists Convention Proceedings*, St. Louis, 1978.

"African Roots of Black Psychology," in Smith et al. (Eds.), *Reflections on Black Psychology*, Washington DC: University Press of America, 1979.

"Homicide Among Black Males: Casual Factors," *Public Health Records*, Vol. 95, November–December, 1980.

"Mental Disorder Among African Americans," *Black Roots*, Vol. 7, No. 2, 1981, pp. 18–25.

"Desegregation in the 80s: Concerns and Challenges for Public Education," *Education Resources Information Center (ERIC) Reports*, February 1981.

"Reconciliation of the African American Woman and Man," *Black Male/Female Relationships*, Vol. 2, No. 2, 1981, pp. 60–65.

"Cultural Expressions of the African American Child," *Black Child Journal*, Vol. 2, No. 2, 1981, pp. 6–15.

"Our Destiny: Authors of the Scientific Revolution," in L. Gary (Ed.), *Social Research and the Black Community: Selected Issues and Priorities*, 1984.

"Paradigms of African American Research," in L. Gary (Ed.), *Social Research and the Black Community: Selected Issues and Priorities,* 1984.

"Nile Valley Origins of the Science of the Mind," in Ivan Van Sertima (Ed.), *Journal of African Civilizations* (Issue on "Nile Valley Civilizations"), 1985, pp. 120–132.

YOSEF A. A. BEN-JOCHANNAN

BOOKS

We, the Black Jews. Puerto Rico: Portuguese and Spanish Pamphlet, 1938.
A discussion that identifies the real Jews.

The Rape of Africa and the Crisis in Angola. New York: Portuguese and Spanish Pamphlets, 1958.
A survey of the European colonial efforts in Afrika and the various fractions in Angola.

An African Nationalist View of Black Power. New York: Congress of Racial Equality, 1966.
Dr. Ben's view on the concept of Black Power.

Black Man of the Nile. New York: Alkebu-lan Books Associates, 1970.
A classic work on the Afrikaness of the ancient Nile Valley.

Africa: Mother of "Western Civilization." New York: Alkebu-lan Books Associates, 1971.
Clearly shows that Afrikans were involved in the creation of the world's major religions.

Cultural Genocide in the Black and African Studies Curriculum. New York: Alkebu-lan Books Associates, 1972.
An explanation of how European educational colonialism is involved in the establishment of an Afrikan curriculum.

A Chronology of the Bible: A Challenge to the Standard Version. New York: Alkebu-lan Books Associates, 1973.
An excellent chronology on the various versions of the Bible, beginning with Afrika's first spiritual text.

The Black Man's Religion: Extracts and Comments from the Sacred Scriptures of the Holy Black Bible. New York: Alkebu-lan Books Associates, 1974.
A critical look at extracts of the Afrikan spiritual texts.

The Black Man's or the "Negro's" Bicentennial Year of ??? from 1619–20 to 1976 C.E./A.D., Vol. I. New York: Alkebu-lan Books Associates, 1976.
A look at the meaning of the bicentennial year on the Afrikan in America.

Influence of Great Myths on Contemporary Life, or the Need for Black Family in Mental Health, Vol. I. New York: Alkebu-lan Books Associates, 1976.
How myths influence the Afrikan family.

Our "Black Seminarians" and "Black Clergy": Without a "Black Theology." New York: Alkebu-lan Books Associates, 1976.
The pitfalls facing American Afrikan ministers without an Afrikan-centered theology.

The Saga of the "Black Marxist Versus the Black Nationalist": A Debate Resurrected. New York: Alkebu-lan Books Associates, 1978.
A critical look at the debate between Marxists and Nationalists.

Tutankhamon's African Roots Haley, Et Al., Overlooked. New York: Alkebu-lan Books Associates and Educational Material Associates, 1978.
Investigating the Afrikan roots Alex Haley neglected to address.

In Pursuit of George G. M. James Study of the Craft and Sisters of the House: "Heaven Is Between a Black Woman's Legs." New York: Alkebu-lan Books Associates, 1980.
A perspective on the beauty of the black woman.

The Alkebu-Lanians of Ta-Merry's "Mysteries System" and the Ritualization of the Late Bro. Kwese Adebisi. New York: Alkebu-lan Books Associates, 1981.
A view of the Afrikans of Ta-Merry and a tribute to Kwese Adebisi.

The African Mysteries System of Wa'set, Egypt and its European Stepchild: "Greek Philosophy." New York: Akebu-lan Books Associates, 1984.
The profound teachings of ancient Egypt and how Greek philosophy evolved from it.

African Origins of the Major "Western Religions." Baltimore, MD: Black Classic Press, 1988.

Re-issue of the 1971 edition, clearly showing that Afrikans are involved in the creation of the world's major religions.

Abu Simbel-Ghizeh Guide/Manual. Baltimore, MD: Black Classic Press, 1989.
An insider's guide to the ancient Abu Simbel-Ghizeh area.

Black Man of the Nile and His Family. Baltimore, MD: Black Classic Press, 1990.
A reissue of Dr. Ben's classic work.

We, The Black Jews. Baltimore, MD: Black Classic Press, 1993
An expanded version of the discussion identifying the real Jews.

JOHN HENRIK CLARKE

BOOKS AND PAMPHLETS

Black–White Alliances: An Historical Perspective. Chicago: Third World Press, 1975.
A critical look at black and white alliances, their successes and failures.

Africans at the Crossroads: Notes for an African World Revolution. Trenton: Africa World Press, 1991.
Insightful essays that lay a foundation for change in the Afrikan world, including a candid account of Clarke's split with *Freedomways* journal.

Christopher Columbus and the African Holocaust. New York: ANB Books, 1992.
A collection of essays that investigate the Christopher Columbus myth and the devastating affect it had on the initiation of the Afrikan Holocaust. Essential to the discussion is the connection between slavery and the rise of capitalism.

Africans Away From Home. Washington DC: Institute of Independent Education, 1992.
An outstanding survey of Afrikans in the Diaspora.

(with ben-Jochannan, Yosef). *New Dimensions in African History: The London Lectures of Dr. Yosef ben-Jochannan and Dr. John Henrik Clarke.* Trenton, NJ: Africa World Press, 1991.
These lectures cover a variety of issues that connect the importance of the Nile Valley civilization to the development of world culture.

Rebellion in Rhyme: The Early Poetry of John Henrik Clarke. Lawrenceville, NJ: Africa World Press, 1991.
A rare collection of poems that reflect Clarke's beginnings as a social thinker, from 1933 to 1948. Book is dedicated to his mentor, Dr. Willis N. Huggins.

African People in World History. Baltimore, MD: Black Classic Press, 1993.
A wonderfully illustrated lecture, prepared especially for teachers and students, that presents short biographies of personalities who influenced the flow of Afrikan history.

My Life in Search of Africa. Ithaca, NY: Africana Studies and Research Center, Cornell University, 1994.
Three special lectures prepared for the Cornell University Africana Studies and Research Center, in which Clarke approaches the topic from several perspectives, philosophically and emotionally.

Who Betrayed the African World Revolution? Chicago: Third World Press, 1995.
  Seven insightful lectures on transition and social change in the Afrikan world.

EDITED WORKS

The Lives of Great African Chiefs. Pittsburgh, PA: *Pittsburgh Courier*, 1958.
  A series of articles Clarke wrote for this renowned black newspaper that are
  indicative of his growing awareness and commitment to the Afrikan
  revolution that swept the continent.

History and Culture of Africa. Hempstead, NY: AEVAC, 1969.
  A series of lectures, presented at the Harlem School of African Culture, on
  Afrikan history and culture to complete the missing pages of world history.

William Styron's Nat Turner: Ten Black Writers Respond. Boston: Beacon Press, 1970.
  A collective response to Styron's fictional account of the life and death of
  black insurrectionist Nat Turner by black writers such as Clarke, John O.
  Killens, Mike Thewell, Ernest Kaiser, Vincent Harding, and Lerone Bennett.

Black Titan: W. E. B. DuBois. Boston: Beacon Press, 1970.
  An exhaustive documentation of the life of a superior scholar/activist.

World's Great Men of Color, Vols. I & II, by Joel A. Rogers. New York: Collier
  Books, 1972.
  Rogers was a peerless researcher of the achievements of black people, and
  Clarke provides an introduction that places many of the controversial
  assertions Rogers makes into proper historical perspective.

Marcus Garvey and the Vision of Africa. New York: Random House, 1973.
  This is a matchless presentation of Garvey's strengths and weaknesses.
  The introduction is as thorough as it is informative.

*Pan-Africanism and the Liberation of Southern Africa: A Tribute to W. E. B.
  DuBois.* New York: United Nations Centre Against Apartheid and the
  African Heritage Studies Association, 1978.
  Part of a series of lectures presented at the United Nations.

*Pan-Africanism and the Liberation of Southern Africa: A Tribute to Paul
  Robeson.* New York: United Nations Centre Against Apartheid and the
  African Heritage Studies Association, 1978.
  Part of a series of lectures presented at the United Nations.

Malcolm X: The Man and His Times. Lawrenceville, NJ: Africa World Press, 1990.
  A path-breaking anthology with brilliant remarks from such writers and
  witnesses of Malcolm's life as Ossie Davis, A. Peter Bailey, Earl Grant,
  Betty Shabazz, and Rev. Wyatt Tee Walker.

New Dimensions in African History: The London Lectures of Dr. Yosef ben-Jochannan and Dr. John Henrik Clarke. Trenton, NJ: Africa World Press, 1991. Introductory lectures planned for the African-Caribbean community in England.

A Century of the Best Black American Short Stories. New York: Hill & Wang, 1993. This book further confirms the existence of a number of talented black writers with fertile imaginations, updating a collection that first appeared in 1966.

Harlem Voices: From the Soul of Black America. Brooklyn: ANB, 1993. A reissue of an anthology, first published in 1970, that documents the history of a storied community and some of its most gifted artists: Langston Hughes, Chester Himes, Ann Petru, James Baldwin, and Leroi Jones are among the contributors.

Harlem U.S.A. Brooklyn, NY: ANB, 1993. Impressions of Harlem, submitted by sociologist Kenneth Clark, authors Alice Childress, Claude Brown, and Julian Mayfield, and others. These articles first appeared in *Freedomways*.

ARTICLES AND ESSAYS

"African History Reconsidered," *Freedomways,* Second Quarter, 1963.

"Black Power and Black History," *Negro Digest,* February 1969.

"The Black Woman: A Figure in World History," *Essence,* May 1971.

"African Perspectives: New Dimensions of an Old Subject," *Freedomways,* Vol. 12, No. 3, 1972, pp. 237–244.

"Cheikh Anta Diop and the New Light on African History," *Freedomways,* Vol. 12, No. 4, 1972, pp. 339–345.

"The Impact of the African on the New World: A Reappraisal," *The Black Scholar,* February 1973, pp. 32–39.

"Kwame Nkrumah: His Years in America" *The Black Scholar,* October 1974, pp. 9–16.

"Africa: Demise of the Golden Age," *The Black Collegian,* May–June 1975.

"The Black Woman in World History," *Black World,* February 1975.

"On the Cultural Unity of Africa," *Black World,* February 1975.

"Twenty Most Important Works by Black Writers," *Black Books Bulletin,* Spring 1975, pp. 22–25.

"African Cultural Continuity and Slave Revolts in the New World," *The Black Scholar,* September 1976, pp. 41–49.

"Africa in Early World History," *Ebony,* August 1976.

"Remembering Arthur A. Schomburg," *Encore,* Vol. 6, No. 3, 1977.

"The University of Sankore at Timbuktu: A Neglected Achievement in Black Intellectual History," *Western Journal of Black Studies,* Vol. 1, No. 2, 1977, pp. 142–146.

"African Culture as the Basis of World Culture," *Présence Africaine,* 1979.

"Ancient Civilizations of Africa: The Missing Pages in World History," in Ivan Van Sertima (Ed.), *Journal of African Civilizations* (Issue on "Egypt Revisited"), 1982, pp. 113–121.

"Toussaint L' Ouverture and the Haitian Revolution," *The Black American,* Vol. 25, No. 44, 1985.

"African Warrior Queens," in Ivan Van Sertima (Ed.), revised edition. *Journal of African Civilizations* (Issue on "Black Women in Antiquity"), 1987, pp. 123–134.

"Nzinga, The Warrior Queen," in Ivan Van Sertima (Ed.), *Journal of African Civilizations* (Issue on "Great Black Leaders: Ancient and Modern"), 1988, 364–369.

"African People on My Mind," in Asa G. Hilliard, III, Lucretia Payton–Stewart, & Larry Obadele Williams (Eds.), *Infusion of African and African American Content in the School Curriculum: Proceedings of the First National Conference.* Morristown, PA: Aaron Press, 1990, pp. 51–59.

"Can African People Save Themselves?" *City Sun,* September–October 1990.

WILLIAM LARUE DILLARD

BOOKS

New Members' Orientation Bible Study. Monrovia: LaRue Christian
Foundation, 1979.
A result of listening with the ears of the mind and heart to the questions
people in the church are asking today, such as agnosticism (belief that God
is beyond human knowledge).

A Burning and a Yearning in My Soul. Monrovia: LaRue Christian Literature, 1981.
A collection of love letters of spiritual enlightenment written by a concerned
pastor for the spiritual growth and development of his parishioners.

Invasion from Outer Space. Monrovia: Joyfully Serving Christ Ministry, 1983.
A futuristic prophesy on eschatology (concerned with the final events of the
world) beginning with the rapture of the church.

From Stagnation to Jubilation Through Spiritual Gift Discovery. Monrovia:
Joyfully Serving Christ Ministry, 1983.
An analyses of the epidemic of spiritual stagnation among the fellowship of
the Saints of God.

Coming and Becoming. Monrovia: Joyfully Serving Christ Ministry, 1986.
A sanctified vessel, well pleasing unto the Lord Christ requiring spiritual
maturing in the Word, Work, and Will of the Lord on a daily basis.

Blacks in Biblical History. Monrovia: Joyfully Serving Christ Ministry, 1988
A booklet on blacks in biblical history.

Revelation Perspective on End-Time Suffering Worldwide. Monrovia: Joyfully
Serving Christ Ministry, 1990.
Attempts to answer abstract philosophical questions unrelated to everyday
living, proclaiming truths to help and encourage our Christian stewardship
of time, talents, and treasury.

Biblical Ancestry Voyage: Revealing Facts of Significant Black Characters.
Monrovia: Ra La-Ven Rue Foundation, 1990.
A classic work tracing the ancestry of significant black figures, based on
historical, social, political, and cultural facts behind the biblical witness.
An area neglected by white biblical scholars who have dominated biblical
research.

LOUIS FARRAKHAN

BOOK

A Torchlight for America, Chicago: FCN Publishing, 1993.
A vision and plan for correcting and building for Afrikans in American.

ROBERT A. HILL

EDITED WORKS

(with Harding, Vincent & William Strickland [Eds.]). *Education and Black Struggle: Notes from the Colonized World* (Monograph No. 2). Cambridge, MA: *Harvard Education Review,* 1973.
An important critical analyses of education and the struggle for liberation of Afrikans in America.

The Marcus Garvey and UNIA Papers, Vol. 1 (1826–August 1919). Berkeley and Los Angeles: University of California Press, 1983.
Each volume of the Marcus Garvey Papers covers a particular historical period of Garvey and the movement. They are a compelling picture of the evolution, spread, and influence of the UNIA, which includes letters, pamphlets, vital records, intelligence reports, newspaper articles, speeches, legal records and diplomatic dispatches. Each volume covers periods in the United States, Afrika or the Caribbean.

The Marcus Garvey and UNIA Papers, Vol. 2 (August 1919–August 1920). Berkeley and Los Angeles: University of California Press, 1983.

The Marcus Garvey and UNIA Papers, Vol. 3 (September 1920–August 1921). Berkeley and Los Angeles: University of California Press, 1984.

The Marcus Garvey and UNIA Papers, Vol. 4 (September 1921–September 1922). Berkeley and Los Angeles: University of California Press, 1985.

The Marcus Garvey and UNIA Papers, Vol. 5 (September 1922–August 1924). Berkeley and Los Angeles: University of California Press, 1986.

The Marcus Garvey and UNIA Papers, Vol. 6 (September 1924–December 1927). Berkeley and Los Angeles: University of California Press, 1988.

The Marcus Garvey and UNIA Papers, Vol. 7 (November 1927–August 1940). Berkeley and Los Angeles: University of California Press, 1991.

Africa for the Africans: The Marcus Garvey and UNIA Papers, African Series,
Vols. 8, 9, 10 (1917–41). Berkeley and Los Angeles: University of California
Press, 1995, 1996.

A Far Cry from Africa: The Marcus Garvey and UNIA Papers, Caribbean Series,
Vol. 11 & 12, (1918–1940). Berkeley and Los Angeles: University of
California Press, 1996, 1997.

(with Bair, Barbara [Eds.]). *Marcus Garvey: Life and Lessons.* Berkeley, CA:
University of California Press, 1987.
An excellent exposure into the life and lessons of Marcus Garvey.

Walter Rodney Speaks: The Making of an African Intellectual. Trenton, NJ:
Africa World Press, 1990.
An outstanding look at one of the world's most important Caribbean
Afrikan scholar/activist.

Pan-African Biography: Its Relevance to the Study of African History. Los
Angeles: African Studies Center/Crossroads Press, 1986.
A critical analyses of Pan-Afrikanism and how it relates to Afrikan history.

(with Rasmussen, R. Kent [Eds.]). *Black Empire* by George S. Schuyler, writing
as Samuel I. Brooks. Boston: Northeastern University Press, 1991.
An outstanding Afrikan-centered serialized fiction of a great new
civilization in modern Afrika.

The Rastafari Bible: (Jah) Version. San Francisco: Harper Collins, 1996
The most comprehensive work on the Rastafari spiritual writings available.

ESSAYS

"Rejoiner: A. W. Singham and the Black Jacobins," *C. L. R. James Symposium*
Documents, University of the West Indies, January 1972.

"Marcus Garvey: The First England Years and After, 1912–1916," in John
Henrik Clarke (Ed.), *Marcus Garvey and the Vision of Africa,* New York:
Random House, 1974.

"Legends in Their Own Time: Walter Rodney, Eric Williams, and Bob Marley,"
Fanon Center Journal, Vol. 1, No. 2, December 1981.

"Dread History: Leonard P. Howell and Millenarian Visions in Early
Rastafarian Visions in Early Rastafari Religion in Jamaica," *Epoche: Journal*
of the History of Religions at UCLA, Vol. 9, No. 1, Fall 1981.

"The Story of Bantu Prophets: An Interview with Bengt Sundkler," *African*
Studies Newsletter, Spring 1983.

"Jews and the Enigma of the Pan-African Congress of 1919," in Joseph R. Washington, Jr. (Ed.), *Jews in Black Perspectives: A Dialogue.* Cranbury: Associated University Presses, 1984.

"The Foremost Radical Among His Race: Marcus Garvey and the Black Scare, 1918–1921," *Prologue: Journal of the National Archives,* Vol. 16, No. 4, Winter 1984.

"C. L. R. James in England, 1932–1938," in Paul Buhle (Ed.), *C. L. R. James: His Life and Work.* London: Allison & Busby, 1986.

Encyclopedia entries, "Cyril Valentine Briggs," "Wilfred Adolphus Domingo," "George Padmore," and "Otto Eduard Gerardus Majella Huiswood," in Bernard K. Johnpoll & Harvey Klehr (Eds.), *Biographical Dictionary of the American Left.* Westport, CT: Greenwood Press, 1986.

"Introduction," *Black Power and Black Religion: Essays and Reviews,* by Richard Newman. West Cornwall: Locust Hill Press, 1986.

" 'Africa for the Africans': The Garvey Movement in South Africa, 1920–1940," in Shula Marks and Stanley Trapido (Eds.), *Politics of Race, Class and Nationalism in Twentieth-Century South Africa.* London and New York: Longman, 1987.

"Before Garvey: Chief Alfred Charles Sam and the African Movement in America, 1911–16," in Robert A. Hill (Ed.), *Pan African Biography: Its Relevance to the Study of African History.* Los Angeles: African Studies Center/Crossroads Press, 1987.

"The Case of Marcus Garvey," in *Mail Fraud Charges Against Marcus Garvey,* Hearing before the Subcommittee on Criminal Justice of the Committee on the Judiciary, House of Representatives, July 28, 1987. Washington DC: Howard University Press, 1990.

"Marcus Garvey: Black Moses," *Compass: A Jesuit Journal* (special issue on "The 1920s"), Vol. 10, No. 1, March/April 1992, pp. 34–35, 50.

"Garvey's Gospel, Garvey's Game," Introduction to *The Philosophy and Opinions of Marcus Garvey,* Vols. 1 & 2. New York: Atheneum, 1992.

"Universal Negro Improvement Association," "Marcus Garvey," "African Brotherhood," "Cyril Valentine Briggs," in Robert O'Meally and Jack Salzman, *The Encyclopedia of African American Culture and History,* Center for American Culture Studies, Columbia University. New York: Macmillan, 1994.

ASA G. HILLIARD III

BOOKS

(with Williams, Larry and Nia Damali). *The Teachings of Ptah Hotep: The Oldest Book in the World*. Atlanta: Blackwood Press, 1987.
The spiritually inspired book presents the 37 instructions of Ptah Hotep, written when he was 110 years old, for Pharaoh Assa Djed-Ka-Ra's son. The work is older than the Bible.

Infusion of African and African American Content in the School Curriculum. Morristown, PA: Aaron Press, 1990.
The importance of inserting global Afrikan content into the current European-oriented school curricula.

Critical Commentaries: The Struggle to Bring True African History into Being. Los Angeles: The Association for The Study of Classical African Civilizations, 1992.
Commentaries stressing the importance of accurate Afrikan historical data.

50 Plus: Essential References on the History of African People. Baltimore, MD: Black Classic Press, 1993.
A must bibliography for the study of Afrikan people.

The Maroons Within Us. Baltimore, MD: Black Classic Press, 1994.
An excellent investigation of the spirit of those who escaped a vicious slave system.

EDITED WORKS

Bibliography on Racism and Scholarship, Atlanta, GA: Wa'set Educational Materials, 1992.

ARTICLES AND ESSAYS

"A Helping Experience in African Education: Implications for Cross-Cultural Work in the U.S.," *Journal of Non-White Concerns in Personnel and Guidance*, 1974.

"The Education of 'Inner-City' Children," in *Demythologizing the Inner-City Child*, Washington DC: National Association for the Education of Young Children, 1976.

"Intellectual Strengths of Minority Children," in *Teachings in a Multicultural Society*. New York: The Free Press, 1977.

"Anatomy and Dynamics of Oppression: The Educators Response," *ERIC Clearinghouse on Urban Education,* Columbia University, 1978.

"Behavioral Criteria in Research and the Study of Racism: Performing the Jackal Function," *Technical Reports I, II, III,* Office of Naval Research, 1980.

"Non-Discriminating Testing of African American Children," paper presented at the Council for Exceptional Children's National Conference on the Exceptional Black Child, New Orleans, 1981.

"The Maroon Within Us: The Lessons of Africa for the Parenting and Education of African American Children," paper presented at Memphis State University, 1982.

"Quality Education in an Urban Environment," paper presented at the University of Houston, 1982.

(and Mona Vaughn–Scott), "The Quest for the Minority," *The Young Child: Reviews of Research,* Vol. 3, 1982, pp. 175–189.

"Psychological Factors Associated with Language in the Education of the African American Child," *Journal of Negro Education,* Howard University, 1983, pp. 24–34.

"The Technology or Politics of Reading: Current Issues in Reading Research on Black Children, Youth and Adults," paper presented at the International Reading Association, Atlanta, 1984.

"Democratizing the Common School in a Multicultural Society," *Education and Urban Society,* Vol. 16, No. 3, May 1984, pp. 262–273.

"The School's Response to Youth Unemployment," *Education and Urban Society,* Vol. 16, No. 3, May 1984, pp. 354–359.

"A Framework for Focused Counseling on the African American Man," *Journal of Non-White Concerns,* Vol. 1, No. 1, April 1985, pp. 1–31.

"Kemetic Concepts in Education," in Ivan Van Sertima (Ed.), *Journal of African Civilizations* (Issue on "Nile Valley Civilizations"), 1985.

"Blacks in Antiquity: A Review," in Ivan Van Sertima (Ed.), *Journal of African Civilizations* (Issue on "African Presence in Early Europe"), 1985.

"Ethnic Participation in Higher Education: Philosophical, Economical, and Political Perspective, U.S.A.," in *Race and Education: A Search for Legitimacy Revisited,* Texas Southern University, 1986.

"The Cultural Unity of Black Africa: The Domains of Patriarchy and Matriarchy in Classical Antiquity," in Larry Obadele Williams & Ivan Van Sertima (Eds.), *Journal of African Civilizations* (Issue on "Great African Thinkers, Vol. I: Cheikh Anta Diop"), 1986.

"Socializing Our Children for the Resurrection of African People," unpublished manuscript, 1988.

"Ancient Egypt: Birthplace of Engineering," paper presented at Georgia Institute of Technology, 1988.

"Kemetic (Egyptian) Historical Revision: Implications for Cross-Cultural Evaluation and Research in Education," *Evaluation Practice*, Vol. 10, No. 2, May 1989, pp. 7–23.

"Wa'set, the Eyes of Ra, and the Abode of Maat: The Pinnacle of Black Leadership in the Ancient World," in Ivan Van Sertima (Ed.), *Journal of African Civilizations* (Issue on "Egypt Revisited"), 1991.

"Fabrication: The Politics and Sociology of Knowledge in the Study of Ancient Kemet," paper presented at Temple University Symposium on Martin Bernal's *Black Athena*, Philadelphia, 1991.

"The Meaning of KMT (Ancient Egypt) History for Contemporary African American Experience," *Phylon*, Vol. XLIX, No. 1/2, 1992, pp. 10–22.

"Bibliography of Racism and Scholarship," Wa'set Educational Materials, Atlanta, 1992.

"Bringing Maát, Destroying Isfet: The African and African Diasporan Presence in the Study of Ancient KMT," paper presented at the Carter Goodwin Woodson Lecture, St. Mary's College, Maryland, 1993.

LEONARD JEFFRIES, JR.

BOOKS

The African Americans: Search for Truth and Knowledge. Philadelphia: Chelsea House, 1988.

(co-author). *A Curriculum of Inclusion: Report of the Commissioner's Task Force on Minorities: Equity and Excellence.* Albany, NY: New York Education Department, 1989.

ARTICLES AND ESSAYS

"A Report on the International Conference: Early Researches in a Global Perspective," *Journal of African Civilizations*, Vol. 3, No. 1, 1981.

"Tribute to Josef ben-Jochannan," *Journal of African Civilizations*, Vol. 3, No. 1, 1982.

"Civilization or Barbarism: The Legacy of Cheikh Anta Diop," *Journal of African Civilizations*, Vol. 3, No. 1, 1982.

"The Essence of Black Studies," *The City College Alumnus*, 1982.

"South Africa in Crisis, No. 17," Geneva, Switzerland: World Council of Churches, 1983.

"Africa: Birthplace of Humanity," *African Commentary*, 1989.

"Reclaiming Nile Valley Civilization," *African Commentary*, 1990.

"Our Sacred Mission," *Critical Commentaries*, 1991.

"Africans in the American Revolution: Repatriates to Africa," in Taiwo Ogunade (Ed.), *Africa and the American Revolution*, New York: Department of Black Studies, City College of the City University of New York, 1994.

DEBORAH MAÁT MOORE

BOOKS

The Pineal Gland and Melatonin: Their Relationship to Blacks. Detroit, MI: Professional Publishing, 1992.
Discussion of the function of the pineal gland and melatonin for Afrikan people.

The African Roots of Mathematics. Detroit, MI: Professional Publishing, 1992.
A pioneering work that shows the Afrikan origin of the mathematical sciences.

Teachers' Resource Guide. Detroit, MI: Professional Publishing, 1993.
An excellent resource guide for teachers of mathematics.

BARBARA A. SIZEMORE

ARTICLES AND ESSAYS

"Social Science and the Black Identity," in James P. Banks & Jean D. Grumbs (Eds.), *Black Self-Concept.* New York: McGraw Hill, 1971, pp. 141–170.

"Is There a Case for Separate Schools?" *Phi Delta Kappan*, January 1972, pp. 218–284.

"Separation: A Reality Approach to Inclusion," in Edgar G. Epps (Ed.) *Race Revelations*, Cambridge, MA: Winthrop Publishers, 1973, pp. 305–331.

"Making the School a Vehicle for Cultural Pluralism," in Madelin D. Stent, William B. Hazard, & Harry N. Rushin (Eds.), *Cultural Pluralism in*

Education: A Mandate for Change. New York: Appleton–Century–Crofts, 1973, pp. 43–54.

"Education: Is Accommodation Enough?" *Journal of Negro Education,* Vol. LIV, 1975, pp. 239–245.

"Educational Research and Desegregation: Significance for the Black Community," *Journal of Negro Education,* Vol. XLVII, No. 1, 1978, pp. 58–68.

"The Four M Curriculum: A Way to Shape the Future," *Journal of Negro Education,* Vol. XLVIII, No. 3, 1979, pp. 314–356.

"Social–Cultural Forces Which Affect Self-Direction and Self-Responsibility of Students," in Delmo Della–Dora & Lois J. Blanchard (Eds.), *Moving Toward Student Directed Learning: A Review of Relevant Research and Promising Practices.* Washington DC: Association for Supervision and Curriculum Development, 1979.

"Shattering the Melting Pot Myth," in James A. Banks (Ed.), *Teaching Ethnic Studies: Concepts and Strategies.* Washington DC: National Journal for Social Studies, 1981, pp. 63–89.

"The Ruptured Diamond: The Politics of the Decentralization of the District of Columbia Public Schools." Washington DC: University Press of America, 1981.

(and Hilliard, Asa G., III [Eds.]), *Saving the African American Child.* Washington DC: National Association of Black School Educators, 1984.

"Pitfalls and Promises of Effective Schools Research," *Journal of Negro Education,* Vol. LIV, 1985, pp. 269–288.

"The Effective African American Elementary School," in George W. Noblit and William T. Pink (Eds.), *Schooling and Social Content, Qualatative Studies.* Norwood: Ablex, 1987, pp. 175–202.

"The Madison School: A Turnaround Case," *Journal of Negro Education,* LVII, 1988, pp. 243–266.

"The Algebra of African American Achievement," in Percy Bates & Ted Wilson (Eds.), *Effective Schools: Critical Issues in the Education of Black Children.* Washington DC: National Association of Black School Educators, 1989, pp. 123–149.

"Curriculum and Effective Schools," in Harvey Holtz et al. (Eds.), *Education and the American Dream.* New York: Bergin & Garvey, 1989, pp. 88–95.

"The Politics of Curriculum, Race and Class," *Journal of Negro Education,* Vol. LIX, No. 1, 1990, pp. 77–85.

KWAME TURE (STOKELY CARMICHAEL)

BOOKS

(and Hamilton, Charles). *Black Power: The Politics of Liberation.* New York: Random House, 1967.
One of the most important books of the sixties that caused a national debate on a new concept of political liberation for Afrikans in America.

Stokely Carmichael Speaks: from Black Power to Pan-Africanism. New York: Random House, 1971.
A strong commentary on the transition from Black Power to Pan-Afrikanism.

"For the African Revolution," *Voices of the African Revolution,* No. 1. London: London Pan-African Association, 1987.
Ture's pinnacle statement on Afrikan revolution.

IVAN VAN SERTIMA

Book

They Came Before Columbus: The African Presence in Ancient America. New York: Random House, 1976.
An historic book that demonstrates the Afrikan influence and presence in the creation of the Americas.

JOURNALS

Van Sertima is the editor of the *Journal of African Civilizations* (New Brunswick, NJ: Transaction Publishers)
The most important journals available on the global presence and achievements of Afrikans throughout the world. A major contributor to developing a new school in Afrikan world scholarship. Issues include:
- *Egypt Revisited,* 1982
- *Blacks in Science: Ancient & Modern,* 1983
- *Black Women in Antiquity,* 1984
- *Nile Valley Civilizations,* 1985
- *African Presence in Early Asia,* 1985
- *Great African Thinkers,* 1986

- *African Presence in Early Europe,* 1986
- *African Presence in Early America,* 1987
- *Great Black Leaders: Ancient & Modern,* 1988
- *Golden Age of the Moors,* 1992
- *Egypt: Child of Africa,* 1995

FRANCES CRESS WELSING

BOOKS

The Cress Theory of Color Confrontation. Washington DC: C–R Publishers, 1970. This small booklet offers an explanation of the renowned Cress Theory.

The Isis (Yssis) Papers: Keys to the Colors. Chicago: Third World Press, 1991. Her best-selling and highly regarded book that is a compilation of all her papers.

ARTICLES AND ESSAYS

"A Conversation with Dr. Frances Cress Welsing," *Essence,* October 1973, pp. 51–90.

"Why Blacks Can't Love," *Essence,* October 1973, pp. 51–53.

"Black Value Systems and Strategies," in Jay Chunn (Ed.), *The Survival of Black Children and Youth,* Washington DC: Nuclossus and Science Publishing Company, 1974.

"When Birth Is a Tragedy: Black Teenage Reproduction," Washington DC: Self-published, 1974.

"Blacks, Hypertension, and the Active Skin Melanocyte," *Urban Health (The Journal of Health Care in the Cities),* 1974.

"An Alternative World Outlook (Commencement Address to Antioch College)," Northwestern University, School of Education, June 24, 1974.

"Speaking Out: On Black Genetic Inferiority," *Ebony,* July 1974.

"The Conspiracy to Make Blacks Inferior," *Ebony,* September 1974, pp. 84–94.

"Black Survival Units and the Economy of the White Supremacy System," *Journal of Afro-American Issues,* Vol. 3, No. 3/4, Summer/Fall, 1975.

"Black Women Moving Towards the 21st Century," *Essence,* December 1975, pp. 50–103.

"Ball Games as Symbols in the White Supremacy System and Culture," *Black Books Bulletin,* Vol. 5, No. 2, 1977, pp. 26–35.

"The Concept and the Color of God and Black Mental Health," *Black Books Bulletin,* Vol. 7, No. 1, 1980, pp. 26–35.

INDEX

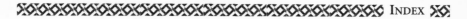

Photo credit: Isidra Person-Lynn

ABOUT THE AUTHOR

KWAKU PERSON-LYNN, a historian, musicologist, writer, broadcast producer, educator, is a native of South Central Los Angeles, California. He received his undergraduate degree from California State University, Dominguez Hills, where he is currently on the faculty in Africana Studies. He obtained his masters and doctorate degrees from the University of California, Los Angeles. He has approximately eighty articles in publication, and *First Word: Afrikan Scholars Thinkers Warriors* is his first book. He is now working on his second book, *On My Journey Now: The Narrative of Dr. John Henrik Clarke,* and on the second volume of *First Word.*

FIRST WORD

is set in MINION, a typeface designed c. 1987 for Adobe by
Robert Slimbach. MINION draws its inspiration from
the typography of the late Renaissance.